Analecta Gregoriana

Cura Pontificiae Universitatis Gregorianae edita

Vol. 136. Series Facultatis Iuris Canonici: sectio B. n. 14

JOHN R. KEATING

THE BEARING OF MENTAL IMPAIRMENT ON THE VALIDITY OF MARRIAGE

AN ANALYSIS OF ROTAL JURISPRUDENCE

Gregorian University Press

Piazza della Pilotta, 4 - Roma

1964

IMPRIMI POTEST

Romae, die 3 Iulii 1963.

R. P. PAULUS MUÑOZ VEGA, S. I.
Rector Universitatis

IMPRIMATUR

E Vicariatu Urbis, die 5 Iulii 1963.

✠ ALOYSIUS, *Card. Provicarius*

TYPIS PONTIFICIAE UNIVERSITATIS GREGORIANAE - ROMAE

PREFACE

Not a few doctoral dissertations have treated the theme of insanity and marriage; and several have taken good account of the developing jurisprudence of the Sacred Roman Rota. But none of these, it seems, has investigated the fundamental problem surrounding this cause of matrimonial nullity: For what intrinsic reason does mental impairment prevent a valid negotiation of the marriage contract? Since the Code of Canon Law does not establish any positive impediment in this regard, the question is one of the natural law itself. The classical axiom that insanity invalidates because it prevents true marital consent, and the recent attempts of canonists to stipulate a legal test of mental ability to place true consent, do not adequately answer the question. The appearance of the psychopathic personality in the matrimonial forum has prompted us to place our investigation on a broader base by asking whether a mental disorder might invalidate the marriage contract regardless of one's ability during the wedding to elicit naturally sufficient consent. Even remaining within the question of ability to give sufficient consent, we are led to ask whether temporary mental disturbance and habitual *amentia* constitute an identical *caput nullitatis*, viz., whether, for example, the marriage of the drunk and the marriage of the schizophrenic are null for the same reason.

Using the rich jurisprudence of the Sacred Roman Rota as a springboard, we have attempted to go beyond in an effort to delineate the invalidating nature of mental impairment of all kinds. The end result, we hope, is a modest attempt to determine the question of law which forty-five years ago the Code of Canon Law did not and, given the elementary status of the sciences of psychiatry and psychology at the time, *could not*, determine.

Not neglecting what canonical writers have contributed in recent years, we thought it best to pay particular attention to the jurisprudence of the Roman Rota, not only because its long line of decisions on this theme suggests many of the problems involved, but also because it has, more than any other source, indicated the avenues of solution. The validity of our conclusions we do not base on the authority of the Roman Rota, but solely on the rational arguments brought forth to sustain them.

A sincere word of gratitude is due to His Eminence, Albert Cardinal Meyer, Archbishop of Chicago, who assigned me to graduate studies in Canon Law and who has kindly enabled me to publish this dissertation; to the Reverend James E. Risk, S.J., professor of Canon Law at the Pontifical Gregorian University and moderator of this dissertation, who directed me with patience and paternal solicitude; to the Very Reverend Peter Huizing, S.J., Dean of the Canon Law faculty, whose suggestions and advice were exceedingly helpful; to the Right Reverend Monsignor Joseph Howard, Rector of the Collegio S. Maria del Lago in Rome, who sustained my efforts with kindness and understanding; to His Excellency, Most Reverend Francis J. Brennan, Dean of the Sacred Roman Rota, who graciously permitted me to examine the unpublished Rota decisions of the last ten years and to cite them in this dissertation.

Rome J. R. K.

July 4, 1963.

TABLE OF CONTENTS

KEY TO THE ABBREVIATIONS

S.R.R. Dec.	*Sacrae Romanae Rotae Decisiones seu Sententiae*
AAS	*Acta Apostolicae Sedis*
ASS	*Acta Sanctae Sedis*
DDC	*Dictionnaire de Droit Canonique*

CHAPTER ONE

PRELIMINARIES TO PROOF AND PRACTICAL QUESTIONS

A pre-Code Rotal decision once mentioned that the difficulty in insanity cases is not with the law but with the facts.[1] Perhaps this was true at a time when few such cases came to the Holy See for adjudication and when the simple criterion of "*sui compos*" or "*non sui compos*" sufficed as a legal norm. But the ever increasing number and variety of "insanity" cases submitted to ecclesiastical tribunals since the promulgation of the Code, plus the incredible progress currently developing in the sciences of psychiatry and psychology, have made urgent a solution to the simple question: whom does the law consider mentally incompetent for valid marriage? In vain will ecclesiastical judges look to the Code for an accurate definition of *amentia* in matrimonial law, for a clear-cut legal test of minimum psychic competence for valid marriage, for a satisfying clarification of the ultimate invalidating force of psychic defect or disorder. It is not surprising, therefore that insanity cases present serious difficulties, not only in the *quaestio facti*, but also, and perhaps even more so, in the *quaestio iuris*.

Article 1. THE *Caput Nullitatis* IN INSANITY CASES.

Unlike the other *capita nullitatis matrimonii*, which have explicit formulations in the Code of Canon Law, the *caput amentiae* is nowhere consecrated in the matrimonial law of Code, either among the diriment impediments of Chapter IV (canons 1067-1080), or among the defects of

---

[1] C. SEBASTIANELLI, Jan. 7, 1918 (Vol. X, 3); also in *AAS*, X (1918), p. 518.

marital consent enumerated in Chapter V (canons 1081-1093). It is not naive, then, to ask, when treating of insanity cases, exactly what the plaintiff is trying to prove. If we answer that one must prove that the contractant was mentally incompetent for true matrimonial consent, we are only stating a truism. The question remains: when is a person to be considered mentally incompetent for true matrimonial consent? A theoretical law cannot be applied to a concrete case unless there is a criterion which the judge can employ,[2] and in insanity cases the critical problem centers about the "legal test" of minimum psychic capacity for valid marriage. Henry Weihofen has this to say when speaking of mental illness and its general bearing in law:

> In short, in each legal situation, the insanity issue really has two parts:
> (1) Was the person mentally ill?
> (2) If so, was the illness such as to satisfy the legal criterion or test?
> Much confusion has been caused by the failure to keep this rather elementary analysis clear.[3].

The omission of a legal test in the Code of Canon Law has thereby remitted not merely the question of fact, but also, to a great extent, the question of law to the ecclesiastical judges themselves, who are left to collect fragmentary indications from the Code, some traditional presumptions of Rotal jurisprudence, and various rules for the evaluation of the conclusions of the canonical experts.

So obscure is this *caput nullitatis* that there is even a dispute whether it belongs to the juridical figure of the

---

[2] LUIGI TAPARELLI S. J., *Saggio teoretico di dritto naturale appoggiato sul fatto* (8. ed.; Roma: La Civiltà Cattolica, 1949), II, n. 1200: "Stabilito un fatto conviene applicarvi il principio *teorico*, il quale, parlando di giudizii, *è la legge*. Ma perchè quest'applicazione sia retta, vuolsi stabilire un *criterio*, col quale possa il giudice confrontar rettamente il *fatto* col *dritto*. Allora finalmente egli sarà in istato di *conchiudere*, cioè di *sentenziare*."

[3] HENRY WEIHOFEN, "The Definition of Mental Illness," *Criminal Psychology*, ed. Richard W. Nice (New York: Philosophical Library, 1962), p. 195.

diriment impediments,[4] the defects of consent,[5] or both,[6] or neither.[7] Consequently, it is not clear whether a marriage which is null by reason of psychic defect or disorder is rectified by simple convalidation according to canons 1133-1135 (diriment impediment), or according to canon 1136 (defect of consent).[8] There is a question whether habitual insanity (*amentia habitualis*) and mental disturbance (*mentis exturbatio*) constitute an identical *caput nullitatis*. For example, it is asked whether schizophrenia and a hypnotic trance render the marriage contract null for the same reason.[9] More radically, the question has recently been raised whether psychic disorder might invalidate the contract not merely because it prevents true consent (*causa efficiens matrimonii*), but also because it creates an objective natural unfitness or ineptitude in the contractant (*causa materialis matrimonii*), rendering him naturally incapable of assuming the essential obligations of the contract; in such a situation an effective exchange of

---

[4] Cf. PIETRO D'AVACK, *Cause di nullità e di divorzio* (2. ed.; Firenze: Cya, 1952), pp. 116-118, 139-140; A. C. JEMOLO, *Il matrimonio nel diritto canonico* (Milano: Vallardi, 1941), n. 46, nota 1; ANNA RAVÀ, "Il *defectus discretionis iudicii* come causa di nullità del matrimonio nella giurisprudenza rotale," *Il Diritto Ecclesiastico*, LXVIII (1957), pp. 359, 383.

[5] Cf. A. DE SMET, "Aliénation mentale en matière de consentement matrimonial," *DDC*, I, col. 416; JAIME M. MANS PUIGARNAU, *El consentimiento matrimonial* (Barcelona: Bosch, 1956), p. 24; JAIME M. MANS PUIGARNAU y ALBERTO BERNÁRDEZ CANTÓN, *Derecho matrimonial canónico* (Barcelona: Bosch, 1959), I, p. 316; R. COLIN PICKETT, *Mental Affliction and Church Law* (Ottawa: University of Ottawa Press, 1952,), p. 144; EUDOXIO CASTAÑEDA DELGADO, *La locura y el matrimonio* (Valladolid-Madrid: Editorial Sever-Cuesta, 1955), p. 1; WILLIAM M. VAN OMMEREN, *Mental Illness Affecting Matrimonial Consent* (Washington, D.C.: Catholic University of America Press, 1961), p. 172; HANS NIKLAUS FÄSSLER, *Die Schizophrenie als Ehenichtigkeitsgrund im kanonischen Recht* (Freiburg in der Schweiz: Paulusdruckerei, 1951), p. 55; DENNIS C. KLEMME, *Lucid Intervals and Matrimonial Consent: Historical Background and Jurisprudence of the Sacred Roman Rota* (Romae: Pontificia Universitas Lateranensis, 1960), pp. 18-19, and, implicitly, the majority of manuals, which suppose insanity as a defect of consent and treat *amentia* under the chapter heading of *De consensu matrimoniali, De vitiis consensus*, and the like.

[6] ERMANNO GRAZIANI, *Volontà attuale e volontà precettiva nel negozio matrimoniale canonico* (Milano: Giuffrè, 1956), p. 92; MATTHAEUS CONTE A CORONATA, O.F.M. Cap., *Institutiones iuris canonici*, III, *De matrimonio et de sacramentalibus* (3. ed.; Taurini: Marietti, 1957), n. 437, nota 5.

[7] JOSEPH BÁNK, *Connubia canonica* (Romae - Friburgi Brisg. - Barcinone: Herder, 1959), p 341.

[8] Cf. D'AVACK, *op. cit.*, p. 117; RAVÀ, *op. cit.*, p. 359.

[9] Cf. *infra*, p. 101 ff.

marital rights and obligations is unthinkable because "*nemo ad impossibile obligari potest.*"[10] Concretely, for example, in the case of the sexual psychopathy called nymphomania, it is debated whether the disorder invalidates because of a defect of internal liberty precluding true consent,[11] or because of a defect of internal liberty precluding an objective possibility of fulfillment of an essential obligation of the contract, namely, marital fidelity.[12] In the latter case, then, the disorder would seem to invalidate like impotence and would prescind from the structural integrity of the act of consent.

The case of the genuine homosexual is even more nebulous. According to some authors, sodomitic acts violate the *bonum fidei* and hence, reserving the right to such acts would vitiate consent. On this premise it is asked whether the marriage contract of the genuine homosexual might be null because of simulation, whether partial or total, whether deliberate or compulsive, or perhaps because of a *vitium mentis* akin to *amentia*.[13] It is not unusual for the Rota to receive such cases where the marriage of the sexual psychopath was attacked in the lower court with a sort of "buckshot" approach wherein four or five possible *capita* are invoked. In at least five recent decisions the legal doubts had to be rearranged in the appeal because they were self-contradictory or obviously inaccurate.[14].

Even the invalidating force of *amentia* in canon 1089, § 3, supervening between the granting of a mandate for marriage by proxy and the eventual celebration of the ceremony, is disputed. The common opinion is that it invalidates because of an automatic extinction of perduring

---

[10] Cf. JOHN R. KEATING, "The *Caput Nullitatis* in Insanity Cases", *The Jurist*, XXII (1962), pp. 394-396.

[11] SEBASTIANO VILLEGGIANTE, "Ninfomania e difetto di consenso," *Il Diritto Ecclesiastico*, LXXI (1960), pp. 315-322.

[12] C. SABATTANI (Neapolitana), June 21, 1957, nn. 3-7 *in iure*, published in part in *Il Diritto Ecclesiastico*, LXXI (1960), pp. 314-322.

[13] GERARDUS OESTERLE, O.S.B., "De relatione homosexualitatis ad matrimonium," *Revista Española de Derecho Canónico*, X (1955), pp. 7-60; idem, "Welchen Einfluss hat die Homosexualität auf die Ehe?" *Oesterreichisches Archiv für Kirchenrecht*, (1961), pp. 305-337; VINCENT P. COBURN, "Homosexuality and the Invalidation of Marriage," *The Jurist*, XX (1960), pp. 441-459.

[14] Cf. *infra*, pp. 22-26.

consent; but another view states that intervening insanity does not automatically destroy consent and that *amentia* invalidates as a strict diriment impediment of the natural law, the same as though incurable impotence had intervened.[15] Because of the undefined invalidating nature of *amentia* some authors hold that the Church can sanate marriages after supervening *amentia.*[16] Others flatly deny it.[17] Finally, authors argue whether this *caput* is reducible to the *caput ignorantiae* so that the governing norm for insanity cases is canon 1082.[18]

Such is the endless confusion and obscurity surrounding this cause of matrimonial nullity. However, we believe that through its elaborations since the time of the promulgation of the Code, the Sacred Roman Rota, especially during the past ten years, has solved many of these questions and has provided solid directional guidelines to a solution of the others.

Section A. The Silence of the Code.

There can be no doubt that the Code itself supposes insanity as grounds of nullity on a much broader scale, beyond the limited scope of canon 1089, § 3. Such a sup-

---

[15] Cf. *infra*, pp. 18-22.

[16] FELIX M. CAPPELLO, S. I., *Tractatus canonico-moralis de sacramentis*, V, *De matrimonio* (7. ed.; Taurini: Marietti, 1961), n. 853, 3°.

[17] PICKETT, *op. cit.*, p. 153; ROBERT J. HARRIGAN, *The Radical Sanation of Invalid Marriages* (Washington, D.C.: Catholic University of America Press, 1938), p. 59; JEAN BERNHARD, "Propos sur la nature juridique de la *sanatio in radice* dans le droit canonique actuel," *Ephemerides Iuris Canonici*, IV (1948), pp. 392-393, and, logically, all those who, commenting on canon 1089, § 3, claim that intervening insanity automatically extinguishes consent, for example, PETRUS Card. GASPARRI, *Tractatus canonicus de matrimonio* (9. ed.; Città del Vaticano: Typis Polyglottis Vaticanis, 1932), II, n. 874; FRANCISCUS X. WERNZ, S. I., et PETRUS VIDAL, S. I., *Ius canonicum*, V. *Ius matrimoniale* (3. ed. a Philippo Aguirre, S. I., recognita; Romae: apud Aedes Universitatis Gregorianae, 1946), n. 459.

[18] Professor d'Avack claims that common doctrine and jurisprudence hold for the affirmative view (*Cause di nullità e di divorzio*, p. 131); Ravà, on the other hand, surveys the field and comes to precisely the opposite conclusion ("Il *defectus discretionis iudicii* come causa di nullità," p. 358). That insanity is not reducible to ignorance is the conclusion of F. LORENC, "De ignorantiae influxu in matrimoniali consensu," *Apollinaris*, XXVI (1953), pp. 348-349. For the contrary view, cf. GERARDUS OESTERLE, O.S.B., "Nullitas matrimonii ex capite ignorantiae," *Consultationes de jure matrimoniali* (Romae: Officium Libri Catholici, 1942), pp. 307-308; JOSIAH G. CHATHAM, "A Primer on Insanity Cases," *The Jurist*, XX (1960), p. 343.

position is contained implicitly in canon 88, § 3, explicitly in canon 1982. [19] Although we may find no specific governing norm it would be incorrect to say that the Code is absolutely silent on the matter. [20]

One might wonder, nonetheless, at this glaring omission. Certainly, it was not due to an oversight on the part of the legislator, for the Code does insinuate this cause of nullity; nor could the legislator be unaware of the long history of insanity cases in ecclesiastical jurisprudence going back at least to the time of Pope Innocent III (1198-1216). [21] The common explanation is that since the natural law itself establishes the invalidating law, there was no need to insert a norm in the Code. One Rota decision reads: "*... per se patet; neque expresse pronuntiandum erat in Codice Juris Canonici.*" [22]

D'Avack attributes the silence to the fact that the legislator probably deemed a specific norm superflous, since due discretion is a requisite of the natural law itself and flows from the general principles regarding juridical acts. [23] Conte a Coronata offers the explanation that the relevant norm of the natural law is already sufficiently declared in canons 1081 and 1082. [24] Banking more on the contractual nature of marriage, Pickett writes:

> Since marriage partakes essentially of the nature of a contract, the natural law itself places it beyond the juridical capacity of those who are not *sui compotes*, making positive legislation to this effect unnecessary. [25]

---

[19] C. WYNEN, Dec. 21, 1937 (Vol. XXIX, 757): "Codex, quamvis impedimentum particulare insaniae non statuerit, tamen indirecte sufficienter innuit insaniam a valide contrahendo arcere. Ita in can. 88, § 3, legitur: 'Infanti assimilantur quotquot usu rationis sunt habitu destituti.' Et in can. 1982 sermo est de 'causis (matrimonialibus) defectus consensus ob amentiam,' in quibus 'requiratur suffragium peritorum, qui infirmum, si casus ferat, eiusve acta quae amentiae suspicionem ingerunt, examinent secundum artis praecepta; insuper uti testes audiri debent periti qui infirmum antea visitaverint.' "

[20] Although d'Avack refers to "this absolute silence of the legislator" (*op. cit.*, p. 115), a Rotal decision could rightly mention: "Minus recte... dictum est de mentecaptis Codicem Juris Canonici silere." C. GRAZIOLI, Nov. 3, 1934 (Vol. XXVI, 710).

[21] C. 24, X, IV, 1.

[22] C. WYNEN, June 3, 1939 (Vol. XXXI, 372).

[23] D'AVACK, *Cause di nullità e di divorzio*, p. 115.

[24] CONTE A CORONATA, *Institutiones*, III, *De matrimonio*, n. 437.

[25] PICKETT, *Mental Affliction and Church Law*, p. 143.

This reason, however, were it true, would mean that the legislator would have done well to omit many norms which are declarations of the natural law. One might argue that the norms on ignorance, error, simulation, contrary intentions, the formulations of canons 1081 and 1082, the impediment of impotence, and many other norms were "unnecessary". To the relief, however, of ecclesiastical judges, whose legal system consists mainly in applying codified norms to concrete cases, the legislator did see fit to formulate the natural law in many instances.

A better reason for the omission seems to be this: at the time of the promulgation of the Code, neither canonical doctrine nor canonical jurisprudence was in a position to provide a reasonable legal test as an accurate formulation of the natural law. The natural law is difficult to penetrate, and all the more to circumscribe with the concise lines of codified law. When the Code was being prepared it was deemed inopportune to "freeze" a legal test of minimum mental competence for valid marriage at a time when ecclesiastical jurisprudence, aided by the fast-developing sciences of psychiatry and psychology, was beginning to investigate more deeply into the ultimate invalidating cause of mental impairment. At the very time of the preparation of the Code there was, in fact, a notable advance in Rotal jurisprudence. Previously, the traditional norm for minimum capacity was the "use of reason" norm; however, it was quickly becoming obvious that the simple use of reason was no criterion of psychic ability to place true matrimonial consent. In retrospect we might say that if the Code had formulated the traditional "use of reason" test, jurisprudence on insanity cases would have been stifled for decades. On the other hand, the omission of a legal test has opened the door to what is perhaps the fastest developing jurisprudence in the history of ecclesiastical matrimonial tribunals. The legislator wisely left it to the judges and the tribunals themselves to investigate the natural law on the nullifying nature of psychic impairment, be it impairment stemming from a psychosis, from mental deficiency, from passing mental disturbances, or, recently, from the obscure mental disorders called the psychopathies. The end result, we think, is a rich jurisprudence and, rare as it might be in system of codified law, a prime example of vigorously developing law.

Section B. Some Irrelevant Norms.

The ecclesiastical judge, it is true, might appeal directly to the natural law itself to substantiate his declaration of nullity by reason of psychic incompetence.[26] Rotal decisions, however, sometimes state that the marriage is null by reason of canon law also.[27] It would be well at this point to analyze some norms of the Code to which Rotal jurisprudence and canonical writers sometimes appeal in an effort to ascertain the nature and extent of this cause of nullity.

1) *Canon 88, §3*: This prescription equates the habitually insane (*quotquot usu rationis sunt habitu destituti*) to infants. Since infants are incapable of marriage, at least by reason of the diriment impediment of nonage, some have claimed that this is the governing norm by which marriages of the insane are rightly declared null. But some observations must be made regarding this canon and its possible application to matrimonial law.

First of all, the definition of *amens* in canon 88, §3, is one who is habitually deprived of the use of reason. It is quite certain, however, and well established in Rotal jurisprudence that a person might habitually enjoy the simple use of reason and yet be *amens* in matrimonial law, for the simple use of reason is no criterion of minimum psychic ability to contract marriage.

Secondly, canon 88, §3, speaks only of the habitually insane and makes no provision for the cases of marital nul-

---

26 "Iure quidem naturali matrimonium contrahere prohibentur." — c. Prior, July 10, 1909 (Vol. I, 87); c. Parrillo, Feb. 16, 1928 (Vol. XX, 58); c. Mannucci, Aug. 8, 1931 (Vol. XXIII, 372); c. Teodori, Jan. 19, 1940 (Vol. XXXII, 83); c. Heard, June 5, 1941 (Vol. XXXIII, 489).

27 "Siquidem illud contraxerint, naturali et canonico iure retinetur nullum." — c. Rossetti, May 10, 1921 (Vol. XIII, 86). "In hanc propterea conclusionem deveniunt Patres, ut licet tempore contracti coniugii Andreas conventus demens, uti forte hodie, dici non posset, eam tamen non haberet mentis discretionem, quae *iuxta ius naturale, positivis praescriptis firmatum,* satis esse ad valide promendum matrimonialem consensum." — c. Felici (Quebecen.), Dec. 3, 1957, in *Monitor Ecclesiasticus,* LXXXIII (1958), p. 55. (Emphasis supplied.)

lity arising from a passing, but actual, deprivation of due discretion.

Thirdly, canon 88, §3, speaks only of the *amens'* juridical capacity regarding strictly ecclesiastical rights and obligations and does not purport to establish his capacity regarding his rights and obligations according to the natural law. [28]

It seems, then, that canon 88, §3, has no application to the marriageable status of the mentally ill. At most, one might grant that it contains an oblique supposition of the legislator of this *caput nullitatis matrimonii.*

2) *Canon 1982*: This canon speaks directly of the necessity of employing experts and expresses the supposition that *amentia* invalidates marriage because of a defect of consent (*in causis defectus consensus ob amentiam*). It seems quite clear, however, that the choice of words "*defectus consensus ob amentiam*" does not rule out the possibility that *amentia* might also invalidate as a strict diriment impediment even to the extent that there be no structural defect of the act of consent. The legislator was merely assuming the settled jurisprudence and doctrine of canonical writers that *amentia* does indeed invalidate by reason of defect of consent. It is noteworthy that the parallel prescription of the Instruction *Provida,* art. 151, omits the phrase "*defectus consensus*".[29] In any case, canon 1982 sheds no light on the comprehension of the term *amentia.*

3) *Canon 1089, §3*: This is the only canon wherein *amentia* is explicitly stated as a cause of nullity. It speaks of supervenient insanity invalidating marriage by proxy, but, once again, does not directly indicate whom the law considers insane or on what precise grounds the marriage is null. [30]

4) *Canon 2201*: Not infrequently do authors purport to borrow principles from penal law for use in the matrimonial forum. Since canon 2201 gives a relatively detailed

---

[28] Gommarus Michiels, O.F.M. Cap., *Principia generalia de personis in ecclesia* (2. ed.; Parisiis-Tornaci-Romae: Desclée et Socii, 1955), pp. 72, 79, 82.

[29] Instructio *Provida,* art. 151: "In causis amentiae unus vel, pro casus gravitate, duo medici deputentur, qui in scientia psychiatrica peculiariter sint versati, cauto tamen ut exclundantur qui sanam (catholicam) doctrinam hac in re non profiteantur."

[30] However, if we are not mistaken, this prescription indicates that *amentia* can invalidate in a way other than by causing a defect of consent. Cf. *infra.* pp. 18-22.

outline of the effect of psychic disorder on penal imputability, it would seem only natural to adapt these prescriptions for application to insanity cases.[31] It seems, however, that such a transfer is hardly legitimate since matrimonial law and penal law, at least on this point, cannot be considered as similar laws in the sense of canon 20 (*a legibus latis in similibus*). For one thing, if we might speak of a "*favor iuris poenalis*", the underlying principle in penal law is that, in doubt, the innocence of the mentally ill is to be upheld. Thus, in case of reasonable doubt about the imputability of a criminal act committed by a person who is mentally ill, the presumption is for lack of imputability.[32] In matrimonial law, on the other hand, the "*favor iuris matrimonialis*" would, in case of doubt about the imputability or sufficiency of consent, hold for the validity of the marriage and hence for the imputability or sufficiency of consent.

Secondly, the legally recognized effects of mental illness on penal responsibility in canon 2201 are formulated in a graduated scale. Penal imputability admits varying degrees, while matrimonial law recognizes only psychic competence or psychic incompetence... the validity or invalidity of the contract.

Thirdly, the provisions pertaining to penal imputability can be purely positive enactments; but marriage of the mentally ill is governed solely by the natural law. Accord-

---

31 CONTE A CORONATA, *Institutiones*, III, *De matrimonio*, n. 437: "Praeterea in defectu specialis expressae iuris positivi dispositionis quae amentium incapacitatem ad matrimonium respiciat, doctrina analogice recurrere solet ad dispositiones circa ipsos amentes latas in iure poenali quae sic sonant: Habitualiter amentes, licet quandoque lucida intervalla habeant, vel in certis quibusdam ratiocinationibus vel actibus sani videantur, delicti tamen incapaces praesumuntur." BÁNK, *Connubia canonica*, p. 345: "Normae iuris criminalis de imputabilitate tantum mutatis mutandis admitti possunt."

32 Cf. canon 2201, § 2. PIUS CIPROTTI, *De iniuria ac diffamatione in iure poenali canonico* (Romae: apud Custodiam Librariam Pont. Instituti Utriusque Iuris, 1937), n. 64: "Quaerunt etiam utrum praesumptio doli alia elidatur praesumptione, quae in can. 2201, § 2, statuitur: *habitualiter amentes, licet quandoque lucida intervalla habeant, vel in certis quibusdam ratiocinationibus vel actibus sani videantur, delicti tamen incapaces praesumuntur*. Quamvis autem illa loquendi ratio satis accurata non sit, certum tamen est praesumptione doli affici solummodo personas capaces; nam antea est inquirendum de capacitate poenali, postea vero, extante capacitate, inquiri potest de imputabilitate."

ingly, penal law may well exonerate as it will, but matrimonial law has no purely positive diriment impediment of psychic incompetence.[33]

5) *Canons 1081 and 1082*: Since insanity is a cause of defective consent, and is often so because it precludes the necessary knowledge required for true marital consent, it is sometimes said, perhaps in too general a sense, that the marriages of the insane are null in virtue of canon 1082. Chatham writes:

> Consent presupposes knowledge. For this reason, according to canon 1082, crass ignorance of the rudimentary nature of marriage precludes consent and invalidates marriage. Insanity, then, which precludes the necessary knowledge of what one is doing also invalidates the marriage contract.
>
> Canons 1801 and 1082 thus contain implicitly the substantive law under which insanity cases are tried. These two canons are a positive restatement of natural law. The natural law, therefore, is the source of invalidity in insanity cases.[34]

It is true that a good number of Rota decisions seem to reduce invalidity to a question of ignorance. Canon 1082 is repeated among the *motiva in iure* in the vast majority of insanity decisions. Yet, there is a large number of decisions for nullity in which there is no question at all of possible ignorance on the part of the defendant; nonetheless, the decision declares nullity "*ob defectum discretionis iudicii*" or simply "*ob amentiam*". That the mentally ill person be ignorant *ad normam can. 1082* might often be the case, but it is purely *per accidens*.

Recent Rotal jurisprudence, it seems, has veered away from a similar "practical" reduction to ignorance and an appeal to the concise norm of canon 1082 to substantiate the sentence. Two very recent Rota sentences are quite clear on the point:

> In propatulo est, homines haud intelligentes quid sit matrimonium, vel matrimonii essentiales proprietates haud percipientes, incapaces esse contrahendi. Sed erraret sane qui cogitaret, quoad requisita ad capacitatem contrahendi, omnia absolvi per illam comprehensionem.[35]

---

[33] MICHIELS, *Principia generalia de personis in ecclesia*, pp. 78-80; FÄSSLER, *Die Schizophrenie als Ehenichtigkeitsgrund im kanonischen Recht*, pp. 54-55.

[34] CHATHAM, "A Primer on Insanity Cases," *The Jurist*, XX (1960), p. 343

[35] C. SABATTANI (Januen.), Mar. 14, 1959, *in iure*.

> Questio defectus discretionis judicii non reducitur ad meram quaestionem ignorantiae. Hoc necesse est statuere in recte dijudicanda causa, quae Nos intentos tenet... Componi ideo potest cognitio sat plena de re matrimoniali cum defectu discretionis judicii...[36]

Certainly, canon 1082 can be a useful negative norm in certain cases. If a person, because of psychic disorder, is incapable of grasping the rudimentary nature of marriage, he therefore is ignorant. *A non posse ad non esse valet illatio*. However, recent Rotal jurisprudence maintains that the cause of invalidity is on the *non posse* level, not on the *non esse* level. The person may *de facto* be ignorant and the marriage is null, to be sure, but not *because* of ignorance *ad normam can. 1082*.[37] In cases, however, where the psychic disorder or defect is not of such a nature or of such gravity as to constitute of itself a cause of nullity, the marriage might legitimately be attacked on grounds verifiable in the psychically competent; in these cases, the mental illness is considered as a *cause* of ignorance, a *motive* for simulation, or an *extenuating circumstance* in relatively grave force or fear.[38]

A very recent Rota decision surveyed the problem created by the silence of the Code and pointed out the only plausible solution:

> IN IURE: C.J.C. in tit. VII, De Matrimonio, libri III, agit quidem (caput V) de consensu matrimoniali, sed non definit capacitatem usu rationis carentium vel mente debilium quod ad matrimonii celebrationem attinet. Declarat tantum — fortasse non recte — satis esse ad nuptias valide ineundas contrahentes non ignorare matrimonium esse societatem permanentem inter virum et mulierem ad filios procreandos: id autem post pubertatem non praesumi (can. 1082).
>
> Plures normas hac in re deficientes sumunt ex praescripto canonis 2201, in quo scriptum legimus:
>
> "§ 1. Delicti sunt incapaces, etc..."
>
> Sed haec ratio explendi lacunam haud est legitima, cum ius poenale, canonicum quoque, peculiaribus regatur normis atque nitatur principiis. Nunc autem norma deficiens sumen-

---

36 C. SABATTANI (Januen.), Feb. 24, 1961, *in iure*, in *Monitor Ecclesiasticus*, LXXXVI (1961), p. 633.

37 Nor may insanity be reduced to the juridical figure of simulation *ad normam can. 1086*. Cf. *infra*, pp. 22-26, on contradictory *capita*.

38 JEMOLO, *Il matrimonio nel diritto canonico*, n. 50; CONTE A CORONATA, *Institutiones*, III, *De matrimonio*, nn. 440, 442.

da est a legibus latis in similibus (can. 20), non in quam maxime diversis.

Legitimum contra est normam deficientem sumere ex praescripto canonis 88, § 3, quod tamen haud est definitum.

Et ideo norma in casu sumenda est a generalibus iuris principiis cum aequitate canonica servatis, a praxi Curiae Romanae, *seu N.S.O.*, et a communi constantique sententia doctorum, seu canonistarum magnae notae.[39]

Presently, if we are not mistaken, the only authoritative source of a true legal test as a reflection of the natural law is to be found in the developing jurisprudence of the Sacred Roman Rota.[40].

Section C. Preliminary Indications of the Invalidating Nature of Psychic Incompetence. *

At the outset it must be stated that the settled jurisprudence of the Sacred Roman Rota has traditionally based the *caput nullitatis* on a defect of consent, namely, on the party's psychic inability to elicit during the wedding ceremony naturally sufficient consent. Thus, if the marriage is null by reason of mental incompetence, it is either because the act of consent was not a human act at all (early jurisprudence), or, if it was a human act, it was not the qualified human act because destitute of the discretion proportionate to the marriage contract itself (later jurisprudence).

---

[39] C. De Jorio (Taurinen.), Dec 19, 1961, *in iure.*

[40] "With the use that diocesan tribunals and the Rota are now making of psychiatric science, it is inevitable that a new synthesis will eventually be evolved that will present canonical principles and jurisprudence in a more adequate relationship to the findings of modern psychiatry. The details of this new synthesis will probably be worked out in the Rota Decisions and summarized by the authors. The source to watch for new developments will be the latest available Rota Decisions . In the meantime the classical passage on insanity as invalidating marriage is probably that of Cardinal Gasparri." — Chatham, "A Primer on Insanity Cases," *The Jurist,* XX (1960), p. 346. On the importance and authority of Rotal jurisprudence, cf. Arthur Caron, O.M.I., "Jurisprudence in Canon Law," *The Jurist,* XVIII (1958), pp. 88-97; Lorenzo Miguélez, Dean of the Spanish Rota, in his presentation to Castañeda's work, *La locura y el matrimonio,* pp. xv-xvii.

* We say "preliminary indications" and treat here only some possible clues to the thesis that mental impairment can invalidate marriage not merely by way of a defect of consent, but also as a strict diriment impediment. We remit to Chapter III our analysis of the recent Rotal jurisprudence on this point.

There are, however, some indications which serve to clarify the invalidating force of *amentia* and which, at least implicitly, seem to suppose *amentia* as a strict diriment impediment that would invalidate regardless of the accidental power of the contractant during the wedding to elicit naturally sufficient consent.

1. The Juridical Figure of *Amentia* in the Code.

Whenever the Code refers to *amentia* it speaks of it as a personal ineptness in the subject whereby he is considered unfit to exercise his rights, place juridical acts, or incur criminal liability. It prescinds from the varying psychological requisites of this or that particular act and regards the mental condition of the *amens* as a lasting disability resident in his person. He is likened to an infant and simply considered *subiectum inhabile* to place juridical acts in general, [41] to act as plaintiff or respondent in court, [42] to acquire a voluntary domicile of his own, [43], to act as sponsor at Baptism [44] or Confirmation, [45] etc. The Code seems to consider the invalidity of acts placed by the *amens* as stemming directly from the natural disability of this type of person, not from a missing psychological quality of the act in question. [46].

---

41 Canon 88, § 3.
42 Canon 1648, § 1.
43 Canon 93, § 1.
44 Canon 765, 1°.
45 Canon 795, 1°.
46 A confirmation of the view that the figure of *amentia* in the Code of Canon Law is an abiding personal disability that abstracts from the psychological requisites of a given act can be drawn from canonical commentaries on canon 12. Basing their opinion on the figure of *amentia* throughout the Code as expressed principally in the general norm of canon 88, § 3, not a few authors interpret canon 12 so that the habitually insane are exempt from ecclesiastical laws even during lucid intervals. Cf. A. VERMEERSCH, S. I., et I. CREUSEN, S. I., *Epitome iuris canonici*, Vol. I (7 ed.; Mechliniae-Romae: H. Dessain, 1949), n. 107; FELIX M. CAPPELLO, S. I., *Summa iuris canonici*, Vol. I (5. ed.; Romae: apud Aedes Universitatis Gregorianae, 1951), n. 74; LUDOVICUS BENDER, O.P., *Normae generales de personis* (Roma-Parigi-New York-Tournai: Desclée & C., 1957), n. 57; JOSEPH A. MCCLOSKEY, *The Subject of Ecclesiastical Law According to Canon 12* (Washington, D.C.: Catholic University of America Press, 1942), p. 189; GOMMARUS MICHIELS, O.F.M. Cap., *Principia generalia de personis in ecclesia* (2. ed.; Parisiis-Tornaci-Romae: Desclée et Socii, 1955), pp. 78-79; idem, *De delictis et poenis*, Vol. I (2. ed.; Parisiis-Tornaci-Romae-Neo Eboraci: Desclée et Socii, 1961), p. 194.

2. *Sanatio in Radice* after Supervenient Insanity.

Certainly, a marriage which is null for defect of consent cannot be sanated, for the essential and indispensable substructure of *sanatio in radice* is lacking, i. e., naturally sufficient consent which is still perduring.[47] There is no doubt, therefore, that a marriage attempted by one under a mental affliction which prevents true consent, cannot be sanated.

But the question is sometimes raised whether a *sanatio in radice* can be granted when a marriage, null from the beginning only because of an obstacle of positive law, is subsequently visited by the misfortune of incurable insanity in one or both of the spouses. The supposition is that they are henceforth unable to repair their marriage by simple convalidation, since one or both of the parties are incapable of renewing true consent at present. Naturally sufficient consent was given in the beginning.

Almost all the authors who posit the question answer simply that a *sanatio in radice* is impossible in such circumstances. The usual reason is that perduring consent is extinguished automatically with the onset of insanity.[48] Cappello, on the other hand, cannot see why a

---

[47] Canons 1139 and 1140. WERNZ-VIDAL-AGUIRRE, *op. cit.*, V, n. 666: "*Quatenus utraque pars in consensu de praesenti perseveret.* Quae condicio adeo constanter apposita non nititur iure humano, sed est mere *declaratoria* iuris divini, ut patet argumentis supra ex natura rei petitis."

[48] STEPHANUS SIPOS, *Enchiridion iuris canonici* (7. ed. recognovit Ladislaus Gálos; Romae-Friburgi Brisg.-Barcinone: Herder, 1960), p. 545: "Si coniugum alteruter in amentiam inciderit, consensus ab initio datus non perseverat." MIGUEL DE ARQUER Y SANTIAGO DE SEMIR, *Derecho matrimonial* (Barcelona: Editorial Poliglota, 1949), n. 196: "...en el caso de locura se extingue automáticamente el consentimiento, como si se tratara de un muerto." CONTE A CORONATA, *op. cit.*, III, n. 688: "Dicendum igitur consensum revocari in amentia perpetua alterutrius coniugis et proinde non posse in tali casu matrimonium in radice sanari." VICENTE MONTSERRAT, *Derecho matrimonial canónico* (Barcelona: Editorial Litúrgica Española, 1961), n. 271: "...porque en el momento de querer hacerse la subsanación no persevera el consentimiento." GASPARRI, *op. cit.*, II, n. 1222: "...revera, cum ex dictis, matrimonium per sanationem in radice fiat validum ex nunc, non concipitur convalidatio matrimonii, quaecumque ea sit, quando una ex partibus incapax est consensus matrimonialis eo prorsus modo quo nec intelligitur eiusmodi matrimonii celebratio." PICKETT, *Mental Affliction and Church Law*, p. 153; G. PAYEN, *De matrimonio in missionibus ac potissimum in Sinis tractatus practicus et casus* (2. ed.; Zi-ka-wei: Typographia T'OU-SE-WE, 1935-36), Vol. II, n. 2607; ROBERT J. HARRIGAN, *The Radical Sanation of Invalid Marriages* (Washington, D.C.: Catholic University of America Press, 1938), p. 59.

sanation cannot be granted. Against Gasparri he states that it is false to say that a sanation can be granted only when a person is actually capable of eliciting true consent; were this reason true, the Church could never grant a sanation while one of the parties is drunk or asleep. Secondly, the mere fact of intervening insanity does not extinguish consent.[49] It is difficult to see how, with the onset of insanity, the afflicted party unwittingly revokes consent.[50].

The practice of the Holy See is quite interesting on this point. In 1889 the Archbishop of Mechlin proposed a case to the Holy Office in which the petitioner requested a *sanatio in radice* of her marriage which had been null because of defect of the Tridentine form. Subsequently, her husband became incurably insane. Solid motives were attached to the petition. The response, dated December 8, 1889, was: *"Sacer hic consessus quoad sanationem in radice non expedire censuit ut concedatur; quod vero ad legitimationem prolis, cum haec per rescriptum Summi Pontificis obtineri possit, oratrix, si ei lubet, recurrat ad S. Congregationem Concilii."*[51]

In the decennial faculties granted by the Propaganda Fide to missionary ordinaries, the following restriction is placed on the faculty of sanating:

---

49 CAPPELLO, *De Sacramentis*, V, *De matrimonio*, n. 853, 3°: "Sententia affirmativa vera videtur, quia argumentum quo nititur opinio opposita non valet. Falsum quippe est, ad valorem sanationis requiri ut eo momento quo ipsa conceditur, partes sint actu capaces consensus matrimonialis praestandi, secus invalide concederetur sanatio eo momento quo pars esset ebria aut dormiens. Sanatio ex dictis id unum exigit, scil. quod consensus coniugalis revera praestitus fuerit et adhuc perseveret seu numquam fuerit revocatus. Iamvero eo ipso quod pars incidit in amentiam, nullatenus mutatur eius voluntas et revocatur consensus, qui naturaliter ac iuridice perseverat. Id applicatur quoque aliis negotiis et casibus, v.g., in ordine ad sacramenta recipienda." This opinion is also upheld by MANS-BERNARDEZ, *Derecho matrimonial canónico*, II, pp. 89-90, and by VINCENZO DEL GIUDICE, *Nozioni di diritto canonico* (11. ed.; Milano: Giuffrè, 1962), p. 303, nota 38.

50 DEL GIUDICE, *ibid.*: "Nell'ipotesi dell'infermità [mentale], invece, la sanatio è possibile, sulla base dell'iniziale consenso e della presunzione semplice della perseveranza del consenso al momento dell'iniziata infermità del coniuge e dell'attuale quiescenza di essa, determinando la legittimità degli effetti ex tunc e per il futuro."

51 *ASS*, XXIII, 333.

Facultas sanandi in radice non extenditur ad casus in quibus supervenerit amentia unius vel utriusque partis. In singulis hisce casibus igitur ad S. Sedem recurrendum erit.[52]

The wording of this restriction not only does not rule out the possibility of such sanation, but seems to indicate that the Holy See simply reserves to itself the concession of a sanation in cases of supervenient insanity.

Finally, the Holy See does grant such sanations.[53] The supposition is that, in spite of supervenient insanity, naturally sufficient consent perseveres.

One might conclude further from the fact of such sanations that insanity cannot be considered a diriment impediment of the natural law, for a sanation cannot be granted while one of the parties is under a diriment impediment which the Church in no way can dispense.[54] However, the Church can and *does* sanate marriages (null from the beginning because of a purely positive obstacle) after incurable impotence has intervened. Apparently, then, the Church can sanate marriages at a time when one or both parties are under a diriment impediment of the natural law.[55]

---

[52] Cf. LUDOVICUS BUIJS, S. I., *Facultates decennales* (Romae: apud Aedes Universitatis Gregorianae, 1961), Fac. n. 30, p. 103.

[53] For a recent example, cf. "Roman Replies" in *The Jurist*, XXII (1962), p. 101. After an attempted marriage, the woman lapsed into an incurable mental condition which left her incapable of eliciting true matrimonial consent necessary for a simple convalidation. The Holy Office received the case in which a petition for a *sanatio in radice* was requested. Cardinal Ottaviani wrote to the Ordinary: "Before granting this favor, this Supreme S. Congregation, considering the petitioner's allegedly incurable condition with the consequent presumption that the parties to this invalid marriage have not been cohabiting, inquires what the specific and urgent reasons are for proceeding to the sanation requested." The requested information was forwarded to the Holy Office and the sanation was subsequently granted (June 26, 1961: Prot. N. 954/61m) under the usual condition: "*dummodo utriusque partis consensus perseveret.*"

[54] WERNZ-VIDAL-AGUIRRE, *op. cit.*, V, n. 666: "Nam ut matrimonium validum fiat, simul consistere debent et *habilitas* et *consensus nupturientium.*" If we are not mistaken, all commentaries without exception place as a necessary requisite for a valid sanation that the obstacle have already ceased or can be dispensed by the Church. Cappello, it would appear, did not advert to this difficulty.

[55] An interesting example of the Holy See sanating a marriage while the man was under the impediment of perpetual impotence, together with an explanation of how the Church can truly sanate such unions, is given by WILHELMUS BERTRAMS, S. I., « De effectu consensus matrimonialis naturaliter validi," *Miscellanea in memoriam Petri Card. Gasparri* (*Apollina-*

In conclusion we might say that although the concept of "persevering consent" is not altogether clear in Canon Law, nevertheless, even in cases of supervenient insanity the principle of canon 1093 holds: "*Etsi matrimonium invalide ratione impedimenti initum fuerit, consensus praestitus praesumitur perseverare, donec de eius revocatione constiterit.*" The authors who hold that the onset of insanity automatically effects a revocation or extinction of perduring consent merely state the thesis but offer no argument in its defense. The precedent of the Church, on the other hand, of sanating marriages after supervenient insanity clearly supposes that insanity can coexist with perduring marital consent, naturally sufficient to constitute valid marriage. This point, we believe, should not be overlooked in an investigation of the ultimate invalidating force of mental incompetence on the marriage contract.

3. The Invalidating Force of *Amentia* in Canon 1089, §3

Salvo meliori iudicio, it seems that the invalidating force of *amentia* as stated in canon 1089, § 3, can be reasonably explained only if it be considered as a strict diriment impediment of the natural law, and not as a cause of defective consent. Canon 1089, §3, reads:

> Si, antequam procurator nomine mandantis contraxerit, hic mandatum revocaverit aut in amentiam inciderit, invalidum est matrimonium, licet sive procurator sive alia pars contrahens haec ignoraverint.

Historically the question of the possible invalidating force of *amentia* intervening between the granting of the mandate and the eventual celebration of the marriage by proxy was treated speculatively by the canonists, but it was by no means an unreal problem in the days of ex-

ris, XXXIII [1960]), pp. 119-138; idem, "De efficacitate consensus matrimonialis naturaliter validi," *Periodica,* LI (1962), pp. 288-300. A contrary position is held by EDUARDO F. REGATILLO, S. I., "Un caso nuevo de sanación in radice," *Sal Terrae,* XLIX (1961), pp. 417-427. Comments Del Giudice (*Nozioni di diritto canonico,* n. 120, nota 35): "Quid, se l'impedimento indispensabile (p. es., di impotenza) sopravvenne al matrimonio invalidamente posto in essere e sia presente al momento nel quale la sanazione si domandi? Si ritiene, da alcuni autori, impossibile la sanazione: ma non sembra tale soluzione sicura, dovendosi aver riguardo al momento del consenso prestato, naturalmente sufficiente e perseverante."

tremely slow communications. It must be noted that canonists uniformly considered the possible invalidating force of intervening insanity solely from the standpoint of consequently vitiated consent. Sanchez posed the problem and answered that intervening insanity would not, of itself, invalidate the marriage since the principal for his part had already done all that was necessary as far as consent was concerned by granting the mandate while sane:

> ... dum contrahit per procuratorem, satis est ut dum mandatum dedit, sui compos esset, nec revocarit, et procurator, dum eius praestat consensum, sit sui compos: ut in caeteris contractibus contingit, quia tunc contrahens non ministrat per seipsum sed medio instrumento.[56]

The authority of Sanchez provided for a fairly wide reception of this opinion.[57] The contrary opinion arose, however, according to which the ensuing marriage would be null, a conclusion based again solely on the status of marital consent. Pontius, followed by a considerable number of notable authors,[58] thought of supervenient insanity

---

[56] THOMAS SANCHEZ, S. J., *De sancto matrimonii sacramento* (Venetiis: apud Nicolaum Pezzana, 1737), Lib. II, Disp. XI, n. 12. "Hinc infertur, si procuratore misso, dans mandatum in amentiam incidat, et talis perseveret, dum procurator nomine suo contrahit, valere matrimonium... sicuti si tunc temporis esset dormiens, valeret matrimonium". — *Ibid.*

[57] Cf. EMANUELIS GONZALEZ TELLEZ, *Commentaria perpetua in singulos textus quinque librorum Decretalium Gregorii IX*, Tom. IV (Venetiis: apud Nicolaum Pezzana 1766), Tit. I, Cap. I, n. 17; ERRICUS PIRHING, S. J., *Jus canonicum*, Tom. IV (Venetiis: ex thipographia Remondiniana, 1759), Tit. I, n. 79; FRANCISCUS SCHMALZGRUEBER, S. J., *Jus ecclesiasticum universum*, Tom. I (Romae: ex typographia Rev. Cam. Apostolicae, 1843-44). Tit. XXXVIII, n. 20; VITUS PICHLER, S. J., *Summa jurisprudentiae sacrae seu jus canonicum* (Augustae Vindelicorum: Veith, 1758), Lib. IV, Tit. I, n. 85; HENRICUS HENRIQUEZ, S. J., *Summa theologiae moralis*, Tom. I (Venetiis: apud Haeredes Melchioris Sessae, 1600), Lib. XI, Cap. IV, n. 4; MARTINUS BONACINA, *Opera omnia*, Tom. I, *Tractatus de magno matrimonii sacramento* (Venetiis: apud Jacobum Thomasinum, 1721), Qu. II, Punct. V, n. 13; AEGIDIUS DE CONINCK, S. J., *De sacramentis et censuris ecclesiasticis* (Lugduni: Sumpt. Claudii Landry, 1619), Tom. II, Disp. XXIV, Dub. IX, n. 70.

[58] BASILIUS PONTIUS, O.S.A., *De sacramento matrimonii tractatus* (Venetiis: apud L. Balilium, 1756), Lib. II, Cap. XV, n. 14; ANTONINUS DIANA, *Omnes resolutiones morales*, Tom. II, *De sacramento matrimonii* (Lugduni: Huguetan-Barbier, 1667), Tract. VI, Resol. 61; IOANNES DE LUGO, S. I., *Disputationes scholasticae et morales de sacramentis in genere* (Lugduni: Sumpt. Iacobi & Petri Prost, 1636), Disp. VIII, n. 108; LUDOVICUS MOLINA, S. I., *De iustitia et iure*, Tom. II, *De contractibus* Moguntiae: Sumpt. Hermanni Mylii, 1614), Disp. 552, n. 7; IOANNES KUGLER, S. I., *Tractatus*

as an equivalent revocation of the mandate and of marital consent, without explaining precisely how this happens. At any rate, this became the common opinion among canonists in the nineteenth century and was thus received into the Code, apparently on the same reasoning. The structure and placement of canon 1089, § 3, would seem to vindicate the reasoning of Pontius that insanity here automatically revokes the mandate and extinguishes consent, since it reads in the same line: "*Si... hic mandatum revocaverit aut in amentiam inciderit...*" Furthermore, the canon was inserted under the chapter heading "*De consensu matrimoniali.*" Cardinal Gasparri, commenting on this canon, says that in such a case "*...consensus in mandante prorsus deficit, sicuti si supremum diem obiisset, ideoque contractus in genere... et matrimonium in specie non intelligitur.*" [59]

Various explanations might be offered why intervening insanity be an obstacle to a valid proxy marriage. It might be said that this is an entirely positive disposition of ecclesiastical law; but such an explanation is out of the question since the whole line of canonical thought preceding the insertion of canon 1089, §3, in the Code considered this effect of the very nature of the situation. The question arose speculatively among canonists, was answered on speculative grounds entirely, became a common opinion, and then was consecrated for the first time in ecclesiastical

---

theologico-canonicus de matrimonio (Norimbergae: Sumpt. Lehmanni, 1713), Pars I, Qu. X; PETRUS GASPARRI, *Tractatus canonicus de matrimonio* (Parisiis: Institut catholique, 1891), n 837; FRANCISCUS X. WERNZ, S. I., *Ius decretalium*, Tom. IV, *Ius matrimoniale* (Prati: Giachetti, 1911), n. 45, nota 107.

[59] GASPARRI, *De matrimonio*, 9. ed. (1932), II, n. 874. WERNZ-VIDAL-AGUIRRE, *Ius canonicum*, V, *Ius matrimoniale*, 3. ed. (1946), n. 459, nota 20: "...nam consensus in mandante per amentiam *deficit* sicut in *mortuo;* deficiente autem consensu in *una* parte matrimonium nec valide *iniri* nec per *sanationem vere convalidari* potest; nec est paritas cum dormiente vel ebrio, in quo usus rationis dumtaxat suspensus est, non extinctus." IOANNES VISSER, C.SS.R., "De matrimonio per procuratorem inito," *Casus conscientiae*, I, *De matrimonio*, ed. P. Palazzini (2. ed.; Romae: Officium Libri Catholici, 1961), p. 117: "Cessat autem mandatum procuratoris... amentia in quam mandans inciderit ante nuptias celebratas, etiam insciis procuratore et altera parte; uti videtur et haec canonis norma confirmat solummodo ius naturale. Amentia autem hoc loco intendi non debet sensu stricte technico, uti illam intendunt hodierni psychologi, sed pro omni morboso defectu intellectus, quo extinguitur (etiamsi temporanee) capacitas dandi validum consensum matrimonialem."

law in 1918 with the promulgation of the Code. Nor has any commentator since the promulgation of the Code claimed that this was purely a positive disposition of the law. As Cardinal Gasparri explained it: " *...consensus prorsus deficit; ideoque... matrimonium non intelligitur.*"

Another explanation might be put forth that it is of the nature of such a proxy negotiation that the principal be *sui compos* at the time of the ceremony. But canonical doctrine is unanimous in stating that if the principal is temporarily *non compos mentis,* asleep, completely drunk, hypnotized, drugged, delirious, etc., at the time of the ceremony, there is no obstacle to a valid marriage. Says Gasparri of such a case: "*Matrimonium valet quia consensus virtualiter perseverat.*" [60]

The third and common explanation is that of Pontius, Gasparri, and Wernz, viz., that intervening insanity is an equivalent revocation of marital consent or its complete destruction. In reply, we might first mention that Sanchez, the most thorough and outstanding canonist on the matter of marriage and insanity, could not see how this could be. And, indeed, there seems to be no intrinsic reason why, *solely from the standpoint of perduring consent,* temporary mental impairment does not invalidate the marriage, while permanent impairment does. The reasons adduced for the contrary position are mainly two: (1) in the case of perpetual insanity intervening, the principal becomes incapable of placing another act of consent; (2) with the intervention of perpetual insanity, the mandate expires the same as though the principal had died. Schmalzgrueber answered by saying that, in the first place, no new act of consent is required; in the second place, there is no parity between death and insanity. [61] It remains to be proved that

[60] GASPARRI, *loc. cit.* This is the commonly accepted reason why drunkenness, sleep, etc., are no hindrance to a valid proxy marriage. Thus, the common interpretation of *amentia* here is *amentia perpetua.* However, it is interesting to note that CAPPELLO *op. cit.,* n. 619, 3, 3°), and BÁNK (*Connubia canonica,* p. 338), and VISSER (*loc. cit.*) hold that even temporary insanity invalidates the marriage, thereby distinguishing temporary *amentia* from *mentis exturbatio* deriving from drunkenness, sleep, drugs, etc.

[61] SCHMALZGRUEBER, *Ius ecclesiasticum universum,* Tom. I, Tit. XXXVIII, n. 20. MICHIELS, *Principia generalia de personis in ecclesia,* p. 83: "Cum ob amentiam non extinguatur personalitas per baptismum acquisita, neque tollantur jura ante amentiam legitime adepta, neque impediatur acqui-

with the onset of perpetual insanity the principal unwittingly revokes has mandate. Finally, if *amentia* necessarily effects a revocation or destruction of consent, the Church could not grant a *sanatio in radice* after incurable *amentia* supervenes, for in this case naturally sufficient consent must be deemed to persevere; and, as stated previously, the Church does grant such sanations.[62]

The simplest and most plausible explanation, it seems, is that *amentia* is a strict diriment impediment of the natural law. Just as if incurable impotence should intervene and invalidate the eventual proxy marriage, so too with insanity. The marriage is null, not because of any vitiation or revocation or destruction of naturally sufficient consent, but simply because the principal is presently under a diriment impediment. He is no longer *subiectum capax iurium et obligationum matrimonialium*. But neither in the case of incurable impotence nor in the case of insanity would naturally sufficient consent be necessarily destroyed. The question of whether psychic disorder need be incurable like impotence in order to render the person incapable of assuming the rights and obligations of the marriage contract will be treated further on.

4. Contradictory *Capita.*

Five recent decisions of the Roman Rota reveal that the appeal was received only after rearrangement of *capita* either because in the lower court two contradictory *capita* had been simultaneously proposed, or because a *caput* offered in the lower court was obviously false and the case was tried on the wrong grounds. Not only does this serve to illuminate the difficulty of finding the apt *caput nullitatis*, but it also helps us to understand, according to Rotal jurisprudence, the real nature of invalidation of *amentia* and its relationship to the invalidating force of simulation.

1) *Coram* Felici (Florentina) April 6, 1954: *Species facti*: the sentence mentions that in the first instance the libellus read: "*ob amentiam viri et quatenus affirmative,*

---

sitio jurium quae acquiri possunt ab infantibus (quibus assimilantur) quaeque per alios sunt exercibilia, ipsis ad normam juris assignandus est *curator* (can. 1648, § 1, 1650, 1651, § 1), qui eos in exercitio jurium auctoritative repraesentat."

[62] Cf. *supra*, p. 17.

ob exclusum ab eo bonum prolis." When appealed to the Rota in second instance the doubts were concorded to read: "*ex capite amentiae viri et, quatenus negative, ex capite intentionis eiusdem contra bonum prolis.*"

2) *Coram* Sabattani (Neapolitana) June 21, 1957. This is a case involving nymphomania. In the court of first instance the case was tried on the grounds of "*ob exclusum bonum fidei ex parte uxoris*" and received a negative decision. Appealed to the Rota, it was seen that this *caput nullitatis* was spurious. How could the nymphomaniac be said to positively exclude what she was incapable of ever assuming in the first place? The power to exclude supposes both the power to exclude and to assume. After extrajudicial examination by experts, the doubts were concorded:

> ... quod mulier bonum fidei rejecerit, potius quam ex positivo voluntatis actu, ex ipsa ineptitudine ad illud servandum ob quamdam abnormem propensionem in res lascivas et psychicam perturbationem, quod ita concordatum fuit: 'An constet de nullitate matrimonii ex defectu discretionis judicii mulieris conventae.' Caput 'exclusio boni fidei' subordinatum manet praecedenti, de eoque agi tantum debet, si novum caput negative dimissum fuerit. [63]

3) *Coram* Ewers (Quebecen.) Oct. 29, 1960. The lower court had tried the case on two equally principal *capita*: (a) *amentia*; b) exclusion of the *bonum prolis*. The Rotal decision observes *in facto*:

> In casu, duplici ex capite contenditur matrimonium nullum esse. At capita, utpote inter se contradictoria, nonnisi subordinate tractari possunt, neque ex utroque nullitas declarari patitur, cum, mentis insania probata, concipi nequeat positivus voluntatis actus quo aliquod essentiale matrimonii bonum excludatur.

4) *Coram* Sabattani (Tridentina) March 24, 1961. The same question came up about the subordination of

---

[63] This decision provides a startling contrast to the traditional jurisprudence of the Rota on insanity. The case was tried on "defect of due discretion" as a strict diriment impediment that prescinds from, or grants, the integrity of the nymphomaniac's act of consent. Independently of the act of consent, she is "*a priori inhabilis ad contrahendum ex eo quod ob suam complexionem iam impossibilis est usus exclusivus corporis.*" Like the impotent person, she is incapable of granting a right or assuming an obligation to an essential marital right (marital fidelity).

amentia and exclusion of the *bonum prolis.* Writes the court:

> Nam coexistentia aeque principalis duorum capitum admitti nequit, cum matrimonium haud possit simul nullum esse ex amentia et ex exclusione boni prolis ex parte unius eiusdemque personae, quae eodem tempore fieret incapax eliciendi consensum et simul capax consensum restringendi seu limitandi, ut ius ad prolem non contineret.

5) *Coram* De Jorio (Taurinen.) Feb. 28, 1962. In the lower court the *dubium* read: "*An constet de nullitate matrimonii ex capite defectus consensus ob amentiam mulieris, id est ob totalem eiusdem mulieris simulationem ex morbo quo laborabat consequentem.*" The Rota observes:

> Optima fuisset formula dubii, si prima tantummodo propositione constitisset, seu quod additum est ad explanandum rem implicavit, non explicavit...
>
> Defensor Vinculi penes N.S.T. animadvertit duo pugnantia capita allata esse ad nullitatem matrimonii evincendam....
>
> Hac aequivocatione nitens Tribunal Pedemontanum sententia die 9 aprilis 1952 lata, declaravit: "Constare de matrimonii nullitate ex capite defectus consensus ob amentiam mulieris, id est ob totalem eiusdem mulieris simulationem ex morbo quo laborabat consequentem."

Observations:

1) *Amentia* (understood as the natural inability to posit true marital consent) and simulation, whether partial or total, are mutually contradictory. A marriage cannot be null on these two grounds simultaneously, nor can *amentia* be reduced to the juridical figure of simulation. It is true, perhaps, to say that simulation means the lack of conformity between the external manifestation of consent and the internal will of the contractant, and this is the situation, in a certain sense, in *amentia* cases. But the juridical figure of simulation supposes the natural ability of the contractant to posit naturally sufficient consent.[64] No

---

64 BÁNK, *Connubia canonica,* p. 341: "De vitiis consensus enim vix moveri potest quaestio, nisi supponetur capacitas seu habilitas naturalis contrahentium." ORIO GIACCHI, *Il consenso nel matrimonio canonico* (Milano: Giuffrè, 1950), p. 47: "Che un matrimonio sia nullo per mancanza del consenso presuppone la capacità psichica a consentire, senza la quale non si può evidentemente scendere ad esaminare se consenso vi fu o no. I matrimoni celebrati sotto l'impulso del terrore, della ipnosi, o di altra costrizione psichica sono dunque nulli non per mancanza di volontà ma per mancanza di capacità."

one can be said to have a positive will to exclude an essential property of marriage, or marriage itself, if he is already unable to construct internally and manifest externally true and sufficient marital consent.

2) *Amentia* (understood not as the psychic inability to give true consent, but as the objective psychic ineptitude, unfitness, incapability of the subject to honor the essential obligations of the marriage contract) and simulation are also mutually exclusive. "*Nemo ad impossibile obligari potest... ius ad impossibile ne concipi quidem potest.*" No one can be said to exclude with a positive will what one is objectively incapable of assuming in the first place. Positive exclusion supposes the power to assume or to exclude.[65] Thus, the incurably impotent man might also make a positive contrary intention *contra bonum prolis.* The marriage is null because of impotence, not because of simulation.[66]

3) "Compulsive" simulation is self-contradictory. A marriage may be declared null by reason of simulation (*ad normam can.* 1086) only if the simulator was psychically capable of eliciting true consent and was, at the same time, a naturally fit subject for marriage, capable of assuming, the essential rights and obligations of the marriage contract. The positive act of exclusion must be a deliberate human act of the will.[67] Arguments, therefore, which

---

[65] SEBASTIANO VILLEGGIANTE, "Ninfomania e cause di nullità matrimoniale," *Il Diritto Ecclesiastico,* LXXI (1960), pp. 162-163: "L'accertamento è di primaria importanza, pacifico essendo che soltanto colui il quale è capace di obbligarsi è anche capace del contrario e cioè capace di simulare, dacché, alla incapacità per fatto oggettivo di assumersi un obbligo, corrisponde logicamente l'incapacità di escluderlo."

[66] The rigt to *actus per se aptos ad prolis generationem* is already objectively non-transferable in the case of the incurably impotent. A subjective contrary intention cannot, therefore, be the effective cause of the non-transference, i.e., of the invalidity of the marriage.

[67] CAROLUS HOLBÖCK, *Tractatus de jurisprudentia Sacrae Romanae Rotae* (Graetiae-Vindobonae-Coloniae: Styria, 1957), p. 129: "Simulatio partialis consistit in intentione animo retenta substantiae matrimonii contraria; in ea duo contrarii quidem sed veri actus voluntatis ponuntur, quibus contrahens vult quidem matrimonium, sed non assumendo obligationem essentialem simul non vult. Qui duo veri voluntatis actus contrarii simul valere nequeunt; posterior enim actus specificus et praevalens destruit priorem genericum a jure requisitum. Consensus partialiter simulatus duobus ex elementis consistit: externis verbis vel signis consensum in totum matrimonialis contractus objectum exprimentibus atque interno vero voluntatis actu, quo unum alterumve bonum matrimonii excluditur."

purport to prove the nullity of marriage contracted by the psychopathic personality (although the psychopath is sometimes described by doctors as a compulsive simulator) on the grounds that he elicited simulated consent as an irresistible effect of his mental disorder, seem ill-founded. Even if it were possible to prove that certain psychopathies, of their very nature, irresistibly lead the contractant to exclude from his consent marriage itself or some essential property of marriage, the juridical figure of simulation would not be verified and canon 1086 could not be considered the governing norm.[68] The marriage might indeed be null, but not by reason of simulation.[69]

Article 2. THE LEGAL DEFINITION OF *Amentia* AND CLASSIFICATIONS OF PSYCHIC DISORDERS AND DEFECTS.

"Insanity" is a legal term. As such, it belongs to the legislator, not to the psychiatrist, to define the concept.[70]

GIACCHI, *op. cit.*, p. 66: "Qui il soggetto, *coscientemente e deliberatamente*, esclude che all'apparenza del matrimonio consegua la sostanza; egli vuole che il matrimonio di cui compie la celebrazione sia mera apparenza, una finzione." Cf. also DINUS STAFFA, "De actu positivo voluntatis quo bonum essentiale matrimonii excluditur." *Monitor Ecclesiasticus*, LXXIV (1949), pp. 164 ff.

[68] Oesterle argues that the marriage of the constitutional homosexual is null by reason of defective, simulated consent. He states that such a marriage could be annulled on three grounds: (*a*) exclusion of marriage itself; (*b*) exclusion of marital fidelity; (*c*) exclusion of the right to conjugal acts. His case for the compulsive simulation of the genuine homosexual is evolved in two articles: "De relatione homosexualitatis ad matrimonium," *Revista Española de Derecho Canónico*, X (1955), pp. 7-60; "Welchen Einfluss hat die Homosexualität auf die Ehe?" *Oesterreichisches Archiv für Kirchenrecht*, (1961), pp. 305-337.

[69] Chap. 3, footnote 169.

[70] WEIHOFEN, *"The Definition of Mental Illness," Criminal Psychology*, p. 194: "Mental illness is a medical concept, and so it would seem self-evident that its definition should come from the medical profession and not from either legislators or judges.

"But mental illness is a phenomenon that the law does recognize and that may have various legal effects. It may render a person irresponsible for his criminal act; it may justify a court order for his involuntary hospitalization; it may render him incompetent to make a will or a binding contract; it may constitute grounds for divorce. However, mental illness in and of itself does not have any of these legal effects. There must be mental illness; but there is always a second requirement, that the illness be of such form or degree as to meet some legal criterion. In a will contest, where the question is whether the testator was

The psychiatrist will enunciate his definitions and classifications of mental illness on the basis of diverse species and etiology; the legislator will formulate the definitions and classifications of mental illnesses only on the basis of their respective effects on juridical responsibility. Because of the pronounced difference in their proper ends, legal and medical definitions of mental illness rarely, if ever, coincide. It is for this reason that legislators have prescinded from medical definitions and have contented themselves with a few simple legal distinctions and concepts which serve the purpose of the law.[71]

If the Code of Canon Law had provided a legal definition of *amentia* in matrimonial law, we would have, equivalently, a statement of the legal test of minimum mental competence for valid marriage. However, there is, in fact, no clear indication in the Code of whom the law considers psychically incompetent for the marriage contract.

In non-matrimonial law the term *amentia* seems to receive in the Code a general descriptive definition that suffices for its purpose, viz., "habitually deprived of the use of reason." In canon 88, § 3, it is stated that those who are habitually deprived of the use of reason after seven years of age are likened to infants and are considered *non sui compotes*. Regarding the subject of Baptism, canon 745 states that the insane are to be considered as infants, *"qui nondum rationis usum adepti sunt..."* (par. 2, 1°). Canon 1648, § 1, employs again the

---

'sane' when he made his will, the question is not merely whether he then had a medically recognized form of mental illness. If not, then of course he was not "insane" in any sense. But even if medical experts agree he was mentally ill, the law asks a further question, which is, broadly, did his mental illness deprive him of sufficient mind to know what he was doing? Did he know it was a will he was executing; did he understand the nature and extent of his property and his obligations toward those persons who are related to him or who have some moral or legal claim upon him?".

[71] C. Parrillo, Feb. 16, 1928 (Vol. XX, 60): "Legislatores, omni aevo, medicorum placita non sunt sequuti in multiformi divisione ac variis nominibus, quibus placuit ac placet mentales infirmitates dispescere ac significare. Cum enim finis legis diversus sit ab eo, quem sibi medici proponunt in variis huiusmodi morbis indagandis, consequens fuit quod lex eam tantum divisionem ac nomina acciperet, quae fini sibi proprio responderent, quaeque diversas species vel subspecies sub se complecterentur." Cf. CASTAÑEDA, *La locura y el matrimonio*, p. 11, nota 11; PICKETT, *Mental Affliction and Church Law*, pp. 1-3; D'AVACK, *Cause di nullità e di divorzio*, p. 185.

general "use of reason" norm when it says: "*Pro minoribus et iis qui rationis usu destituti sunt, agere et respondere tenentur eorum parentes aut tutores vel curatores.*" Finally, it is clear that penal law uses the simple "use of reason" criterion to measure criminal imputability in the mentally ill. Canon 2201 states that they are incapable of delicts who are *actually* without the use of reason (§ 1), or who are habitually insane (§ 2); imputability is lessened or extinguished by mental disturbance according as the use of reason is diminished or altogether destroyed (§ 3); the feeble-minded, i.e., those who have an imperfect use of reason,[72] are less liable for criminal acts.

Michiels, in collating various canons of the Code which have to do with the mentally ill, concludes that the legislator distinguishes two categories of the mentally unsound:

1) those who are deprived entirely of the use of reason, whether haibtually or only momentarily;

2) those who are not entirely devoid of the use of reason, but who, either habitually or momentarily enjoy the use of reason imperfectly or less fully.[73]

Whenever Canon Law recognizes special legal effects in the case of the mentally ill, whether they concer their criminal liability, their subjection to ecclesiastical laws, their juridical capacity in general or in particular, it assigns universally, it seems, a mere "use of reason" test.

Section A. THE CONCEPT OF *Amentia* IN MATRIMONIAL LAW.

In matrimonial law the term *amentia* is used twice, once regarding intervening insanity in proxy marriages (can. 1089, § 3), and again regarding the necessity of employing experts in nullity cases of defective consent because of insanity (can. 1982). It might be expected that the term as used in these two canons would retain the general, though univocal, meaning which it has throughout the Code, viz., the habitual deprivation of the use of reason. Indeed, at the time of the promulgation of the

[72] Cf. J. NOVAL, O.P., "De semi-amentibus et semi-imputabilitati obnoxiis utrum revera existant aut in iure poenali ecclesiae agnoscantur," *Jus Pontificium,* IV (1924), p. 82.

[73] MICHIELS, *Principia generalia de personis in ecclesia,* p. 72.

Code, this might well have been true. But in the developing jurisprudence of the Roman Rota, it soon became clear that the "use of reason", though perhaps an adequate criterion for capacity to stand as sponsor at Baptism or Confirmation, to act and respond in court by oneself, to be criminally responsible, etc., was, in fact, no adequate test of psychic competence to marry validly. In matrimonial jurisprudence the term *amens* began to be extended so as to include those who, although enjoying the habitual and actual use of reason, were for one reason or another, still mentally incapable of eliciting true matrimonial consent sufficient to contract marriage. As the increased number and variety of cases submitted to the Rota were adjudicated, there was a profoundly more extensive, and intensive, investigation of mental illness. All the time, it seemed, the term *amentia* was growing further and further away, not only from the clinical concept of insanity, [74] but even from the Code's generic concept.

Even some recent commentaries give a definition of *amentia* in matrimonial law which is identical to its acceptance throughout the Code. [75] Some authors who have dwelt on the point have concluded to an extremely wide definition. For example, Allers, Ravà, and Bánk would include in the term any and all psychic defects or disorders by which marriage is null, whether it be a question of a psychosis, mental deficiency, a psychopathy, a passing mental disturbance caused by drunkenness, hypnosis, fever, etc. [76] This, of course, is not a definition, but a nega-

---

[74] BÁNK, *Connubia canonica*, p. 349: "..ob progressum scientiae psychiatriae permagnum, notio iuridica notioque psychiatrica 'amentiae,' seu mentis morbi ab invicem sensim sine sensu magis magisque discrepant."

[75] E.g., EDUARDUS F. REGATILLO, S.I., *Ius sacramentarium* (3. ed.; Santander: Sal Terrae, 1960), n. 1316: "*Amentia* est habitualis defectus usus rationis ea aetate qua iuxta naturam adesse deberet; seu insania circa omnia."

[76] RUDOLPH ALLERS, "Annulment of Marriage by Lack of Consent because of Insanity," *The Ecclesiastical Review*, CI (1939), p. 340: "This is the general term for all kinds of mental ailment causing an incapacity of responsible action and correct thought." RAVÀ, "Il *defectus discretionis iudicii* come causa di nullità del matrimonio nella giurisprudenza rotale," *Il Diritto Ecclesiastico*, LXVIII (1957), II, p. 396: "Avvertiamo pertanto, al fine di evitare ogni eventuale confusione, che il termine *amentia*, da noi usato nel corso del lavoro, deve essere assunto, dopo quanto abbiamo detto, nella sua unica accezione valevole in sede giuridico-matrimoniale,

tive description, for it does not tell us a criterion of who is psychically incompetent. A very recent Rotal decision attributed this all-inclusive meaning to *amentia*:

> Quando deficit hujusmodi maturitas judicii sufficiens ad matrimonium intelligendum vel eligendum, sive id proveniat ex habituali alienatione animi, sive ex exturbatione transeunti, sive ex psychica debilitate, habetur *amentia in sensu contractuali*... vel adest illa sufficiens discretio iudicii, vel non adest. Si prius, habetur sanitas; si alterum *amentia* simpliciter.[77]

However, the court seems to be aware that this acceptance of *amentia*, at least in Rotal jurisprudence, is somewhat novel, for it continues: "Reapse, *si acceptatur definitio supra tradita* (n° 2, a), evidenter locus amplius non est amentiae sic dictae 'semiplenae,'..."

General Rotal jurisprudence, it seems, has kept to a middle course, extending the term beyond "the habitual deprivation of the use of reason," but not so much as to include cases of passing mental disturbance. And only rarely is feeble-mindedness referred to as "*amentia*."[78]

As an all-inclusive phrase that embraces all the possible mental disorders and defects by which marriage can be null, the Rota regularly uses "*defectus discretionis iudicii matrimonio proportionatae.*" "Due discretion," therefore, is convertible with psychic competence, while "defect of due discretion" is convertible with psychic incompetence for valid marriage. "*Unica mensura sufficientis consensus est discretio judicii matrimonio proportionata*".[79] When due discretion is lacking for

---

e cioè nella sua accezione più vasta di alienazione, perturbazione ed alterazione mentale che, nelle svariatissime forme indicate ed illustrate dalla scienza medica, influisce, più o meno sensibilmente, sulla capacità intellettiva e volitiva dell'individuo producendo, a seconda dei casi, l'invalidità o meno del consenso e quindi l'invalidità o meno del matrimonio." BÁNK, *Connubia canonica*, p. 341: "Amentia ergo designat omnes species infirmitatis mentis vel animae, quibus matrimonium invalidari potest."

[77] C. Sabattani (Januen.), Feb. 24, 1961, in *Monitor Ecclesiasticus*, LXXXVI (1961), pp. 632, 633.

[78] C. Bejan (Atrebaten.), Oct. 25, 1958, *in iure*: "Omnibus illis in casibus in quibus defectus consensus eliciti in matrimonio tribuitur exturbationi vel debilitati mentis, causa matrimonialis potius quam sub specie amentiae, iudicio submittitur ob singularem causam deficientis internae libertatis." Cf. also c. Massimi, July 28, 1928 (Vol. XX, 318).

[79] C. Sabattani (Januen.), Feb. 24, 1961.

causes ranging from full-blown psychoses to passing inadvertence, marriage is null. When due discretion is present, from the standpoint of psychic competence, the marriage is valid.

Conclusions:

1) The term *amentia* in the Code has a general meaning of "habitual deprivation of the use of reason."

2) In matrimonial law the Rota uses the term mainly with the same acceptance, preferring other terms in the case of mental debility or passing mental disturbance, e.g., *vitium mentis, morbus mentis, mentis debilitas, defectus internae libertatis, defectus debitae discretionis,* etc.

3) The phrase "due discretion" is all-inclusive, is strictly a legal phrase, and is undefined except that it includes all psychic disorders and defects whereby marriage is null.

4) The term *amentia* in canon 1089, §3, has probably been extended. Whereas, when the Code was promulgated it was probably understood as referring to those who completely lost the use of reason, now it is rather clear upon the elucidation of Rotal jurisprudence, that it includes those who retain the mere use of reason, but who, at the time of the proxy ceremony, have been rendered naturally unfit for marriage by the strict diriment impediment of defect of due discretion — *subiectum incapax assumendi iura et obligationes essentialia contractus maritalis* — even if, perchance, they still be capable of eliciting marital consent naturally sufficient to initiate the bond in the normal person. Their status at the time of the proxy ceremony is that of the person in whom incurable impotence has supervened.

5) The term *amentia* in canon 1982 now extends to cases of nullity wherein the person, although possessing the the use of reason, was incapable of eliciting true matrimonial consent. But it does not seem to include cases of nullity by reason of defect of consent due to passing mental disturbance, for example, cases pleaded on the grounds of lack of consent due to drunkenness, drugs, hypnosis, etc. There is no juridical obligation to employ experts in

these latter cases.[80] On the other hand, the phrase "*defectus consensus*" does not seem to be restrictive. In other words, the legislator is not ruling out the necessity of employing experts in cases of invalidating *amentia* which do not involve a defect of consent. Thus, experts are necessary in cases of psychic disorder which, while invalidating the contract, do not necessarily render consent defective.[81]

Section B. The Legal Classification of Psychic Disorders.

It is precisely because of the irrelevance of medical distinctions and classifications of various mental disorders that the Code has seen fit (in penal law, where alone it treats *ex professo* of the effects of mental illness on imputability) to rescrict itself to a simple tripartite division. Canon 2201 distinguishes habitual insanity (§2), mental disturbance (§3), and mental debility or feeble-mindedness (§4). These three concepts can conveniently comprehend all possible psychic disorders or defects, whatever be, medically speaking, their etiology, species, duration, or gravity.

[80] C. Jullien, Feb. 23, 1935 (Vol. XXVII, 79): "Utrum vero in casu determinato tota defecerit deliberatio debita, an remanserit sufficiens lumen intellectus visque voluntatis, iudicis est aestimare, et quamvis non agatur de amentia proprie dicta [this case was one involving a plea of insufficient consent because of drunkenness and morphinism], ad quam dignoscendam lex iubet uti opera peritorum, iudex prudenter potest decernere ut periti conclusiones tradant de natura et gravitate factorum quae adducuntur ad ostendendum, quod contrahens non habuit in actu celebrationis usum rationis sufficientem."

Pickard, it would seem, fails to make this distinction. Judging from his extremely wide definition of *amentia* in canon 1982, he would logically require the use of experts in cases of alcoholic intoxication, narcotic euphoria, etc., including these causes of nullity within the term *amentia*. He writes: "So general is the term that it would embrace not only the many types of mental illness, as one generally understands them, but also characteristic types of mental deficiency... From these considerations the writer concludes that the proper interpretation of *amentia* in canon 1982 points to some form of mental disorder or abnormality which may render a person incapable of giving true matrimonial consent." — William M. Pickard, *Judicial Experts: A Source of Evidence in Ecclesiastical Trials* (Washington, D.C.: Catholic University of America Press, 1958), pp. 161, 162.

[81] C. Sabattani (Neapolitana), June 21, 1957.

1) *habitualiter amentes*: comprises all the possible mental disorders which are *per se* permanent and total;

2) *mentis exturbatio*: comprises all mental aberrations which are *per se* temporary, whether they totally or partially incapacitate.

3) *mentis debilitas*: comprises all mental defects which *per se* partially incapacitate, whether permanently or momentarily. [82]

D'Avack assumes this trichotomy of penal law and adapts it for use in the matrimonial forum, stating that such a transfer is not only legitimate, but highly feasible:

> Of all the various classifications, for my part, I still think it preferable to hold, by all means, to the basic tripartition of the Code itself, which, at least in penal law where alone it treats *ex professo* of the defect of the use of reason and its effects on imputability, distinguishes in canon 2201:
>
> a) habitual insanity; ...
> b) mental disturbance, ...
> c) mental debility... [83]
>
> Finally, I am convinced that as far as the problem of insanity in general is concerned, and that of insanity as a cause of marriage nullity in particular, the best thing that can be done in the field of law would be to adopt the system which the Code itself uses in penal law... [84]

Such a classification, as was pointed out by Ravà [85] and repeated in a recent Rotal decision, [86] cannot be legitimately

---

[82] Cf. D'AVACK, *op. cit.*, pp. 140-141; RAVÀ, *op. cit.*, pp. 393-394; MICHIELS, *Principia generalia de personis in ecclesia*, p. 72; idem, *De delictis et poenis*, I, pp. 190 ff; GENNARO J. SESTO, *Guardians of the Mentally Ill in Ecclesiastical Trials* (Washington, D.C.: Catholic University of America Press, 1956), pp. 41-42.

[83] *Loc. cit.*

[84] *Ibid.*, p. 187.

[85] *Op. cit.*, pp. 395-396.

[86] C. Sabattani (Januen.), Feb. 21, 1961, *in iure*: "Tricotomia, in canone 2201 contenta, varios dispescens mentis defectus diversosque imputabilitatis gradus, rei matrimoniali per se aptari nequit... Triplex distinctio in re poenali merito operatur, quia imputabilitas gradus nonnullos pati potest. Eadem distinctio, e contra, nihil prodest in regione contractuali, et praesertim in materia matrimoniali, quia coniugium validum vel irritum est juxta quod adsit vel desit validus consensus. Non datur tertium, quoad matrimonium. Ideo tricotomia supra relata regere non valet consensum nuptialem. Hic enim non agitur de imputabilitate actus, sed de sufficientia consensus." (*Monitor Ecclesiasticus*, LXXXVI [1961], pp. 631-632.)

transferred to matrimonial law. Penal law, which admits varying degress of imputability, rightly attaches specific effects to a mental disorder, according as it is habitual insanity, mental disturbance, or mental debility. Matrimonial law admits no such variation or gradation of psychic competence for valid marriage. The basic question in insanity cases is: was the person possessed of the minimum degree of psychic competence required for valid marriage? This prescinds not only from the fact whether the impinging mental infirmity was schizophrenia, manic-depressive psychosis, etc., but also from the above-stated "legal" classification of *amentia habitualis, mentis exturbatio,* and *mentis debilitas.* Any attempt to formulate the bearing of mental illness on the validity of the marriage contract, based solely on the specific differentiating factors of these three types, and not on their common effect (i. e. diminution or deprivation of due discretion,) is bound to be artificial, extrinsic, and inaccurate. Thus, we sometimes find such misleading maxims as: "*Ebrietas non invalidat matrimonium nisi sit perfecta, seu nisi ebrietas usum rationis adimat ex toto; mentis debilitas per se matrimonium non invalidat; amentia non invalidat nisi sit habitualis et continua,* etc." [87]

If the trichotomy is inept in delineating the *quaestio iuris,* it can be, nonetheless, quite useful in the *quaestio facti.* [88] In procedural law this legal classification can be very practical, if not at times necessary, in ascertaining the juridical effect of the mental illness on the validity of the bond. The pactical application of principles and the correct use of personal presumptions can vary according as the psychic disorder is *amentia habitualis, mentis exturbatio,* or *mentis debilitas.* For example, the presump-

---

[87] One finds such "rules" even in the commentaries of first-rate canonists. For example. CAPPELLO, *De matrimonio,* n. 579: "Alii censent amentiam semiplenam sive imperfectam impedire actum humanum ideoque obesse validae celebrationi matrimonii. Quae sententia, perspectis gravissimis officiis matrimonialis contractus eiusque perpetuitate et indissolubilitate, certa videtur... Contra nonnullos tenendum videtur, etiam eos qui *monomania* laborant, praesertim si haec praecise circa rem uxoriam versetur, inhabiles esse ad matrimonium contrahendum." REGATILLO, *Ius sacramentarium,* n. 1316: "Unde non solum amentia plena et furor, qui omnino usum rationis adimit, matrimonium dirimit; sed et ea quae infra semiamentiam vel semifurorem plus minus posita est."

[88] Cf. RAVÀ, *loc. cit.*

tions of perpetuity and continuity are valid in cases of habitual insanity, but hardly so in cases of mental disturbance. The hereditary factor might provide admissible evidence in cases of mental deficiency, but not in cases of passing disorders.

Hence, the mere classification of mental illness made in canon 2201 can be legitimately and usefully adopted in procedural law in matrimonial cases; but the transference, *mutatis mutandis,* of the legal effects upon imputability which penal law ascribes to the various types of mental disorder, may in no wise be legitimately made with the purpose of filling the lacuna of the Code by formulating similar substantive law in the matter of marriage and insanity.[89]

Article 3. THE GENERAL STRUCTURE OF PROOF.

The general structure of juridicial proof will be quite different depending on whether mental illness is considered as a cause of inability to elicit an integral act of marital consent, or rather as a natural disability residing in the subject whereby he is radically unfit for the state of matrimony, incapable by nature to assume the essential obligations of the marriage contract. If, in the juridical scheme of causes of nullity, *amentia* is considered as a defect of consent, the stream of proof will be directed solely towards the moment when consent was expressed. The person's mental condition is contrasted exclusively against his actual ability to bring to bear all the cognitional and volitional elements necessary to elicit an integral act of consent, an *actus exsistens,* a qualified human act which, legitimately manifested, would suffice, of itself, to generate the marriage bond. The testimony of witnesses, the examinations of the experts, the *praesumptiones hominis* (which play so great a role in cases of this type),[90] and all other elements of proof will aim ultimately at answering the

---

[89] Cf. *supra,* p. 9.

[90] Instructio *Provida,* art. 174: "Praesumptionibus *hominis* est potissimum locus in causis, quae spectant ad consensus defectum. Ad eas constabiliendas instructoris est curare, ut circumstantiae proferantur in lucem, quae matrimonium praecesserunt, comitatae vel secutae sunt."

pivotal question: at the very moment of contracting, was this person mentally capable of eliciting an act of marital consent naturally sufficient [91] to initiate the marriage bond? Antecedent and subsequent *amentia* will have no direct bearing on the possible invalidity of the bond; rather, they usually enter the case as necessary adjuncts in establishing the fact of concomitant, incapacitating *amentia*. Lucid intervals and remissions could change the whole picture. If the marriage is null, it will be because of a defective act of consent, an *actus inexsistens*, by its very nature insufficient to effect the contract. The *caput nullitatis* will be based on a *lex irritans* [92] of the natural law; because "*consensus erat irritus*" there was no effective cause of the marriage bond.

On the other hand, if insanity be considered a diriment impediment, the natural integrity of the act of marital consent will not be the criterion of a valid marriage. The person's mental condition will be a cause of nullity, not necessarily because it incapacitates for the act of consent during the wedding ceremony, but because it renders the person fundamentally unfit for the *state* of matrimony. Regardless of his ability to construct naturally sufficient consent during the wedding, was he then, given his natural disability, an apt subject for the state of matrimony, a *subiectum capax effective assumendi iura et obligationes essentialia contractus matrimonialis?* Even

---

[91] The question is almost universally phrased: "Was this person capable of eliciting *valid* consent?"' The phrase "naturally sufficient" seems preferable to the term "valid," a term which gives the impression that the act of consent was not only structurally integral in itself, but moreover generated its proper legal effect, viz., the marriage bond. The Code never calls consent "valid" or "invalid"; it would seem that this very question of terminology led the legislator in canon 1139, § 1, to omit the term "valid" when speaking of the sanation of marriages wherein consent had been "naturally sufficient but juridically inefficacious," lest he speak of "valid" consent to an "invalid" marriage. The *dubium* in insanity cases, moreover, is not simply whether the bond was null, but whether it was null because of defective consent, regardless of the possibility of another obstacle to validity by reason of a diriment impediment or defect of canonical form.

[92] Laws are "*irritantes*, sensu stricto, si directe respiciant ipsum *actum* a quolibet positum seu qualitatem aut circumstantiam ex parte ipsius actus requisitam (v.g. in can. 572, § 1, n. 3 et 1094)." — MICHIELS, *Normae generales juris canonici*, I (2. ed.; Parisiis-Tornaci-Romae: Desclée et Socii, 1949), p. 320.

if, given the peculiar nature of his psychic disorder, or given a true lucid interval, the person could and did elicit an integral act of consent capable of generating the contract, nevertheless his naturally sufficient consent was inefficacious because *aliunde* his disability prevented an effective exchange of rights and obligations. As the incurably impotent man, though he consent with a clear mind and full deliberation, cannot initiate the bond because he is incapable of giving an essential right and assuming an essential obligation of marriage, so also the psychically disordered man (who perhaps consciously and with clear mind and full deliberation gives consent) is naturally incapable of giving an essential right and assuming an essential obligation of matrimony. For example, the sexual psychopath afflicted by grave and incurable nymphomania may well know the substance and obligations of marriage and yet may be, willy-nilly, incapable of an effective assumption of the essential obligation of marital fidelity; she is psychically incapable of assuming a *perpetual* obligation because she compulsively needs one consort after another; or she is psychically incapable of an *exclusive* obligation, being irresistibly drawn to indulge in extramarital affairs. The simple axiom, "*nemo potest ad impossibile obligari,*" [93] is equally applicable to the marriageable status of the physically impotent and the psychically incompetent. Correlatively, a "right" to what is impossible is simply inconceivable.

In the juridical scheme of nullity causes, accordingly, *amentia* would be likened to the diriment impediments, especially that of impotence which also derives from the natural law. [94] The *caput nullitatis* would be grounded in a defect of personal capacity, sanctioned by a *lex inhabi-*

---

[93] Reg. 6 in VI°.

[94] The inherent similarity between insanity and impotence, recognized in early canonical writings, is evident in the fact that marriage necessarily supposes in the contractants both *capacitas corporis* and *capacitas animi.* "Impossibilitas coeundi vel conveniendi alia est animi tantum, alia corporis tantum, alia utriusque; animi tantum ut in furiosis, corporis ut in frigidis et maleficiis impeditis, utriusque ut in pueris et puellis." — BERNARDUS PAPIENSIS, *Summa de matrimonio,* III, n. 10 (ed. Laspeyres; Ratisbonae: apud G. Iosephum Manz, 1860, p. 301). Cf. also RUFINUS, *Summa super decretum Gratiani,* C. XXVII (ed. Singer; Paderborn: Schöningh, pp. 433-434)

litans [95] of the natural law. The marriage is null because the person was not *iure habilis.* [96]

The traditional jurisprudence of the Sacred Roman Rota has always, until very recently, sought the source of nullity in the contractant's mental inability to elicit during the wedding naturally sufficient consent. Hence it is that an analysis of general Rotal jurisprudence on insanity cases must be restricted to the structure of proof which supposes "insanity" solely as a defect of marital consent.

Section A. Some Inherent Difficulties in the *Quaestio Facti.*

Some recent writers have stated that the proof of *amentia* is easier to establish than proof of the normal defects of consent enumerated in *Caput V* of the matrimonial law of the Code. D'Avack writes:

> In the specific case of insanity, however, in reality it presents a good deal less difficulty than the defects of consent, in as much as in such a case the *defectus intellectus et voluntatis in ordine ad matrimonium* of the contractant is not the result of his conscious intellectual awareness or of a free and wilful deliberation, as is the case with the defects of consent; but it is solely the outcome of an unconscious and involuntary, intrinsic incapacity due precisely to the mental alienation. Thus, it is enough to ascertain the existence of this exterior disturbing factor to be in a position thereby to deduce immediately the existence of the related *defectus consensus* of the afflicted person, without having to investigate further about his effective state of mind or positive intention, without having to make a direct search of his effective internal will as contrasted with his manifested will, which constitutes the crucial point in cases of defect of consent. [97]

---

[95] Laws are "*inhabilitantes,* si directe respiciant agentis *personam* seu qualitatem aut circumstantiam ad ejusdem capacitatem agendi requisitam, ita ut nonnisi indirecte invalidetur actus, quia scilicet a tali persona ad eum ponendum absolute vel relative inidonea fuit positus (v.g. in can. 1067, § 1, 1072, 1075, 1076)." — Michiels, *op. cit.,* pp. 320-321.

[96] Canon 1035: "Omnes possunt matrimonium contrahere, qui *iure non prohibentur.*" Canon 1081, § 1: "Matrimonium facit partium consensus *inter personas iure habiles* legitime manifestatus...».

[97] *Cause di nullità,* p. 155. Ravà, *op. cit.,* p. 399: "Sempre in linea generale avvertiamo anche che minori difficoltà comporta l'accertamento dell'esistenza dell'*amentia* all'atto della celebrazione del matrimonio, rispetto a quelle che comporta l'accertamento dei vizi del consenso in genere."

It is indeed true that in simulation cases, for example, it is difficult to prove the existence of a positive contrary intention, a positive exclusion which is within the power of the contractant to make or not to make, and this need not (in fact, *cannot*)[98] be proved in insanity cases. But this one "advantage" hardly makes insanity cases less difficult than simulation cases. For one thing, in insanity cases, as explained above,[99] there are obscurities not only in the question of fact, but also in the question of law. And even in the question of fact, insanity cases involve peculiar difficulties not encountered in ordinary cases of defect of consent.

a) *Borderline cases.*

A basic difficulty in insanity cases is that, naturally enough, all are what we might call "borderline" cases. On the principle that no sane person wants to marry a lunatic, rarely will a case be presented to an ecclesiastical tribunal which involves a person who was openly insane on the wedding day. If the law prohibited only unmistakable psychotics from valid marriage, marriage tribunals would rarely, if ever, handle an insanity case:

> At, si eos tantummodo a contrahendo jus arcuisset, vix, et ne vix quidem, ex hoc capite causae pertractandae in Nostro foro darentur: etenim, nonnisi pari amentia laborans ad tales sibi coniugio copulandos se disponeret.[100]

The fact that an incapacitating mental disorder might well remain indiscernible to others at the time of the wedding has been acknowledged since the time of Decretal Law. In his famous decretal *Dilectus* Pope Innocent III (1198-1216) declared null the marriage of Opizo and Rufina, "*ignorans quod Opizo esset furiosus*".[101] The

---

[98] Cf. *supra* the section on contradictory *capita*, pp. 22-26.

[99] Cf. *supra*, pp. 1-5.

[100] C. Mattioli (Quebecen.), May 6, 1953. However, at least one case has come before the Rota in which the plea was "*ob amentiam utriusque partis*"; c. Pinna (Romana), Mar. 21, 1959, in second instance, and c. Doheny (Romana), Mar. 16, 1962, in third instance. Both Rotal sentences ruled "*constare de matrimonii nullitate ob amentiam viri tantum.*" The final decision added: "*vetito autem utrique parti transitu ad alium matrimonium, inconsulto H.A.T.* ».

[101] C. 24, X, IV, 1.

glossator asked how Rufina could have possibly consented to marry a lunatic; either she was a very silly girl, or, what is much more probable, she was reasonably unaware of Opizo's affliction: "*Saepe enim furiosi sunt constituti in conspectu umbratae quietis, nec tamen sunt mentis sanae, licet videantur.*" [102] It was precisely upon this observation of the glossator that later canonical doctrine and jurisprudence built its basis to extend the nullity of the bond to all cases involving not only an *alienatio furiosa,* but also any form of *insania quieta,* that is practically speaking, to all forms of insanity without distinction. This was a logical extension since the *mens legis,* that is, the basis for the nullity recognized in the *Dilectus,* did not reside in the manner in which the alienation manifested itself (whether manic or depressive), but rather in its effects on the intellect and will of the afflicted person. It is only to be expected that insanity cases encountered in ecclesiastical tribunals treat of "*insania quieta.*" [103] On the other hand, not everyone who behaves strangely, is insane. [104] Drawing the line between "sane" and "insane" is an almost impossible task, even for the experts. Henry Weihofen writes:

> A century ago, "mental disease" was a fairly clear concept; all such disease was thought to be the product of lesions in the brain. Today, psychiatrists recognize that many mental disorders seem to be wholly functional; a post-mortem examination shows no organic pathology of any kind. So long as organic pathology was assumed to be involved, it was possible to regard the mentally ill as clearly distinct from those who were "sane". But since the recognition of functional disorders, and especially since Freud, the view that there is a clear, qualitative division between the sane and the mentally ill has largely been abandoned in favor of the

---

[102] Glossa in v. *Furore.*

[103] 'Unde nil mirum si quis appareat adhuc sua posse apte agere et ordinare negotia, qui tamen ad matrimonium censeri incapax debeat."; c. Teodori, Jan. 19, 1940 (Vol. XXXII, 83).

[104] "Qui indole abnormi praediti sunt, saepe quidem morose agere solent ponendo actus qui admirationem vel risum provocant, sed ideo nondum sunt nec vocari possunt suae mentis haud compotes. Etenim eorum abnormitas non provenit ex deficiente usu rationis aut ex defectu libertatis, sed illi ita agunt partim ex malignitate vel morositate, partim ex ira cum sensu vindictae coniuncta, partim ex mera levitate vel ex desiderio aliter agendi ac ceteri homines."; c. Wynen, Oct. 20, 1948 (Vol. XXXX, 374).

quantitative view, that there is no such clear line between the two; there is rather an unbroken continuum from normal to abnormal. But if there is no longer merely black and white, but a continuous shading from one to the other, it becomes apparent that asking the medical expert where he draws the line between two shades of gray is not quite like asking him whether a bone is or is not fractured.[105]

b) *Indirect proof.*

The nature of mental defect is such that it does not admit direct proof of its existence and relation to a given act.[106] *Amentia* is an internal affliction whose effects on external behavior can indeed be perceived by the senses, but whose effects on the *psychic ability to construct true marital consent* cannot be ascertained by the senses directly:

> Probatio directa non est possibilis; est enim amentia morbus in mente latens, qui sensibus non percipitur; sed admittitur probatio indirecta, quae conficitur recurrendo ad coniecturas et praesumptiones verbis et factis innixas, quae sanae menti repugnant; ab effectibus enim causa rite deducitur.[107]

Thus, all proof of *amentia in ordine ad matrimonium* will be indirect in the sense that from the external evidence of the damaging effects of this affliction on the person's general thought and behavior, one can conjecture or presume the nature and degree of its damaging effect on the faculties and powers employed in positing marital consent. Such conjectures and presumptions, it is true, must be built on external *facts* perceptible and verifiable by the senses; nevertheless, as the Dean of the Spanish Rota has observed, "Though not difficult to construct in some cases, in others they leave a strong sense of uncertainty."[108]

Indirect proof through conjectures and presumptions is often rendered even more difficult because of the unreliability of the testimony of witnesses in this type of marriage case. There is the common belief that the ad-

---

[105] WEIHOFEN, *op. cit.*, p. 198.

[106] "...potest sane medicus *directe* excludere fluxum veri seminis, non vero validi consensus." — c. Sabattani (Januen.), Mar. 14, 1959, *in iure.*

[107] C. Rossetti, May 10, 1921 (Vol. XIII, 88).

[108] MIGUÉLEZ, in his presentation to Castañeda's *La locura y el matrimonio*, p. XII.

mission of insanity in one member of the family carries with it a shameful stigma for the entire family; often too, because of the intimate bond between members of the same family, the abnormalities of one will be benignly attributed to other causes.[109] If there are other members of the family who are planning marriage, their marriage chances might be ruined.[110] Sometimes a financial reason can color the testimony of the family.[111]

The testimony of the accusing partner must be carefully weighed also. It is usually the case that he is accusing the validity of the marriage on the grounds that the defendant was insane on the wedding day, athough he himself, who was probably most interested in ascertaining the normal mental condition of his future spouse, suspected nothing at the time. Athough the Rota certainly accepts the adage that love is blind,[112] and hence the

109 "Hi enim ad vindicandam sanitatem mentis necessarii sui trahuntur praeter quam affectu erga ipsum, proprio quodam commodo, cum debilitas mentis unius, iudicio vulgi, in probrum ipsius familiae convertatur." — c. Felici (Quebecen.), Dec. 3, 1957, *in iure*, in *Monitor Ecclesiasticus*, LXXXIII (1958), p. 51. "In causis, quae promoventur ob insaniam unius ex coniugibus — animadverterunt Patres — non valde consideranda esse, generatim loquendo, testimonia quae redduntur in foro a consanguineis infirmi, vel ab ipso infirmo: sive quia agitur de personis incompetentibus, sive quia consanguinei difficillime percipiant naturam et gravitatem similium morborum, in quibus, jure vel injuria, dedecus maximum conspicitur pro tota familia." — c. Filipiak (Parisien.), Nov. 15, 1957.

110 "Addatur morbum, de quo in themate, cum membrum unum alicuius familiae offendit, cetera rubore ac verecundia quadam frequentissime afficere: ob facilem nempe, ac rationabilem timorem, quo omnes agitantur, communem aestimationem amittendi, tamquam a progenie infecta descendentes et impuro sanguine dotati. Et id quam maxime contingit cum de eadem familia sunt (prout in casu) aliae puellae matrimonio mox collocandae, vel nuper collocatae: quibus periculum incumbit vel quod sponsus eas derelinquat, vel quod mariti dilectio attenuetur." — c. Mattioli (Quebecen.), May 6, 1953, *in facto*, in *Monitor Ecclesiasticus*, LXXX (1955), p. 622.

111 "Quam maxime autem eiusmodi manifestationes peritum a Tribunali ecclesiastico designatum [familiares] celant, quia ex declaratione nullitatis matrimonii magnum damnum oeconomicum et morale paterentur. Nam, matrimonio nullo declarato ex dementia uxoris, domestici tenentur eam alere et eiusdem deliramenta ferre." — c. De Jorio (Taurinen.), Dec. 19, 1961, *in iure*.

112 "Neque mittendum est aliquas ingenii abnormitates minoris fieri momenti ad amante, quinimo et in bonum sensum verti, iuxta illud Horatii: 'amatorem quod amicae turpia decipiunt caecum vitia, aut etiam ipsa haec delectant.' (Serm. I, 3, 38-40)." — c. Felici (Quebecen.), Dec. 3, 1957, *in iure*, in *Monitor Ecclesiasticus*, LXXXIII (1958), p. 51.

partner should not be expected to evaluate correctly mental abnormalities in his fiancée, nonetheless, the partner, in search of liberty now, will often feel free to opine the mental condition of his spouse at the time of the wedding, judging from subsequent behavior. The evaluation of the symptoms belongs rather to the court experts.

But even the experts' estimation of the mental condition of the defendant is not always built on solid footing. For one thing, the conclusions of the experts will always be *a posteriori.* Only in light of the subsequent course of the illness does the expert find himself in a position to "project" into the past and conjecture the effects of the affliction on the defendant's power of due discretion at the time of the ceremony. It sometimes happens that the experts build their projection upon "facts" which have not been proved judicially,[113] or they might hold "legal" notions which are false, having too wide a conception of what is demanded for true matrimonial consent.[114] Athough the experts chosen by the ecclesiastical tribunals will usually be men of sound prin-

---

[113] "At periti possunt quandoque ex aliquibus factis insaniam deducere, quae tamen ad normam iuris plene evicta non sunt: quo in casu iudex nec potest nec debet eorum conclusiones amplecti." — c. Parrillo, Feb. 16, 1928 (Vol. XX, 71). "Contingere enim potest ut peritus, cuius scientia extra dubium ponitur, conclusiones tamen deducat ex factis quae iuridice non sint probata, aut quae, ambiguitate quadam involuta, possint, attentis aliis a perito non consideratis, conducere ad alias conclusiones." — c. Jullien, Dec. 16, 1936 (Vol. XXVIII, 771).

[114] For example, in the decision c. Many, Aug. 11, 1913 (Vol. V, 562-573), the expert thought that the law demanded that the person have an ethical and religious appreciation of marriage. The sentence c. Grazioli, Feb. 16, 1928 (Vol. XX, 57-81), relates that the expert demanded for valid marriage "the plenitude of human personality, the full use of the mental faculties." The decision c. Wynen, Feb. 27, 1937 (Vol. XXIX, 169-196), rejected the conclusions of the expert who demanded that the person have the power of logical reflection and differentiation of the various aspects of marriage, its goodness and usefulness. In the celebrated decision c. Wynen of Feb. 25, 1941 (Vol. XXXIII, 144-168), the experts demanded a special power of ethical, social, and religious evaluation of marriage. In all these cases the opinion of the experts was rejected as a false legal notion of true marital consent. A very recent Rotal sentence states: "Subveniunt equidem periti, sed hi quandoque accidit ut indulgeant doctrinis vanis et peregrinis, quin id persentiant, et saepius, cum putent iuridice necessarium quod ethice tantum requiritur, ut sua ipsorum probitate decipiantur." — c. Fiore (Romana), May 16, 1961, *in iure.*

ciples, it can sometimes happen that some court psychiatrists hold a philosophical doctrine which too readily admits the extinction of responsibility and free will.[115] Even in the strictly medical sphere, doctors can make mistakes,[116] and the danger is greater in the still groping science of psychiatry.[117] Different backgrounds deriving from contrasting schools of psychiatry can lead court experts to contradictory conclusions from an identical starting point, i. e., from the judicially proved facts.[118] It is not, of course, the part of the judge to settle medical controversies; in case of conflicting medical opinions, he has the not altogether easy task of evaluating them, adhering to that which is the more reasonable and better informed,[119] expressing, at the same time, the reasons which

---

115 "Nevertheless, in certain psychiatric groups, it has become a sign of modernity and scientific maturity to go all out for determinism, to believe that man is a helpless victim of his genes and his environment. To subscribe to this is a symbol that one is not dragging one's scientific heels. The more sage leaders of American psychiatry, however, have accepted the fact that man is not without freedom of choice." — MANFRED S. GUTTMACHER, "The Psychiatric Approach to Crime and Correction." *Criminal Psychology*, p. 115.

116 "Nam, inter omnes constat medicos non raro errare et inter se discrepare cum in morbis corporis tum in aegritudinibus mentis dignoscendis." — c. Wynen, Mar. 1, 1930 (Vol. XXII, 136).

117 "In re autem psychologica facilis errandi aperitur via et multis arbitriis materia subiecta esse potest." — c. Felici (Quebecen.), Dec. 3, 1957. "...cautissime consideranda sunt vota psychiatrorum, qui nihilominus declarant defuisse aliquod elementum essentiale validi consensus. Siquidem adaequate describere actiones facultatum spiritualium hominis, iam theorice est res ardua, quae per plus quam duo millia annorum, ab Aristotele usque ad hodiernam diem, occupavit et etiam nunc occupat mentem virorum maxime acutorum et perspicacium, speculationi metaphysicae et investigationi vere deditorum. Neque minus difficile est in casu practico alicui homini, sufficienti intelligentia communi ac libero arbitrio praedito, abiudicare facultatem ponendi actum vere humanum, saltem quoad obiectum determinatum de quo agitur, v.g. matrimonium." — c. Wynen, Feb. 25, 1941 (Vol. XXXIII, 152).

118 "...immo augetur difficultas ex eo quod non raro diversarum scholarum psychiatrae eamdem non participant sententiam hac in re..." — c. Lefebvre (Quebecen.), Apr. 7, 1960, *in iure*.

119 "Non est quidem iudicis controversias in re medicali dirimere, est autem videre quaenam ex diversis sententiis melius rationi et hodiernis theoriis accommodatur." — c. Rogers (Neo-Eboracen.), Dec. 1, 1960, *in facto*. "Dissentientibus vero inter se peritis super casu specifico, non illico concludendum est rem non probari, sed iis assentiendum, qui melius videntur informati vel, ceteris paribus, illis qui magis matrimonio favent." c. Lefebvre (Drepanen.), Oct. 17, 1959, *in iure*.

moved him to accept or to reject the conclusions of the experts. [120]

c) *"A posteriori" proof.*

It is a fact that insanity does not ordinarily strike a person suddenly. *"Regulariter ad amentiam pervenitur sensim sine sensu."* Usually the symptoms and pathological manifestations come to light only after a more or less extended period of latent "incubation" during which the person gradually loses his power of due discretion. Thus, athough the principle holds that insanity is presumed to exist only from the moment in which it is positively ascertained, nevertheless, given the nature of the psychic defect, and given the *curriculum vitae* of the person's thought and behavior patterns from before the wedding to the present, the mental status of the contractant is usually established through a conjectured "projection" into the past. In fact, it not unusually happens that such an *"a posteriori"* proof is the only possible way to ascertain the defect of due discretion concomitant with the wedding.

> Exinde, non mirum est quod judicium certum solummodo a posteriori generatim proferri possit; cum, nempe, singula facta, quae, varii quidem ponderis. et aliquando exigui, inter temporis lapsus longe diversos contigerant, sub luce finalis ruinae, in sua veritate appareant, ac manifesto constet ipsa nil aliud fuisse quam passus, communi ac latenti impetu positos versus unius eiusdemque morbi phasem terminalem. [121]

Often it happens that abnormal manifestations of thought and behavior which took place prior to the wedding, are, at that time, highly ambiguous signs at best. Only in light of the subsequent course of the illness can they be reduced to a certain diagnosis. [122] Add to this that usually a case will be started in the tribunal only many years after the wedding. [123] If we stop to think exactly what is the point to

---

[120] Instructio *Provida,* art. 154; canon 1804, § 2.

[121] C. Mattioli (Quebecen.). May 6, 1953, *in iure,* in *Monitor Ecclesiasticus,* LXXX (1955), pp. 618-619.

[122] "Ea enim quae nuptias praecesserunt non sunt aestimanda nisi lumine adhibito eorum quae subsecuta sunt... » — c. Bejan (Quebecen.), Feb. 26, 1959, *in iure.*

[123] One Rotal decision had to do with a case that was started twenty-four years after the wedding (c. Pinna, Oct. 30, 1958); another, after

be elucidated, we see that it is a rather tenuous thing at best to prove or bring to light, namely, the quality of an internal act that took place many years previous, banking only on conjectures and presumptions. That such cases are difficult in the question of fact there can be no doubt, and Rotal decisions have pointed up the fact repeatedly.[124]

Section B. *Praesumptiones Hominis* AND THE *Favor Matrimonii.*

Probably in no other type of marriage case does proof rest more heavily on personal presumptions. This can present a problem, both theoretical and practical, when some of the basic personal presumptions seem to militate against the validity of the bond in direct antithesis to the "queen" of presumptions, the *favor matrimonii.* The seeming conflict is best exemplified in the personal presumption of continuity, so often employed in insanity cases with decisive emphasis. The presumption of continuity is usually stated thus:

> In dubio utrum matrimonium tempore amentiae initum sit, an in lucido intervallo, censetur initum tempore amentiae, quia agitur de morbo natura sua perpetuo et insanabili, ideoque praesumitur durare omni tempore. Unde, probata amentia antecedenti et subsequenti, etiam amentia concomitans iure admittenda est.[125]

---

twenty-seven years (c. Wynen, Mar. 1, 1930); in another, the expert made his report thirty-two years after the wedding (c. Jullien, July 30, 1932).

[124] "Iudicium proferre circa talem incapacitatem in casu particulari est res ardua." — c. Teodori, Jan. 19, 1940 (Vol. XXXII, 84). "In praxi itaque de tali incapacitate decernere, negocium est difficilis solutionis." c. Mannucci, Aug. 8, 1931 (Vol. XXIII, 373). "Utcumque autem certum sit amentes qua tales arceri a valido matrimonio contrahendo, nihilominus saepe difficile est morali cum certitudine discernere, an certus quidam homo in contrahendo sui non compos fuerit, aut habitu aut saltem actu. Siquidem difficultas talem quaestionem dirimendi provenit partim ex eo, quod agitur de morbo mentis qui non semper, ne a peritis quidem, facile cognosci potest; partim ex eo, quod nonnisi in casibus rarissimis aliquis homo mente sanus nuptias inire praesumit cum comparte, cuius infirmitas mentalis est conclamata et certa. Generatim potius accidit, ut amentia alicuius coniugis tempore demum vitae coniugalis manifesta fiat et ut consequens accusatio matrimonii ex parte alterius coniugis nitatur assertione coniugem infirmum iam tempore nuptiarum vere amentem fuisse. Quod eruere, saepe sane arduum est." — c. Wynen, June 3, 1939 (Vol. XXXI, 372-373).

[125] CAPPELLO, *De matrimonio,* n. 580, 3°.

Hence, if there is doubt whether the person lacked due discretion for valid marriage at the time of entering the contract, the judge may presume that he *did* lack due discretion, if it is proved that both before and after the wedding the person certainly lacked due discretion because of a chronic mental disorder or disease. Yet, it would seem that in light of the *legal* presumption of the *favor matrimonii*, the judge must hold for the validity of the bond when there is doubt about the existence of an effective cause of nullity; consequently, it seems, he should hold for the presence of due discretion at the time of the wedding as far as his ultimate decision is concerned.

Accordingly, Oesterle calls the presumption of continuity an "exception" to the *favor matrimonii*, since in the settled jurisprudence of the Roman Rota, it seems to override the legal presumption of the validity of the bond.[126] Others, perhaps, might attribute its predominance to equity in the sense that the judge, motivated by the "*lex suprema, salus animarum*", may, when the validity of the marriage is doubtful, rule for invalidity and allow a second marriage when the peculiar circumstances or spiritual necessity of the partners seem to call for it.[127]

On the general relationship between legal presumptions and personal presumptions which pertain to doubtful marriage cases, Doheny writes:

> The value and force ascribed to presumptions of law by the law itself cannot be rendered nugatory by any doubt or any *praesumptio hominis* arising from circumstances, inferences, or indications. Such arbitrary procedure would mean that the judges were preferring their own conjectures on an uncertain matter to the probable and legally recognized conjecture of the law itself. As is to be expected, the presumption established and recognized by the law itself always supersedes and even supplants a *praesumptio hominis*, unless the contrary is definitely proved, as Reiffenstuel aptly observes: "*Praesumptio juris praevalet praesumptioni hominis hancque tollit nisi contrarium illius probetur.*"[128]

---

[126] GERARDUS OESTERLE, O.S.B., "De praesumptionibus in jure matrimoniali," *Revista Española de Derecho Canónico*, IV (1949), p. 9.

[127] Cf. K. L. RECKERS, "De favore quo matrimonium gaudet in iure canonico," *Ephemerides Iuris Canonici*, VI (1950), p. 533.

[128] WILLIAM J. DOHENY, *Canonical Procedure in Matrimonial Cases*, Vol. I, *Formal Judicial Procedure* (2d ed.; Milwaukee: Bruce, 1948), p. 423. The final citation is to Reiffenstuel, *Ius canonicum*, Lib. II, Tit. XXIII, n. 92

An anonymous author in an article entitled "Incipit lamentatio vinculi" states under n. 64: *"Contra iuris praesumptionem praesumptio hominis vix admittitur."* [129] A recent Rota decision, however, rebuked the lower court for being influenced by this article, saying that if this principle were true, then it is unintelligible why the *favor matrimonii* and other legal presumptions that militate for validity would not overrule *all* contrary proofs. The Rota states that legal presumptions *de iure simpliciter* yield to contrary evidence, and personal presumptions can well present contrary evidence. [130]

Certainly, it will sometimes happen that two presumptions — the one a legal presumption, the other a personal presumption, both equally applicable in a single case — will be directly opposed. Which one should prevail? [131] We think that the question, stated thus, is incorrectly stated.

The judge may, with the help of legitimate personal presumptions, attain to moral certitude of the invalidity of the marriage. In such a case, the *favor matrimonii* cannot be invoked. One cannot say that personal presumptions prevail over, supersede, or override the *favor matrimonii* in such a case, for the *favor matrimonii* does not even enter a case unless, after all the admissible evidence has been evaluated (including that gained by personal presumptions), there is still a *reasonable* doubt in favor of validity. [132] Certainly, the existence of *amentia* at the very moment of the wedding must be rigorously proved in court, as all causes of nullity must be; it is never presumed but must be proved. *As long as such proof has not been positively produced,* the general presumption of the *favor matrimonii* is operative. [133]

---

129 *Apollinaris,* XII (1939), p. 381.

130 Cf. c. Wynen, May 6, 1941 (Vol. XXXIII, 370).

131 Even with the question stated thus, the above-mentioned Rotal decision quoted Schmalzgrueber with approval: "Si praesumptio hominis validior et verisimilior est, contra iuris etiam praesumptionem praevalet." — *Ius ecclesiasticum universum,* Lib. II, Tit. XXIII, n. 38.

132 Instructio *Provida,* art. 172: "Dubium sive iuris sive facti, quod faveat matrimonio, debet esse prudens, seu probabili fundamento nixum, ut praesumptioni pro matrimonii valore locus sit."

133 LUDOVICUS BENDER, O.P., *Dubium in Codice Iuris Canonici* (Romae: Desclée & C., 1962), p. 91: "Animadvertendum tamen strenue est quod can. 1014 tantummodo praebet normam agendi circa ipsam matrimonii

There are two extremes which must be avoided in this delicate matter. On the one hand, the *favor matrimonii* is not to be minimized in insanity cases. D'Avack states (inaccurately, it seems), that once the existence of *any* chronic mental disorder has been positively established, one should immediately presume that it constitutes an effective cause of nullity; the burden of proof rests with him who asserts the validity of the bond and the *favor matrimonii* becomes inoperative.[134] On the other hand, one must not be misled by certain phrases found both in Rotal jurisprudence and in canonical writings which seem to demand extraordinary contrary proof before the *favor matrimonii* becomes inoperative.[135] While the legal presumption of canon 1014 is *iuris simpliciter*, it is incorrect to apply the division of "slight, probable, or violent" to *any* legal presumption. Moreover, as Flatten points out, phrases such as "*nisi concludentissimis argumentis contrarium probetur*", or "*evidentibus argumentis probare*", do not place a limitation on the scope of admissible proofs, nor do they suppose that more than the normal measure of moral certitude be demanded:

> Id tantum dicitur illis phrasibus, ad probandum contrarium, uti pro qualibet, absque exceptione, judiciali probatione, argumenta concludentia requiri quibus judex omni prudenti eximatur dubio et morali instruatur certitudine. Verbis igitur illis probatio obscura vel insufficiens rejicitur; non probatio exigitur potioribus aucta qualitatibus.[136]

---

validitatem, *stante dubio.* Canon non praebet normam agendi quoad actus, quorum effectus est *ipsius dubii* solutio."

[134] "...una volta dimostrata positivamente l'esistenza di una qualunque *amentia habitualis,* la presunzione del *favor matrimonii* viene senz'altro meno e l'*amentia* si presume *a priori* costituire un'*amentia in actu matrimonii, in ordine ad matrimonium* e *in gradu proportionato matrimonio,* cioè appunto di natura tale da configurare un impedimento ed una correlativa causa di nullità del vincolo matrimoniale." — D'AVACK, *Cause di nullità,* p. 184.

[135] E.g., "nisi contrarium *concludentissime* evincatur, nisi contrarium *manifestissime* constet, etc." Thus Holböck speaks of the *favor matrimonii*: "Haec praesumptio regina est aliarum praesumptionum, nullaque ratio habenda est de oppositis exceptionibus, quando illae non sunt adeo perstringentes et efficaces, ut concludentissime evincant praetensam matrimonii nullitatem " — *Tractatus de jurisprudentia Sacrae Romanae Rotae,* p. 43.

[136] HENRICUS FLATTEN, "Qua libertate iudex ecclesiasticus probationes appretiare possit et debeat," *Miscellanea in memoriam Petri Card. Gasparri* (Romae: Pontificia Universitas Lateranensis, 1960), p. 204. Flatten

Hence, the *favor matrimonii* becomes inoperative when the weight of contrary evidence, as duly evaluated by the judge, effectively excludes all reasonable and prudent doubt of the invalidity of the bond; legitimately employed personal presumptions which seem to militate against the validity of the marriage, are a contributing factor to the "weight of evidence". And in insanity cases, they are an essential factor. But in no sense are they rightly called "exceptions" to the *favor matrimonii.*

Section C. "Objective" and "Subjective" Legal Criteria.

The problem of the invalidating force of mental impairment on the marriage contract can be considered from two sides, as, in fact, Rotal jurisprudence has considered it. There is question of the objective psychic disorder which impinges, and the subjective faculties which are impinged upon. Thus, in establishing a legal criterion, one might consider the affliction itself and ask what objective qualities it must present in order that it invalidate marriage; or one might consider the subject and ask what minimum discretion he must retain in order to be mentally competent for valid marriage. The first criterion might be called, for lack of better terminology, the "objective" criterion; the second, the "subjective" criterion.

a) *The "objective" test.*

The general problem of relating a state of mind to a particular act, or rather, of ascertaining the effects of mental impairment on the imputability of juridical acts, is resolved in a threefold characteristic of the mental disorder: 1) the person must be shown to have been laboring under the psychic disorder *at the very moment* when

---

quotes Eichmann-Mörsdorf: "Erroneum est, praescriptum canonis 1869, § 4, ita intellegere, ac si ad dirimendas lites quibus Jus favet, major requireretur gradus certitudinis moralis; utut haec opinio valde divulgata sit, tamen quavis basi legali caret. Heic ut alibi simplex certitudo moralis sufficit." — Eduard Eichmann und Klaus Mörsdorf, *Lehrbuch des Kirchenrechts auf Grund des Codex Juris Canonici,* III (8. ed.; Paderborn, 1954), p. 176, nt. 4.

he placed the act; 2) it must be shown that the disorder had *a causal connection* with the act in question so that either the act would not have been placed except for the disorder, or, at least, the act was somehow the product of the disorder; (3) at that moment the disorder or defect was *serious to such a degree* as to render the act invalid or the criminal act unimputable.[137]

Although in insanity cases the question is not precisely about the *imputability* of the act of consent, but about its *sufficiency*, nonetheless, these general principles have been applied to marital consent both by Rotal jurisprudence and by canonical writers.[138] The result is what we might call the "objective" test. In order that psychic disorder or defect have truly invalidating force upon marriage, effectively preventing sufficient consent, it must present the following three characteristics simultaneously:

1) *Amentia concomitans*: The mental affliction must be proved to have existed at the very moment when consent was manifested. Neither antecedent nor subsequent insanity has any direct bearing on the possible invalidity of the bond; they usually enter the case as indispensable indications of the fact of concomitant insanity.

2) *Amentia matrimonialis*: The disorder or defect must be of such a nature that it impinges upon that sphere of mental activity which has to do with eliciting matrimonial consent. Thus, perhaps, a certain disorder might affect the thought and behavior of a person in the area of job, school, social relationships, etc., but not affect the psychic process of constructing marital consent.

3) *Amentia perfecta seu plena*: The disorder must affect the "matrimonial" sphere of thought and behavior at the time of the wedding to such a degree that the ability to elicit true matrimonial consent is precluded. The gravity of the disorder is of paramount importance.

Such an "objective" test cannot prescind from the "subjective" requirements on the part of the contractant,

---

137 Cf. MICHIELS, *Principia generalia de personis in ecclesia*, pp. 74-75.

138 Cf. D'AVACK, *Cause di nullità*, pp. 150 ff.; CHARLES LEFEBVRE, "*Demence*," *DDC*, IV, col. 1108; FÄSSLER, *Die Schizophrenie als Ehenichtigkeitsgrund im kanonischen Recht*, pp. 51-52; CONTE A CORONATA, *Institutiones*, III, *De matrimonio*, n. 438.

for how can a mental disorder be judged "perfect" unless we know what the indispensable minimum psychic capacity is which must remain intact? Or how can a mental defect be judged "matrimonial" — a vague term at best, even in the commentaries which treat our material at length — unless we know precisely what psychic powers are essential in the internal formation of, specifically, matrimonial consent? Ravà could easily conclude, therefore: "In other words, it is never possible to ascertain the existence of *amentia* when only the objective elements are taken into account." [139]

b) *The "subjective" test.*

The subjective test will be founded on an analysis of the minimum psychic powers which may not be missing in the formation of true matrimonial consent. In this regard, there are negative norms and positive norms. A negative norm states what may not be missing. Thus, the mental ability to understand the rudimentary nature of marriage as stated in canon 1082, §1, provides a negative norm. If a person is incapable to this extent, he is certainly mentally incapable of marrying. But the fact that a person does have this fundamental power does not indi-

---

139 RAVÀ, "Il *defectus discretionis iudicii* come causa di nullità del matrimonio nella giurisprudenza rotale," *Il Diritto Ecclesiastico*, LXVIII (1957), II, p. 422.

Writes d'Avack: "Come invero ho già avuto occasione di rilevare, nel diritto in generale ed in quello canonico matrimoniale in particolare, l'accertamento di quella che può essere stata la *maturitas judicii* dell'*amens* riguardo ad un qualunque atto in genere e al matrimonio in specie, deve raggiungersi attraverso un'indagine non solo obbiettiva, ma anche e sopratutto subbiettiva, cioè deve desumersi non soltanto da quella che risulta essere la natura e la gravità obbiettiva dell'*amentia* stessa in quel dato momento, ma insieme e sopratutto sia dall'analisi delle personali qualità intellettive e volitive di quel singolo individuo che ne è affetto, sia dall'esame della natura e caratteri del'atto specifico che esso va a compiere o ha già compiuto. È evidente infatti che una medesima species di *amentia*, pur presentando il medesimo grado obbiettivo di gravità, può poi per un soggetto costituire una semplice *amentia imperfecta* e per un altro invece una vera *amentia perfecta*, così come può nel medesimo soggetto essere tale rispetto a determinati atti e non esserlo invece rispetto ad altri." — *op. cit.*, p. 186.

C. Bejan (Quebecen.), Feb. 26, 1959, *in iure*: "Quaecumque fuerit natura et gravitas infirmitatis mentis, semper manet solvenda quaestio: utrum die celebrati matrimonii, pars morbo revera ita laboraverit ut consensum validum emittere nequiverit."

cate that he is thereby mentally capable of valid marriage. There are other powers required that a person be mentally competent for marriage. A positive norm, on the other hand, states the mental competence which is *necessary* and *sufficient* for valid marriage.

Rotal jurisprudence has elucidated several negative norms but has not been content with only that. For a negative norm does not draw a line between psychic competence and psychic incompetence. If we are not mistaken, the most recent jurisprudence of the Sacred Roman Rota has pointed out the elements of a truly positive legal test of minimum psychic competence for valid marriage. A positive test is decisive and universal and unique. If a person meets this test, he is psychically competent; if he fails to meet this test, he is psychically incompetent.

The Rota has come upon this positive subjective test through the evolution of the notion of "due discretion". Although in early jurisprudence the term "discretion" was used in various restricted senses, it now seems settled in jurisprudence that "due discretion" serves as the unique test of minimum mental competence.[140] Such a legal test can prescind from all the "objective" qualities of the mental disorder; as long as the disorder deprives the contractant of "due discretion" the marriage is null, whether he suffers from *amentia habitualis, mentis exturbatio,* or *mentis debilitas,* whether he is afflicted by a psychosis, psychoneurosis, mental deficiency, or a psychopathy, whether "*amentia*" or "*dementia*", whether congenital or accidental, whether terminal or initial in its development, whether "perfect" or "imperfect".

In Chapter II we shall treat of the objective test. Although it is insufficient in itself as a legal test, yet its description reflects well the developing jurisprudence of the Roman Rota, various relevant controversies, and the formation of many presumptions which are vital in the adjudication of insanity cases. In Chapter III we shall attempt to outline what appears to be the positive legal test of minimum psychic competence, based on the most recent developments in Rotal jurisprudence.

---

140 "Unica mensura sufficientis consensus est discretio judicii matrimonio proportionata..." — c. Sabattani (Januen.), Feb. 24, 1961, *in iure.*

Scholion 1. REGARDING SIMPLE CONVALIDATION.

At first sight it might seem a dangerous oversight on the part of the Rota that no account is taken of the possibility of a private convalidation of marriage impugned on the grounds of mental incompetence at the time of the wedding. It would seem that convalidation in many instances is possible merely by cohabitation or intercourse performed with marital affection during a lucid interval or after the cause for the mental incompetence has ceased. Bossio writes:

> If the marriage was solemnly celebrated according to the Tridentine form and the impediment of insanity was occult, and if the sane partner did not revoke consent elicited in the beginning, I would judge that the marriage is convalidated by the act of copula performed with marital affection or by mutual cohabitation... The reason is that, in this case, internal consent is enough on the part of the insane spouse and such cohabitation with marital affection is equivalent to internal consent. [141]

A pre-Code Rotal decision spoke on the point when the question was brought up by the Defender of the Bond. Doheny writes:

> Finally, there could have been no question of private convalidation of the marriage by Nuntius alone after his illness without an explicit manifestation of his consent according to the juridical form required by the Church: "Quando enim ex una parte defectus consensus est etiam externus, et ita quidem ut sit publicus, seu iuridice probari possit in foro externo, tunc ad revalidandum matrimonium non sufficit renovatio consensus implicita. aut etiam explicita, sed requiritur ut renovetur consensus coram parocho et testibus, uti communiter docent Canonistae. Quod cum in casu nostro factum non fuerit, matrimonium remanet in sua nullitate." [142]

This case, however, is no real indication of the general problem; much less does it argue for the fact that insanity causes always a defect of consent which is exter-

---

[141] *De matrimonii contractu tractatus* (Venetiis, 1643), Cap. IIII, n. 60, as quoted by Castañeda, *La locura y el matrimonio*, p. 39.

[142] DOHENY, *op. cit.*, I, p. 771, citing the decision c. Sebastianelli of Mar. 23, 1914 (Vol. VI, 151).

nal and public. This particular case was such that Nuntius moreover gave no external indication of consent during the wedding, either by word or by some equivalent sign. He acted simply like a dead man, partially unconscious from typhoid fever. Hence, not only was there an internal defect of consent, but there was no legitimate manifestation of consent.[143]

How must a marriage, null because of mental impairment, be convalidated? Professor d'Avack states that the answer depends on whether *amentia* is considered a diriment impediment or a defect of consent:

> The acceptance of one or the other qualification, besides having a direct systematic value, presents also an indirect practical repercussion as far as the institute of convalidation is concerned, that is, the repair of null marriages. As we shall see, when a marriage, invalid because of a diriment impediment, is to be convalidated, it is necessary that when the impediment ceases or is dispensed there be given ordinarily a renewal of consent by both of the contractants (cann. 1133-1135); on the other hand, when it is a question of convalidating a marriage null by reason of a defect of consent, it is enough that consent by renewed only by the partner who did not consent, or who had consented invalidly, so long as the original consent of the other partner perdures.[144]

However, it does not seem to us that the convalidation of such marriages is reducible so simply to one or another canon in the Code, depending on how one considers *amentia* in the juridical scheme of causes of nullity. First, whether simply as a defect of consent or as an impediment as conceived by d'Avack (i. e., the psychic inability to elicit true consent), there is always involved, in either case, a defect of consent. Since there can be no marriage without true consent, the partner in question must supply

---

143 "Animadvertendum tamen est secundum consensum tunc tantum sufficere quoties defectus consensus fuerit *mere internus* seu non externe manifestatus, i.e., non perceptibilis ab aliis ex signis, modo agendi aliisve elementis externis. Quoties defectus consensus sit etiam manifestatus externe, iste consensus virtualis insufficiens novo actu non substituitur consensu virtuali sufficienti, nisi novus actus seu novus consensus etiam *externe sit manifestatus,* imo in forma iuridica si defectus sit simul externus et publicus seu sic ut probari possit in foro externo." — LUDOVICUS BENDER, O.P., "Convalidatio matrimonii et defectus consensus," *Monitor Ecclesiasticus,* LXXXI (1956), p. 487.

144 *Cause di nullità,* p. 117.

sufficient consent as an essential constitutive element of marriage. Secondly, d'Avack's conception of *amentia* as an impediment does not seem to constitute a strict diriment in the language of the Code; hence, canons 1133-1135 do not seem to be applicable to the convalidation of marriages invalidly contracted by the "insane".[145]

Hence, since the defect of consent by reason of insanity is internal (i. e., there is no external manifestation of the defect during the ceremony), canon 1136, § 2, seems to be the governing norm for convalidation: "... *satis est ut pars quae non consenserat, interius consentiat.*" Furthermore, such consent can be given tacitly, e. g., by long cohabitation or by intercourse performed with marital affection.[146]

This brings us back to our original question why the Rota does not check into this possibility of easy convalidation, and why the Defender of the Bond does not offer this as an objection. The answer, it seems, lies in the fact that in order to convalidate his marriage, a person must be aware that he is in an invalid union and wishes hereby to make it valid. Rota decisions have often quoted the words of D'Annibale:

> Utrum is qui consensum supplet aut renovat, scire debeat, actum vel consensum a se praestitum (atque ideo et matrimonium) nullius momenti fuisse? Utique: alias, cum *nil volitum quin praecognitum,* non videretur consentire... absurdissimum foret, contrahere matrimonium eum, qui ignorat se matrimonium contrahere.[147]

Very rarely will it happen that partners living in an invalid union will be in a position to convalidate their marriage privately without instruction, for example, from a confessor. No one can unwittingly convalidate his marriage; that a person did in fact know of his invalid union and that he did knowingly and willingly convalidate it is a fact to be proved. The convalidation of marriage is not

---

145 Cf. *infra,* Chap. III, Part. II, Art. 3.

146 "A nemine ignoratur matrimonium nullum, ex defectu consensus interni, revalidari posse non modo per expressionem veri ac validi consensus, sed etiam per consensum tacitum: verbigr., per longam pacificam cohabitationem vel per copulam maritali affectu positam et libere acceptatam." — c. Mattioli (Platien.), May 25, 1955.

147 D'Annibale, *Summula theologiae moralis,* III, n. 483.

presumed.[148] Given these conditions, therefore, it is clear that private convalidation is a rare possibility and hence the practice of the Rota is quite reasonable.

Scholion 2. Is Marriage Consummated only by Conjugal Copula which is a Human Act?

The question might arise concerning the possibility of obtaining a dispensation *super rato* in cases wherein the marriage itself cannot be declared null for mental disorder, but wherein perhaps the valid marriage remained unconsummated because conjugal intercourse was not performed *modo naturali, modo rationali,* or *modo humano,* i. e., as a truly human act. It is asked whether a minimum degree of psychic competence or a minimum degree of actual consciousness is required during the first conjugal copula in order that the marriage be consummated and that, therefore, the specific juridical effects attributed to consummation might effectively arise. Immediately we think of marriages "consummated" by an insane spouse, or while one or both of the partners are unconscious because of intoxicating drink, the use of narcotics, aphrodisiacs, etc.

There has been a controversy on this point since 1947. In that year the Rota adjudicated a case in which the validity of the marriage was impugned on the grounds of functional impotence in the man; subordinately, in case of a negative decision regarding nullity, it was asked wheth-

---

148 "Admittendum autem non arbitramur, cohabitationem per undecim annos inter sponsos protractam, et copulam spontanee ab Anna admissam, potuisse, in casu, defectum consensum sanare. Ut enim Anna hoc facere posset, oportuisset quod illa nullitatem sui matrimoni cognovisset, illudque voluisset revalidare; et id probari deberet, quia revalidatio matrimonii non praesumitur." — c. Cattani Amadori, Mar 1, 1913 (Vol. V, 194). This case was tried on the grounds of invalidating fear. It should be noted too that neither party was bound to the Tridentine form. In another case involving a plea of fear, the Rota recently stated: "...inepte prorsus aestimaretur quis sanare seu convalidare aliquid voluisse, quod sanum prorsus ac validum (esto erronee) reputat... sicut 'scientia aut opinio nullitatis matrimonii consensum matrimonialem necessario non excludit' (c. 1085), ita, a pari, scientia aut opinio validitatis, consensus integritatem, vel validitatem, vel convalidationem, per se, non secumfert... Per hoc, iam clarissime innuitur renovationem ne concipi quidem posse, ubi scientia seu conscientia nullitatis consensus prorsus desit." — c. Mattioli (Platien.), May 25, 1955.

er the fact of inconsummation was proved and whether a dispensation *super rato* should be requested of the Holy Father. According to the evidence produced, it was established that the man could not ordinarily attain to conjugal intercourse because of a functional disorder preventing erection. On one occasion, however, through excessive use of the aphrodisiac called Yohimbina, erection was brought about; at the same time the drug deprived him of his senses. Acting like a wild man, he attained to marital intercourse. This was the only time he took the aphrodisiac and the only time he could achieve conjugal copula.

The Rota, on October 15, 1947, confirmed the negative decision of the lower court regarding nullity on the grounds of functional impotence, but answered affirmatively to the subordinate doubt concerning the fact of non-consummation, since the one act of intercourse performed was not a human act. Advised of the peculiar circumstances of the case, the Holy Father in audience on November 16, 1947, declined the concession and referred the case to the Congregation of the Holy Office, which in this particular case acted as the extraordinary delegated court of appeal in the solution of the following question:

> An matrimonium haberi debeat inconsummatum, si essentialia copulae elementa posita sint a coniuge, qui ad unionem sexualem non pervenit nisi adhibitis mediis aphrodisiacis, rationis usum actu intercipientibus?

The reply of the Holy Office, dated February 2, 1949, was: "*Negative.*"[149] Thus, the decision of the Rota was reversed.[150] Hürth and Lazzarato immediately commented on the reply, explaining that the act of consummation requires only the material placing of conjugal copula, no matter how or under what circumstances the material

---

149 Reported in *Periodica*, XXXVIII (1949), p. 220.

150 The decision c. Grazioli of Aug. 8, 1939 (Vol. XXXI, 496), had declared: "Quodsi tantum per violentos inhumanosque conatus a parte viri foret continenter obtinenda penetratio ac copula a muliere, non posset dici innaturali hac ratione haberi vera consummatio consequenterque vera potentia coeundi: quemadmodum non per remedia extraordinaria, violenta vel vitae discrimen secum ferentia diceretur adesse possibilitas sanationis ex hisce defectibus, quorum quidem perpetuitas aliud constituit requisitum ut habeatur impotentia matrimonium canonice dirimens."

union is achieved.[151] Staffa summons the weight of the more common opinion of canonists, both before and after the Code, in support of the reply.[152] Marcone proposed the thesis that since the act of consummation is a juridical act, it must necessarily be a deliberate human act.[153] Del Corpo replied that the act of consummation is not a juridical *act*, but a juridical *event* or *fact*.[154]

If it be fairly settled that the mere material act of intercourse consummates a valid marriage, it is not so certain that the ability so to consummate a marriage necessarily argues to potency. This may seem a strange statement when we are used to seeing potency defined in terms of ability to consummate a marriage.[155]

In his comments on the Holy Office reply of February 2, 1949, Hürth discusses a question left undecided, he states, in the reply itself, whether a man who could arrive at sexual union only through the use of aphrodisiacs as actually deprive him of the use of reason should be regarded as potent or impotent.[156] Staffa argued that the reply did answer this question since "*ab esse ad posse valet illatio*," i. e., from the fact that such a person does achieve consummation, he is therefore capable of placing *actus per se aptos ad prolis generationem*.[157] Lazzarato drew two

---

151 FRANCISCUS HÜRTH, S.I., "Dubia matrimonialia. III: Dubium circa consummationem matrimoni," *Periodica*, XXXVIII (1949), pp. 220-227; DAMIANUS LAZZARATO, "De copula artificiosa semel tantum admissa," *Ephemerides Iuris Canonici*, IV (1948), pp. 470-472. (Although dated 1948, this number was issud in 1949 after the reply of the Holy Office.)

152 DINUS STAFFA, "De impotentia et consummatione matrimonii," *Apollinaris*, XXVIII (1955), pp. 391-399.

153 JOSEPH MARCONE, "An matrimonium consummetur actione tantum hominis," *Monitor Ecclesiasticus*, LXXXII (1957), pp. 631-656. Marcone interprets the Holy Office reply as restricted only to those who *actu* are deprived of the use of reason; such a situation allows for a virtual intention to perform the conjugal act, which suffices for consummation. But with regard to the habitually insane, there is no virtual or habitual intention which might account for a truly juridical act. *Ibid.*, pp. 650-652.

154 AEGIDIUS DEL CORPO, "Actus hominis et actus humanus in consummatione matrimonii." *Monitor Ecclesiasticus* LXXXIII (1958), pp. 303-313. Cf. also CAPPELLO, *De matrimonio* (7. ed., 1961), n. 383; REGATILLO, *Ius sacramentarium* (3. ed., 1960), n. 1050 bis.

155 JOHN McCARTHY, "The Impediment of Impotence in the Present-day Canon Law," *Ephemerides Iuris Canonici*, IV (1948), p. 120: "So we can define impotence as the incapacity to consummate marriage."

156 HÜRTH, *op. cit.*, pp. 224 ff.

157 STAFFA, *op. cit.*, p. 395: "Quia impotens non est qui mediis aut remediis indiget ad matrimonium consummandum, impotens dicendus

conclusions from the reply of the Holy Office: (1) the insane man really consummates marriage even though it not be a human act; (2) the sadist who can arrive at sexual union only by previously inflicting great punishment upon his wife is to be considered potent, for he attains to the material act of perfect copula.[158] A Rotal decision of 1957, published in part the same year in *Monitor Ecclesiasticus*, brought to light a follow-up reply of the Holy Office regarding the original case of the marriage consummated with the use of aphrodisiacs which left the man unconscious during the act. The Holy Office was asked whether this case could be tried further on the grounds of impotence in the man. The private reply, dated May 9, 1951, stated: "*Causam sub aspectu impotentiae viri pertractari iam non posse.*"[159]

A remarkable marriage case was presented to the Worcester Tribunal for dissolution because of non-consummation or nullity because of psychic impotence.[160] It was impossible for the bride to have marital relations unless she was placed under the influence of drugs to the extent that she became unconscious or semi-conscious. The case was referred to the Sacred Congregation for the Sacraments which answered by sending the opinion of its consultor "which this Sacred Congregation adopts as its own since it is based on clear and sound reasoning." The *votum* of the consultor holds to the opinion that the conjugal act consummative of marriage need not be a human act.

---

non est qui, ob nervorum infirmitatem, vaginismum, impedimentum in vagina existens, vel aliud obstaculum aut morbum, copulam perficere nequit nisi utendo remediis valde excitantibus, aut nisi cum maxima difficultate vel gravissimis doloribus... vel post repetitos ac violentus conatus." The reasons adduced to show that a man who can attain to intercourse only by unconscious acts is potent seem to be: (1) he can place the essentials of erection, penetration, and ejaculation within the vagina; (2) "*ab agere ad posse valet illatio;*" (3) if the reply stated the marriage was consummated, it implicitly stated it to be a valid marriage and hence the man is implicitly ruled potent, for only a valid marriage can be consummated; (4) "*secus enim neque plurimis copulis, e.gr. in statu ebrietatis, aut cum invita, dicendum esset matrimonium consummari.*" — *Ibid.*, p. 399.

158 LAZZARATO, *op. cit.*, pp. 471-472.

159 Contained in passing in the decision c. Felici of Mar. 26, 1957, published in *Monitor Ecclesiasticus*, LXXXII (1957), p. 271.

160 Cf. T. LINCOLN BOUSCAREN, S. J., and JAMES I. O'CONNOR, S. J., *The Canon Law Digest, 1960 Supplement* (Milwaukee: Bruce, 1961), under canon 1118.

With regard to possible impotence, the consultor states that it is difficult that functional or psychic impotence be proved to be perpetual, an essential note of the diriment impediment. But this is a question for competent medical men to decide in a given case. "In view of these premises and considerations, the matrimonial process can be instituted in the said case after the matter has been attentively examined and after the opinion of some prudent and conscientious specialist in the matter has been sought."[161] The supposition is that if this condition is antecedent and perpetual, it constitutes the diriment impediment of impotence.

A Rotal sentence handed down December 30, 1949 (i. e., after the first reply of the Holy Office) states that a person who can place the material act of perfect copula only through intolerable pain to his partner, might well consummate the marriage; but the impediment of impotence cannot thereby be excluded.[162] Another very recent Rota decision upheld the principle of existing impotence if the person can attain to sexual union only through intrinsically evil means, provided this condition is proved to be antecedent and perpetual.[163]

---

161 The response is dated Aug. 2, 1958.

162 "Notandum demum est ad validitatem contractus requiri ut copula fieri possit modo naturali et humano. Non sufficit ergo eiaculatio seminis ad ostium vaginae etiamsi fecundatio sequatur, nec sufficit depositio seminis intra vaginam per violentiam viri non obstantibus resistentiis et intolerabilibus doloribus mulieris. Talis enim inhumanus modus agendi, etsi materialem matrimonii consummationem causat, impotentiae impedimentum excludere nequit; nam sicut nemo iure tenetur ad operationem chirurgicam subeundam quae secum fert periculum vitae, ita nemo iure tenetur ad copulam admittendam quae necessario secum fert dolores qui intolerabiles sunt." — c. Heard, Dec. 30, 1949, *Ephemerides Iuris Canonici,* VII (1951), p. 363. Cf. the comments of Giuseppe Spinelli, "In tema d'impotenza femminile per intollerabilità della copula," *Il Diritto Ecclesiastico,* LXII (1951), pp. 267-271, wherein also this decision, not subsequently published in *Sacrae Romanae Rotae Decisiones seu Sententiae,* is published in part. Cf. also Gerardus Oesterle, O.S.B., "Vera impotentia a parte mulieris?" *Il Diritto Ecclesiastico,* LXIII (1952), pp. 43-51.

An earlier Rotal decision had stated: "Quodsi tantum per violentos inhumanosque conatus a parte viri foret obtinenda penetratio ac copula a muliere, non posset dici innaturali hac ratione haberi vera consummatio consequenterque vera potentia coeundi." — c. Grazioli, Aug. 8, 1939 (Vol. XXXI, 496).

163 "Ideo, vere impotens dicendus esset: nam, id re vera nos posse teneri debet, quod jure possumus, scilicet absque Dei offensione et legis moralis injuria." — c. Mattioli (Chicagien.), Mar. 24, 1960.

In conclusion it must be said that potency and impotency, as canonical concepts, may not be resolved in the notion of the stark physical ability or inability to arrive at sexual union. As canonical concepts they have a necessary bearing on the ability of a person to enter the marriage contract. As such, they must be conceived in the order of *rights* and *obligations*. He is potent who is capable of assuming the *right and obligation* of placing *actus per se aptos ad prolis generationem;* he is canonically impotent who cannot assume the *right* and *obligation* of placing *actus per se aptos ad prolis generationem.* Hence it is that a person who can attain to material union only through sinful measures or through intolerable pain is impotent, provided the condition be antecedent and incurable by ordinary means. Thus it seems that the sadist or masochist who can arrive at sexual union only by self-mutilation or infliction of pain or mutilation on the partner is impotent; so too is the psychoneurotic who can attain to material union only through violence, trauma, or intolerable horror. Finally, it seems that he who can attain to intercourse only while unconscious or otherwise mentally deranged is also impotent, for no one is considered to possess a *right* which can be honored only by *actus hominis,* nor does a person assume an obligation *sub gravi* which can be fulfilled only by the acts of a brute.

CHAPTER TWO

PSYCHIC DISORDER OR DEFECT WHICH INVALIDATES

On the premise that mental disorder can invalidate the marriage contract in so far as it prevents the afflicted person from eliciting true and sufficient consent (the indispensable efficient cause of the marriage bond), ecclesiastical jurisprudence has developed a structure of proof defining the objective qualities of mental impairment which are necessary and sufficient to preclude true marital consent. According to classical Rotal jurisprudence, mental impairment of all types invalidates marriage if it presents concurrently three characteristics:

1) *Amentia concomitans.* Mental defect or disorder must be proved to have existed concomitantly with the expression of consent.

2) *Amentia matrimonialis.* It must be proved to have affected the specific sphere of psychic activity which produces marital consent.

3) *Amentia perfecta seu plena.* It must be proved to have been of such gravity as to effectively deprive one of the minimum degree of discretion required for placing sufficient consent.

Article 1. AMENTIA CONCOMITANS

Since the crucial point centers on the person's ability or inability to posit naturally sufficient consent for the marriage contract, it is clear that only that mental disorder is immediately relevant which exists at the very moment when the manifested will of the two parties is joined in a bilateral accord to initiate the bond. It is precisely at this moment when true and sufficient consent, which no human power can supply, may not be lacking without invalidating the contract. Mental illness prior to the wedding (*amentia antecedens*) has no direct bearing on the possible invalidity of the bond, nor, what is more important, does mental illness that follows the wedding (*amentia subsequens*).[1] Antecedent and subsequent insanity are important judicially only as a basis to establish the fact of concomitant insanity, which alone can exert an invalidating force on the contract.[2]

Historically some doubts were raised on this point. Some thought that concomitant insanity would not invalidate marriage if the afflicted person had previously made the requisite intention to marry before he fell ill; his virtual intention subsisting with the malady, it was said, would suffice.[3] This opinion, which neglected to consider that the legitimate manifestation of internal consent must likewise be a human act in order to engender the bond both as contract and sacrament, was short-sighted and short-lived. But the analogous problem of the possible invalidating force of insanity intervening between the granting of a mandate and the eventual celebration of marriage

---

1 "Hii, qui matrimonium sani contraxerunt, et uni ex duobus amentia, aut furor, aut aliqua infirmitas accesserit, ob hanc infirmitatem coniugia talium solvi non possunt." — *Decretum magistri Gratiani* (ed. Friedberg, 1959), c. 25, C. XXXII, q. 7.

2 "Ad irritandum vero matrimonium, non sufficit quod amentia praecesserit, vel sequatur ipsum matrimonium, sed requiritur quod sit amens tempore quo contrahit." — FRANCISCUS DE VICTORIA, O.P., *Summa sacramentorum Ecclesiae* (Venetiis: s.n.t., 1579), n. 287.

"Ut autem ex tali capite matrimonium dici possit nullum, requiritur, ut sive amentia sive dementia in actu exstiterit momento quo ipsum matrimonium fuit contractum." — c. Pecorari, Aug. 10, 1943 (Vol. XXXV, 709). "Praeterea amentia concomitans ea est, quae hominem afficit ipso tempore celebrationis matrimonii. Ideo amentia antecedens et amentia subsequens per se matrimonium non invalidant." — c. Morano, Dec. 21, 1935 (Vol. XXVII, 696). "Neque nullitas matrimonii evincitur ex eo quod, post contractas nuptias, in coniuge amentia, vel dementia, plena seu perfecta aliquando manifestetur, sed probare concludenter oportet matrimonii tempore contrahentem iam plene seu perfecte amentem vel dementem evasisse." — c. Massimi, Oct. 29, 1924 (Vol. XVI, 372).

3 Gonzalez Tellez gives the impression that such an opinion was widespread: "Illud tamen dubitari solet an matrimonium celebratum a furioso qui, antequam in furorem inciderit, animum habuit illud contrahendi, validum sit." — *Commentaria perpetua*, Lib. IV, Tit. I, Cap. 24, n. 4. He answered negatively along with the common opinion. Cf. SANCHEZ, *De sancto matrimonii sacramento*, Lib. I, Disp. VIII, n. 20; PONTIUS, *De sacramento matrimonii tractatus*, Lib. IV, Cap. I, n. 12; LUGO, *Disputationes scholasticae et morales de sacramentis in genere*, Disp. VIII, n. 108.

by proxy presented new difficulties since in this case true consent had already been legitimately manifested. This dispute, which widely divided canonical writers from the time of Sanchez, was settled definitively in 1918 by the Code in favor of the invalidating force of insanity concomitant with the proxy ceremony.[4] If we except the peculiar case of *sanatio in radice* after supervenient insanity, the rule is unanimously upheld in canonical doctrine and jurisprudence that only that insanity has nullifying force which subsists at the moment of the negotiation of the marriage contract itself. It is not required, however, that the insanity be *manifest* at that time; otherwise marriage tribunals would rarely handle an insanity case.[5]

Section A. Relevant Personal Presumptions.

Basic to the adjudication of insanity cases is the presumption of sanity: a person is presumed to be sane and to possess due discretion for valid marriage until the contrary be proved. Thomas Sanchez, who is reponsible for so many of the axioms and presumptions cited in the insanity cases of the Rota, wrote:

> Dubitabis tamen, quae praesumatur in dubio? Dicito sic: quando non constat, eum, de quo tractatur, antea furore correptum esse, non praesumitur furiosus. sed sanae mentis: ... et ratio est clara, quia natura ipsa homines sanae mentis producit, quare asserenti aliquem insanum esse adversatur praesumptio, quae a natura ipsa descendit.[6]

---

[4] Canon 1089, § 3. Cf. *supra*, Chapter I, pp. 18-22.

[5] "Quod amentia — rectum usum rationis voluntatisque exercitium praepediens — in ipsomet actu celebrationis matrimonii manifestetur, certe non requiritur." — c. Quattrocolo, Mar. 10, 1944 (Vol. XXXVI, 150). From the very nature of the situation it is to be expected that insanity cases involve what the decretists and decretalists called "*insania quieta*" as opposed to "*alienatio furiosa.*"

[6] Sanchez, *op. cit.*, Lib. I, Disp. VIII, n. 17. Roman Law had stated it thus: "Quilibet praesumitur esse talis, qualis naturaliter esse debet seu solet." (C. 6, 36, 5). Rotal jurisprudence repeats the presumption often. "Praesumptio stat pro eo, quod omnis homo sit mente sanus, donec contrarium certo probetur." — c. Wynen, June 3, 1939 (Vol. XXXI, 383). "Iure praesumitur pro sana mente, et amentia probetur oportet per actus univocos qui eam concludant; ideoque non sufficiunt nec leves nec aequivoci." — c. Jullien, May 9, 1936 (Vol. XXVIII, 305). "Omnis homo praesumitur esse sanae mentis, usque dum contrarium certo sit demonstratum. Quamobrem assertio, certum quendam hominem non esse vel non fuisse sui compotem, stricte probanda est." — c. Wynen, Mar. 1, 1930 (Vol. XXII, 134).

The specific presumption, in the case of marriage already contracted, is reinforced by the general presumption of the *favor matrimonii*. In case of prudent doubt of a person's ability to elicit sufficient consent, these presumptions must guide the decision.

Since alleged concomitant insanity is nearly never manifest at the time of the marriage ceremony and since the damaging effect of mental illness on due discretion cannot be measured directly, ecclesiastical jurisprudence has resorted mainly to two presumptions, classical since the time of Decretal Law, as aids in establishing the objective existence or subsistence of mental aberration at the very moment of the expression of marital consent — the presumption of *perpetuity* of mental illness, and the presumption of *continuity* of mental illness.

a. *The presumption of perpetuity.* On the basis that insanity constitutes a pathological state which, by nature, is neither transitory nor curable, but rather permanent and incurable, the afflicted person, once he is recognized as insane, is presumed to be insane thereafter. *Semel furiosus, semper furiosus.*[7] The burden of proof rests with him who asserts the contrary; the presumption yields to judicial proof that the afflicted person effectively recovered his sanity. Hence, if it is proved that the contractant, prior to his marriage, was insane, the presumption stands for the subsistence of the disorder at the time of the wedding.

As Sanchez himself pointed out, an essential requisite to the legitimacy of the presumption of perpetuity is that the preexisting disease or disorder was truly habitual and chronic prior to the wedding, and not a passing seizure or outbreak of *mentis exturbatio*. As an indication of its chronic nature Sanchez said that if the condition lasted a

---

[7] "Et ratio est, quia cum furoris morbus suapte natura perpetuus, insanabilis, ac desperatus sit, praesumitur durare omni tempore..." — SANCHEZ, *op. cit.*, Lib. I. Disp. VIII, n. 17. "...unde constito de perpetuo coniugis furore, illud sane consequi videtur nullitatis vitio matrimonium infectum iri ob consensus deficientiam" — S. PALLOTTINI, *Collectio omnium conclusionum et resolutionum*, Tom. XII, v. *Matrimonium*, § 3, n. 7. 19.

month or a year it could be considered chronic and incurable; thus the presumption of perpetuity is operative.[8]

The presumption of perpetuity may not be used generally in reverse, but, according to Rotal jurisprudence, it is admissible as an adminicle in cases of congenital mental diseases, or if the disorder becomes manifest very shortly after the wedding.[9]

In itself, the presumption of perpetuity as applied to insanity cases has a limited utility. For one thing, what medieval doctors considered incurable is today, often enough, curable by ordinary treatment. Dr. Henry Davidson writes:

> Psychopaths and homosexuals are hardly ever cured. I have never known of a homosexual who was reconverted to normal sexual channels. I have never seen a single reliable report of a cured psychopath. Alcoholism offers a better chance. The group known as "Alcoholics Anonymous" has an astonishing record of rehabilitation. With the insane, our batting average is somewhat better. There is enough chance of recovery to make treatment worth while. Deeply entrenched or deteriorated psychotics rarely reach the criminal courts, and with early psychotics the outlook is more promising. To be sure, the well preserved paranoiac is resistant to treatment, but other early psychotics may improve considerably under modern mental hospital therapy. In round numbers, ratio of recovery in early psychotics runs from 30 to 50 per cent — which is pretty good considering that insanity has traditionnaly been considered "incurable".[10]

The notable difference between the American school of psychiatry and the Continental school as regards the curability of schizophrenia and the possibility of true remissions has been highlighted in some very recent Rotal decisions. One decision, adhering to the opinion which holds the incurability of schizophrenia rejected the tenet of the

---

[8] SANCHEZ, *op. cit.*, Lib. I, Disp. VIII, n. 17: "Quod autem procedit, si probatum fuerit furorem durasse quodam continuo tempore, ut anno, mense: secus si probatur in aliquibus actibus furiosum fuisse: non enim praesumitur permanere furorem." Quoted with approval in c. Lega, Feb. 13, 1913 (Vol. V, 144).

[9] Cf. SANCHEZ, *loc. cit.;* DE SMET, *De sponsalibus et matrimonio*, n. 522 bis, nota 4; c. Parrillo, Feb. 16, 1928 (Vol. XX, 75-76).

[10] Dr. HENRY A. DAVIDSON, "The Psychiatrist's Role in the Administration of Criminal Justice," *Criminal Psychology* (ed. Richard W. Nice), pp. 27-28.

American school as "improbable".[11] The very next day, however, another Rotal decision was handed down in which the court warned of the proper use of the presumptions of perpetuity and continuity in schizophrenia cases: "*Idque eo vel magis obtinet, quod non pauci psychiatri, praesertim ex America Septentrionali, denegant naturam degenerativam et insanabilem schizophreniae, et admittunt intervalla, non tantum remissionis, sed plenae sanationis.*" [12]

Another liability of the presumption of perpetuity is that it be accorded more strength than the facts on which it rests warrant. The dictum of d'Avack that the presumption prevails even though there be positive doubt of the malady's subsistence seems an overstatement. [13] The force of the presumption is to dispel legitimately any positive doubt; if positive doubt should remain about the legitimate use of the presumption, it is the presumption which must yield, not the positive doubt which could not be legitimately dissolved.

Furthermore, the presumption of perpetuity will rarely be applicable in insanity cases strictly by itself. Never, practically speaking, will concomitant insanity be conjectured solely from the established fact of antecedent insanity without any regard for the subsequent course of the disorder after the wedding. It is almost always the case that the nature and gravity of the antecedent and concomitant insanity are diagnosed solely in light of the subsequent signs and symptoms. Thus it is that the presumption of perpetuity finds its usefulness mainly as the necessary substructure for the all-important presumption of continuity. [14]

---

[11] "Recentius vero, quidam sunt psychiatri, ad scholam americanam pertinentes, qui admittere videntur veras curationes in quibusdam speciebus schizophreniae; sed hodieque saltem, eorum sententia non videtur attigisse veram probabilitatem, saltem pro casibus gravioribus." — c. Lamas (Neo-Eboracen.), Oct. 21, 1959. Cf. JOHN E. MCGOWAN, "Fundamentals of Psychiatry in Relation to the Ecclesiastical Tribunal," *The Jurist*, XVI (1956), pp. 251-266.

[12] C. Sabattani (Neo-Eboracen.), Oct. 22, 1959.

[13] *Cause di nullità e di divorzio*, p. 157.

[14] "Probata enim amentia, pro ea praesumptio militat, donec contrarium probetur... praesertim si etiam post matrimonium coniux nova amentiae signa praebuerit, ex quo sane nova oritur praesumptio, ut eius amentia medio quoque tempore perdurarit; probatis namque extremis,

b. *The presumption of continuity.*

Once insanity is positively established as existing in the subject at two distinct periods, its subsistence is presumed during the interval:

> Quodsi constet de amentia seu de dementia antecedenti simul et consequenti matrimonium ipsum, iure deducitur et concomitantem exstitisse.[15]

The presumption of continuity was first a tenet of medical science and then entered ecclesiastical jurisprudence.[16] Some authors erroneously call it a *legal* presumption in matrimonial law,[17] but neither the Code nor Rotal jurisprudence has considered it as established by law. Indeed, in penal law the Code in canon 2201, §2, does presume the continuity of mental illness even when the habitually insane is known to enjoy lucid intervals or appears sane in certain lines of thought and behavior. All authors admit that this is at least a *praesumptio iuris simpliciter.* Some consider it a *praesumptio iuris et de iure,*[18] while a few

---

et media praesumitur probata dementia... Unde constito de perpetuo coniugis furore, illud sane consequi videtur, nullitatis vitio matrimonium huiusmodi infectum iri, ob consensus deficientiam." — SALVATOR PALLOTTINI, *Collectio omnium conclusionum et resolutionum,* Tom. XII (Romae: Typis S. Congr. de Prop. Fide, 1886), v. *Matrimonium,* § 3, nn. 10-11.

"...probata namque amentia, pro eadem militat praesumptio, praesertim si post matrimonium quoque coniux nova amentiae signa dederit." — c. Teodori, June 9, 1942 (Vol. XXXIV, 468).

15 C. Pecorari, Aug. 10, 1943 (Vol. XXXV, 709). Cf. also c. Many, Aug. 11, 1913 (Vol. V, 565); c. Lega, Feb. 13, 1913 Vol. V, 144); c. Many, June 27, 1916 (Vol. VIII, 209); c. Rossetti, Mar. 16, 1921 (Vol. XIII, 51); c. Prior, Aug. 17, 1922 (Vol. XIV, 319-320); c. Florczak, June 29, 1923 (Vol. XV, 132); c. Mannucci, Aug. 8, 1931 (Vol. XXIII, 373); c. Grazioli, July 1, 1933 (Vol. XXV, 408); c. Wynen, Jan. 13, 1938 (Vol. XXX, 31).

"Quartus demum est casus, quo amentiae status iam probatus, vel firmatus fuerit, non accidenaltiter, atque ad modicum tempus ex aliqua corporis infirmitate, sed simpliciter, atque per tempus notabile; et tunc, dum a communiter accidentibus, ista infirmitas, postquam contracta est, esse solet incurabilis, certa conclusio videtur, atque fere omnes concordant, ut praesumptio stet pro continuatione furoris vel amentiae." — JOANNES BAPTISTA DE LUCA, *Theatrum veritatis et justitiae,* Tom. IX, *De testamentis* (Lugduni: Cramer & Perachon, 1697), Disc. XXXVIII, n. 2.

16 "Probatio indirecta subministratur a praesumptione, quae antea est scientiae medicae, postea iurisprudentiae canonicae." — c. Bonet (Romana), June 3, 1957; c. Sabattani (Januen.), Mar. 14, 1959.

17 Cf. D'AVACK, *Cause di nullità e di divorzio,* p. 180; DOHENY, *Canonical Procedure in Matrimonial Cases,* I, *Formal Judicial Procedure,* p. 827.

18 Cf. NOVAL, "De semi-amentibus et semi-imputabilitati obnoxiis," *Jus*

authors hold that it is an absolute principle, not merely a legal presumption.[19]

In matrimonial law, however, there is no such *legal* presumption concerning the marriage capacity of the habitually insane.[20] The natural law alone is the governing norm on the psychic competence for valid marriage. The presumption of continuity is a *presumptio hominis* legitimately conjectured by ecclesiastical judges from the settled doctrine of medical science. That the law itself has raised the medical conjecture to the status of a legal presumption in penal law serves to illumine its legitimacy also in matrimonial law. A rotal decision *coram Florczak* outlined the solid reasons why the personal presumption of continuity is legitimate in the matrimonial forum:

> Haec enim praesumptio, etsi quoad rem matrimonialem in Codice J. C. formaliter inscripta non sit, tamen legitime coniicitur tum ex lege lata de habitualiter amentibus qui licet in certis actibus sani videantur, delicti tamen incapaces praesumuntur (can. 2201, § 2), tum ex receptissima in foro et apud probatos scriptores interpretatione veteris illius iuris quod Codex J. C. refert de hoc impedimento ex capite defectus consensus ob amentiam, tum denique ex ipsa natura eiusmodi morbi. Nam "cum furoris morbus suapte natura perpetuus, insanabilis et desperatus sit, praesumitur durare omni tempore, et illa dilucida intervalla sunt per accidens, ideoque minime praesumuntur."[21]

To employ the presumption validly, three things must be proved: (1) the illness certainly existed before the marriage; (2) the illness certainly existed after the marriage;

Pontificium, IV (1924), p. 83; GERMANUS-JOSEPH PELLEGRINI, C.P., *Jus Ecclesiae poenale*, I, *De delictis* (Neapoli: D'Auria, 1962), p. 96.

19 REGATILLO, *Institutiones iuris canonici*, II, n. 794; MICHIELS, *De delictis et poenis*, I (2. ed., 1961), p. 194.

20 Cf. KLEMME, *Lucid Intervals and Matrimonial Consent*, p. 15; FÄSSLER, *Die Schizophrenie als Ehenichtigkeitsgrund im kanonischen Recht*, p. 55.

21 C. Florczak, June 29, 1923 (Vol. XV, 132), with the final citation from Sanchez, probably the most commonly cited passage in early Rotal sentences dealing with *amentia*. The full passage reads: "Tandem si furiosus lucida habeat intervalla, cum dubitatur an actus tempore furoris, an sanae mentis gestus fuerit, *Enriq. L. 11. de matrim. c. 4, n. 3,* ait in dubio praesumi rationis usum, dicendum tamen est praesumi tempore furoris gestum esse. Et ratio est, quia cum furoris morbus suapte natura perpetuus, insanabilis, ac desperatus sit, praesumitur durare omni tempore, et illa dilucida intervalla sunt per accidens, ideoque minime praesumuntur." — *De sancto matrimonii sacramento*, Lib. I, Disp. VIII, n. 17.

(3) the nature of the illness is such that it is chronic and does not allow long intermittent remissions.[22] Since it is a personal presumption, and not a legal presumption, its strength will vary according to the strength of the facts on which it rests. Thus, for example, if univocal signs of the mental aberration are evident immediately before and immediately after the wedding, the presumption of concomitant aberration is very strong;[23] if the external symptoms are ambiguous or are evident only at periods distant from the time of the wedding, the presumption of continuity obviously loses force.[24]

Following are three examples of the application of the presumption of continuity made by recent Rotal decisions to schizophrenia, paranoia, and manic-depressive psychosis. It is interesting to note the specific adaptations of the application, depending on the precise nature of the mental disorder. Schizophrenia is a general dissociative process which, according to classical medical opinion, does

---

22 "At si extremis primum deficit, alterum solum non suffragatur ad praedictum effectum." — c. Parrillo, Feb. 16, 1928 (Vol. XX, 71). "Si igitur constat de longis intervallis lucidis, non amplius applicari potest principium: 'Probata amentia antecedenti et subsequenti matrimonium, iure et amentia concomitans deducitur' nam hoc principium valet tantum, si tum brevi ante tum brevi post nuptias amentia certo adfuerit." — c. Wynen, June 3, 1939 (Vol. XXXI, 374). Doheny, commenting on a Rotal decision handed down in 1921 writes: "The sentence of the diocesan tribunal declared in favor of the nullity of the marriage. However, it based its decision on the presumption that once insanity is proved to exist before and after the marriage, the insanity at the time of the marriage may be presumed. The presumption, however, was placed on a false basis, as real insanity had not existed; from which it follows that the presumption cannot be validly invoked in the case." — *Canonical Procedure in Matrimonial Cases*, I, p. 816.

23 "Quod si ex adverso brevi ante et fere immediate post contractum matrimonium, imo si in ipsamet matrimonii die et in actu celebrationis nuptiarum indubia insanae mentis indicia prodiderint, tunc nullitas actus sic gesti per se evidentissime patet." — c Quattrocolo, June 23, 1928 (Vol. XX, 259).

24 "Quare non sufficit ostendere aliquem contrahentem multo tempore, forsan pluribus annis, ante nuptias impetum morbi mentalis passum fuisse, ut eius matrimonium dici queat initum in absoluta mentis deordinatione seu in statu amentiae; neque aliud tenendum est, si idem contrahens diu post nuptias alium vel similem impetum morbi habuerit, cum unum vel alterum factum singulare nondum constituat habitum, multo minus habitum absque lucidis intervallis tempore intermedio." — c. Wynen, June 3, 1939 (Vol. XXX, 375). Writes Sanchez. "Similiter praesumitur furiosus quoad actus, qui paulo post furoris tempus aguntur, non autem quoad illos, qui longo intervallo distant." — SANCHEZ, *loc. cit.*

not admit true lucid intervals in its progressive deterioration of the mental faculties; paranoia consists in a systematic delirium centered about a certain nucleus or theme; manic-depressive psychosis does admit true remissions between the alternating periods of mania and depression.

Schizophrenia: "Probatio indirecta subministratur a praesumptione, quae antea est scientiae medicae, postea jurisprudentiae canonicae. Datur enim in casu idem morbus, in duobus sane temporibus, cuius species praesens non est nisi reformatio in peius speciei tunc exsistentis. Si attente res conspiciatur, videntur ipsa themata delirantia eadem esse, necessario graviora in praesenti statu... Hoc statuto, scientia medica quae schizophreniam novit uti morbum 'processualem' seu progredientem fataliter in peius, deducit haec non constituere nisi duo momenta eiusdem morbi. Quoniam vero hic morbus, iuxta eandem scientiam, necessariam deliberationem et libertatem ad contrahendum non permittat, tunc intervenit jus, et hoc tribuit criterium, quod, probata amentia in duobus temporibus extremis, amentia in ipso tempore intermedio *praesumitur*." [25]

Paranoia: "Et, sicuti in schizophrenia, admissa amentia ante et post nuptias, praesumitur amentia concomitans, ita in paranoia, admisso delirio systematico praesertim circa rem uxoriam, capacitas contrahendi, plerumque ob defectum libertatis, adempta praesumitur, cum argui nequeat integritas functionis circa illum nucleum, cui delirium insidet." [26]

Manic-depressive psychosis: "Etenim, cum nuptiae celebratae sint...post duos annos a secunda infirmitate, praesumptio dementiae momento matrimonii non datur; tamen, cum sive ante sive post nuptias indubie in dementiam incidisset, *fundata habetur possibilitas* quod etiam momento contractus vir insaniret. Hoc sane probandum est, et constare censuerunt Patres sive ex ideis delirantibus quibus ipse eo tempore laborabat, putans se esse Napoleonem, sive e discessu inexplicabili quem per quadrantem fecit, immediate ante nuptias, sive e modo ejus agendi in re conjugali." [27]

---

[25] C. Bonet (Romana), June 3, 1957.
[26] C. Sabattani (Januen.), Mar. 14, 1959.
[27] C. Heard (Rhedonen.), Jan. 8, 1959.

Section B. The Problem of Lucid Intervals.

Intimately connected with the presumption of continuity is the question of lucid intervals, a question passionately discussed in the past and in the present, both in the science of medicine and that of law. Peculiar, however, to the science of law is the consideration of the lucid interval under a twofold aspect: (1) lucid intervals as a question of *law;* (2) lucid intervals as a question of *fact.* The failure to keep distinct the *quaestio iuris* from the *quaestio facti* with regard to the legal relevance of lucid intervals has caused an apparent opposition between canonical authors which, in fact, does not exist.

Already in Decretal Law stress was placed on the need to distinguish carefully true lucid intervals from only apparent lucid intervals. "*Saepe enim furiosi sunt constituti in conspectu umbratae quietis, nec tamen sunt mentis sanae, licet videantur.*" [28] Upon this observation of the glossator later canonical doctrine made the distinctions between *alienatio furiosa* and *insania quieta,* between *umbrata quies* and the true *lucidum intervallum.*

At law the concept of lucid interval is relative and is measured against the psychic requirements of a specific juridical act placed during the period of alleged recovery of juridical capacity. Thus in matrimonial law a true lucid interval is a period during which a person, otherwise habitually destitute of the psychic ability to elicit sufficient consent, regains temporarily at least the minimum degree of discretion required for true marital consent. Hence, during this interval he is capable of marrying validly.

As far the question of law is concerned, it has been the unanimous opinion of canonists from the earliest times that if a person should actually marry during a true lucid interval, the marriage is valid. [29] Rotal jurisprudence,

---

[28] C. 24, X, IV, 1, glossa ordinaria ad v. *Furore.*

[29] "...tunc furiosus per dilucida intervalla redit ad sanam mentem, et tunc si contrahat, tenet..." — *Ibid.* The gloss to *Neque furiosus* in the Decree of Gratian reads: "quia non possunt consentire. Possunt tamen si habeant dilucida intervalla." — c. 26, C. XXXII, q. 7. Sanchez notes that, although valid, a marriage celebrated during a lucid interval would be illicit: "Observandum tamen est, quamvis habitu furiosus, si intervalli lucidi tempore ducat uxorem valide contrahat, peccare tamen con-

in the theoretical line of the question of law, holds this principle without exception.[30]

The question of fact, i.e., whether in a given instance a person actually did recover his ability to elicit true consent, is really a medical problem, not a legal problem. But it is a problem which enters the judicial decision; the judge must ultimately hold that a period of remission at the time of the wedding was either merely apparent or a true lucid interval during which the party effectively regained due discretion. It is in this area that the somewhat confusing opinions have arisen among authors, some claiming that the law "does not admit lucid intervals", others claiming that the law "does admit lucid intervals".

Medical science, in the line of general principle, has held for the presumption of merely apparent lucid intervals without the effective recovery of due discretion. Some writers[31] and even some Rotal decisions, failing to keep distinct the question of law from that of fact, speak as though this medical opinion was poorly founded and should not be admitted.[32] But canonical jurisprudence and doctrine have, in fact, always held and assumed the same presumption, i.e., that periods of apparent recovery from an otherwise habitual incapacity are merely apparent and not real. True lucid intervals are "accidents" and are

---

trahendo, quia idoneus non est ad prolem educandam." — *De sancto matrimonii sacramento*, Lib. I, Disp. VIII, n. 18.

[30] The decision c. Many, Aug. 11, 1913, recalls that this is commonly accepted doctrine, citing Sanchez, Wernz, D'Annibale and Gasparri. "Si amens habeat lucida intervalla et in his matrimonium contrahat, matrimonium validum est." — Vol. V, 564. "Quare si mentecapti matrimonium in iis quae vocantur lucida intervalla ineant, validum illud contrahere possunt." — c. Grazioli, July 27, 1929 (Vol. XXI, 333). "...intervalla lucida sunt per accidens, nec praesumuntur, atque omnino distinguantur oportet vera intervalla dilucida quibus mentis compotes fiunt (can. 754, § 2), ab intervallis lucidis falsis, seu umbratis cum fucata veri specie, ob quae infirmi videntur sanae mentis, quamvis non sint." — c. Jullien, July 5, 1947 (Vol. XXXIV, 398).

[31] "*Lucida intervalla* in mente captis saepe dantur; quare, si in hisce matrimonium contrahant, valide contrahere possunt, etsi contrarium neotherici teneant." — Regatillo, *Ius sacramentarium*, n. 1316.

[32] "Mentecapti namque habent et quae vocantur lucida intervalla, in quibus possunt etiam quandoque valide contractus inire et proinde etiam matrimonium, etsi hodie iuxta complures medicos etiam in ipso lucido intervallo habeatur latens quaedam amentia." — c. Grazioli, Apr. 24, 1931 (Vol. XXIII, 153).

never presumed; in fact, there is a positive presumption against them.

> Lucida, quae dicuntur, intervalla, nonnisi per accidens censentur haberi... Accidentia autem non praesumuntur, sed probari debent... Neque praesumuntur lucida intervalla cum amentes ex vitio naturae nunquam convalescant... Praesumptio stat pro eo, quod non habentur.

These axioms are nothing more than restatements of the presumption of continuity.

When must the presumption of continuity yield to the fact of a true lucid interval? Practically speaking, the classical enunciation is that of Cardinal Gasparri: *"Perpendendae igitur sunt omnes casus circumstantiae: si, omnibus rite consideratis, intervallum adeo lucidum fuerit et intervallum lucidum adeo longum, ut consensus matrimonialis sit certus, standum est pro consensus validitate, secus pro nullitate."* [33] The interval must be proved to be long, truly lucid, truly rehabilitating for sufficient marital consent. Relying on the solid conclusions of psychiatric science, recent Rotal sentences seem to demand nothing short of clear, compelling proof of rehabilitation:

> Quae conclusio plene consentanea est praesumptioni a jurisprudentia N. S. O. admissae, incapacitatis praestandi validum consensum — tempore intermedio — a coniuge de cuius insania antecedenti et subsequenti nuptias plene constet, nisi *omnino probetur* intervallum adeo lucidum fuisse ut de recuperata *perfecta valetudine mentis dubitari nequaquam liceat.* [34]
>
> ... neve obliviscatur tenues remissiones non semper restituere plenam integritatem psychicam, nisi de intervallo adeo lucido nec brevi agatur quod discretionem iudicii *perfecte in integrum restituerit.* [35]

---

[33] GASPARRI, *Tractatus de matrimonio,* II, n. 785.

[34] C. Pinna (Basileen.), Jan. 13, 1959 (Schizophrenia). An earlier decision seems to lay down a severe condition before admitting a true lucid interval: "Certo certius si aperte ac incontrovertibiliter probetur in tempore medio insaniam omnino cessasse, coniugii validitas impeti nequit." — c. Caiazzo, July 30, 1940 (Vol. XXXII, 614).

[35] C. Pinna (Romana), Mar. 21, 1959 (manic-depressive psychosis). A rule of thumb indicating the existence of a true lucid interval is given in a Rotal decision which stated: "Qui omnes suas actiones ac verba per considerabile tempus prudentiae regulis conformet." — c. Wynen, Jan. 13, 1938 (Vol. XXX, 13).

In the last analysis, not only in medicine, but also in the field of the Church's matrimonial law, the famous question of lucid intervals, at least today, is much less important than one would be led to believe from the prominence it receives in canonical commentaries. The lucid interval is treated as an exception whose existence in a concrete case is usually extremely difficult to prove judicially against the general presumption of ecclesiastical jurisprudence and dominant medical opinion concerning the continuity of mental disease and defect.

Article 2. Amentia Matrimonialis

The second condition which must be judicially verified in order to establish the invalidating force of mental illness on the marriage contract is that the disease or disorder affected the contractant in the specific area of psychic discretion for marriage (*in re matrimoniali*), as opposed to other areas of thought and behavior. The supposition is that a mental defect or disorder may produce abnormalities in certain restricted categories of ideas or activity, but leave intact the afflicted person's discretion in the field of marriage. In this regard we have the celebrated distinction between *amentia* and *dementia*. A person is *amens* if he is irresponsible in everything; he is *demens* if irresponsible only in certain lines of thought and behavior. The distinction is based on the classical medical distinction between the manias and the monomanias.

Bánk points out that the terms *dementia* and *demens* never occur in the Code,[36] and Michiels states that it is not clear whether the Code even admits the distinct concepts.[37] An apodictic argument for the affirmative opinion cannot be drawn from canon 2201, §2: "Habitualiter amentes, licet quandoque lucida intervalla habeant, vel *in certis quibusdam ratiocinationibus vel actibus sani videantur,* delicti tamen incapaces praesumuntur." In this canon the legislator is speaking of those who are insane but who appear sane only in certain sectors; the concept of *demen-*

---

[36] Bánk, *Connubia canonica,* p. 342, nota 3.
[37] Michiels, *Principia generalia de personis in Ecclesia,* p. 82.

tes of matrimonial jurisprudence is just the opposite, viz., sane in most spheres but insane "*in certis quibusdam ratiocinationibus vel actibus.*" In the practical order, admitting the existence of *dementes*, there is no doubt, says Michiels, that according to the mind of the legislator *dementes* come under the dispositions set for *amentes*. Hence, their legal status in the Code is identical.[38]

In the theoretical order pertaining to the *quaestio iuris*, the concepts and principles are simple and clear:

1) "In iure canonico insania distingui solet inter amentiam atque dementiam. Amentiae nomine appellatur insania circa omnia obiecta atque negotia; nomine dementiae donatur insania circa quaedam tantummodo obiecta vel negotia."[39]

2) "*Demens*, in his, quae ad dementiam ipsius pertinent, aequiparatur amenti."[40]

3) "Patet igitur consensum praestitum ab amente esse semper invalidum, consensum vero praestitum a demente esse invalidum, si dementia vertatur circa obiectum contractus."[41] "Iuris praeterea est firmissima regula quod dementia, quae circa unum tantum vel alterum obiectum fertur, non est impeditiva matrimonii, nisi quando fertur in ipsum matrimonium."[42]

The conflicting opinions arise when we enter the question of fact: Do monomaniacs as conceived in the legal notion of *dementes* really exist? Sanchez mentioned the controversy that existed on the point during his time. Some denied the possibility of a restricted or partial insanity, arguing on philosophical grounds that the intellectual faculty of man is spiritual and one.[43] Sanchez called the problem an "*egregium dubium*" and, arguing from philosophy, physiology, law, and experience itself, held for

---

[38] *Ibid.*

[39] C. Morano, Apr. 30, 1935 (Vol. XXVII, 282).

[40] GASPARRI, *op. cit.*, II, n. 785.

[41] C. Morano, Apr. 30, 1935 (Vol. XXVII, 282).

[42] C. Quattrocolo, Nov. 17, 1932 (Vol. XXIV, 455).

[43] "Omnis potentia eodem modo respicit omnia sua obiecta, ut visus omnes colores, et si circa unum obiectum vitietur, eodem vitio quoad reliqua laborabit; ergo si ex imaginativae laesione intellectus quoad aliquod obiectum deficit, perperam ratiocinando, deficiet quoad reliqua, et ita vel in omnibus, vel in una re delirabit." — FRANCISCUS *a* VICTORIA, O.P., *Relectiones theologicae* (Lugduni: Landry, 1587), I, 92, n. 19.

the real existence of *dementes.*[44] Supported by the immense authority of Sanchez, the concept of *demens* as reflecting a reality entered ecclesiastical jurisprudence so that Michiels can say:

> No matter what the psychiatric theory might be, it is certain that the tradition of moralists, the doctrine of canonists, and especially ecclesiastical jurisprudence always, even in most recent times, admit the existence of *dementes* or monomaniacs and their juridical capacity in those areas which evidently lie outside their delirium.[45]

Michiels confesses that "most modern psychiatrists do not admit the existence of *dementes*", a fact admitted likewise by canonists fifty years ago[47] and widely insisted upon today.[48] There is ample evidence that Rotal jurisprudence has not only leaned towards this position but, at least recently, has definitely adopted it. Paranoia, which in early canonical doctrine and jurisprudence, was always given as

---

44 "His tamen minime obstantibus credo verius esse inveniri saepe delirantes in aliqua speciali materia, ac proinde in illa rationis, liberi arbitrii, meriti, atque demeriti expertes, sed naturaliter brutorum instar imaginatione duci; in aliis vero ratione uti, et libere operari, capacesque esse merendi, et demerendi, ac subinde posse fateri, alia sacramenta recipere, sponsalia, ac matrimonium celebrare." — *De sancto matrimonii sacramento*, Lib. I, Disp. VIII, n. 23.

45 MICHIELS, *De delictis et poenis*, I, p. 184.

46 *Ibid.*, p. 183.

47 Amanieu upbraids some authors who allowed themselves "to be intimidated" by the modern psychiatrists: "Des auteurs contemporains se sont cependant laissés intimider par les affirmations des psychiâtres, cf. Gasparri... Pérries. Cappello qui professe nettement l'opinion opposée à la tradition." — AMANIEU, "Aliénation mentale en matière de nullité de mariage," *DDC*, I, col. 439.

48 Cf. IOANNES CHELODI, *Ius matrimoniale iuxta Codicem Iuris Canonici* (3. ed.; Tridenti: Libr. Edit. Tridentinum, 1921), n. 109; idem, *Ius canonicum de personis* 4. ed. curavit Pius Ciprotti. Vicetiae: Edit. S.A.T., 1957), n. 91; De Smet, *De sponsalibus et matrimonio,* n. 522 bis, nota 5; WERNZ-VIDAL, *Ius canonicum*, Tom. VII, *Ius poenale ecclesiasticum*, n. 64; NOVAL, "De semi-amentibus et semi-imputabilitati obnoxiis," *Jus Pontificium*, IV (1924), p. 82; GASPARRI, *Tractatus de matrimonio*, II, n. 785; CAPPELLO, *De matrimonio*, n. 579. Finally, de Arquer and de Semir write: "Nowadays this conception of the paranoias or monomanias, in the sense of partial responsibility, i.e., responsibility is retained in the areas outside the theme of the delirium, is rejected by all the modern psychiatrists. They affirm, rather, that these mental illnesses affect the entire personality, morbidly permeating it. Certainly in the case of full-blown paranoia, the delirious idea constitutes the paranoid's center of interest; it dominates his faculties; it regulates his behavior and exercises a compulsive influence on all his activity and decisions. Since evidence of full deliber-

the classical example of *dementia* in that its damaging influence is restricted to a systematic nucleus of ideas, is now definitely acknowledged to belong to the category of *amentia*, not *dementia*:

> IN IURE: ... Delirium plene possidet paranoicum, eius personalitatem ita permeat et invadit ut sit unica cogitandi agendique via et forma. Eapropter omnino improprie paranoia inter monomanias adscribi assolet: non enim unam vel aliam facultatem inficit sed totam, uti diximus, personalitatem... Quoad monomanias autem, quibus improprie, uti diximus, paranoia accensetur, censent plurimi hodie doctores iuris, iuxta opinionem psychiatrorum, monomaniacos "ita esse intellectu perturbatos ut numquam satis constet de eiusdem recto usu" ne in ea quidem materia quae videtur maniae subtrahi... non haberi scilicet unquam necessariam discretionem.
>
> IN FACTO: ... Verum tamen in nostro convento delirium affecerit, ante nuptias, omnes eius actus communes vel sub forma exaggeratae ambitionis, vel sub forma suspicionis, desponsionis, timoris, vix fieri potuit ne delirium ipsum affecerit contractum matrimonialem... Ergo cum constet ex actis Carolum tempore matrimonii delirio paranoico iam esse affectum, delirium autem ipsam turbasse matrimonialem provinciam, concludendum est, iuxta concordem peritorum deductionem, eum non elicuisse valide matrimonialem consensum. [49]

The same Ponens reiterated this thesis in another decision:

> Autumant quidam paranoiam esse inter monomanias recensendam: id non satis respondere psychiatrorum conclusionibus iam demonstratum est in citata *Florentina*, coram me Ponente... sine difficultate concludi potest Titiam tempore quo factum est matrimonium, delirio affectam fuisse paranoico, non tantum generico, sed ipsam rem matrimonialem attingenti, atque tali ut nequiret ipsa consensum matrimonialem validum, nempe cum debita discretione et deliberatione, emittere. [50]

The older opinion that *dementia* has invalidating force "only if" it affects the province of marriage has been tempered many times in Rotal jurisprudence to read "at least if, especially if, not only if..."

---

ation in such persons is never had, their capacity to marry is greatly to be doubted." — *Derecho matrimonial*, n. 208.

[49] C. Felici (Florentina), Apr. 6, 1954. Cf. the excerpt of this decision published in *Monitor Ecclesiasticus*, LXXIX (1954), pp. 585-590.

[50] C. Felici (Romana), July 12, 1955.

Coram Grazioli, April 24, 1931: "... *saltem si* insaniant circa rem uxoriam." [51]

Coram Jullien, March 13, 1937: states that in case of doubt, presume that the *dementia* did affect "*rem matrimonialem.*" [52]

Coram Jasanik, July 24, 1941: states with approval "Attamen quod dementes attinet, etiamsi eorum monomania circa rem uxoriam non versetur, secundum modernos medicos nunquam certo de plena eorum deliberatione constat, ita ut de eorum capacitate ad validum contractum ineundum dubitandum sit." [53]

Coram Teodori, June 9, 1942: "Non solum amentes, sed etiam dementes seu monomaniaci, *praesertim si* dementia sit circa rem uxoriam, consensu matrimonialis incapaces evadere possunt." [54]

Coram Pecorari, August 10, 1943: "Si monomania sese referat ad alias res, disputant doctores, utrum demens sit capax matrimonii ineundi. Plures moderni medici dicunt nunquam certo constare de plena deliberatione; et proinde valde dubitandum esse de capacitate huiusmodi personarum ad validum contractum ineundum. Huic sententiae videtur adhaerendum esse, attenta praecipue peculiari natura et gravitate contractus matrimonialis." [55]

Coram Felici, May 22, 1956: "Monomaniae autem, nisi respiciant ipsam rem sexualem et matrimonialem, *vel nisi gravissimae sint,* intactam relinquunt discretionem et voluntatem necessariam ad verum matrimonium contrahendum." [56]

Finally, Cardinal D'Annibale, who is responsible for the technical terminology of *amentia* and *dementia,* and who has always been regarded as one of the foremost proponents of the thesis of the real existence of *dementes* and their unaffected competence in matters outside the nucleus of their aberration, [57] has recently been reinterpreted with approval by the Rota as, in fact, an opponent to the classical tenet of Sanchez. Openly subscribing to the modern medical opinion, and citing D'Annibale for support, the sentence reads:

---

51 *S.R.R.Dec.,* Vol. XXIII, 153.
52 *S.R.R.Dec.,* Vol. XXIX, 210.
53 *S.R.R.Dec.,* Vol. XXXIII, 668.
54 *S.R.R.Dec.,* Vol. XXXIV, 467.
55 *S.R.R.Dec.,* Vol. XXXV, 708.
56 *Florentina* — cf. *Monitor Ecclesiasticus,* LXXXI (1956), pp. 264-267.
57 D'Avack calls him "uno dei massimi assertori di tale tesi." — *Cause di nullità e di divorzio,* p. 174. Amanieu states that D'Annibale energetically reproved the "new" opinion: *Nolumus abduci doctrinis variis et peregrinis.* — "Aliénation mentale en matière de nullité de mariage," *DDC,* I, col. 439.

Nostri, profecto, constanter distinxerunt inter amentiam et dementiam, animadvertendo: "Amens seu furiosus dicitur is, qui insanit quoad omnia: dementem dixerim eum, quam graeco vocabulo monomaniacum vocant, idest qui insanit circa unam rem tantum, vel alteram." (D'Annibale, Summ. Theol. Mor., P. I, n. 31, p. 25.

Sed statim subiungitur: "Nihilominus. quidam hodierni psychiatrici dementiae et amentiae eandem vim esse contendunt, rati numquam ex parte laedi organum virtutis imaginativae" (L.c., p. 26, nota 18).

Et jure merito praecl. A. talem sententiam amplexari videtur, quae nostro tempore communis est inter psychiatros. Quis enim validum haberet matrimonium illius hominis, de quo idem A., loco citato, refert? Illius nempe, qui "postquam judicibus omnia bene et recte respondisset, jussus acta conscribere, subscripsit his verbis: Jesus Christus"?... [58]

The effort of earlier jurisprudence to fit various medical species of mental illness into a legally conceived tripartite division of *amentia, dementia matrimonialis*, and *dementia non-matrimonialis* and to apply the appropriate principles, was both unrealistic and unnecessary. The controversy concerning the invalidating force of *dementia*, although sometimes stated as a controversy of law, is a controversy of medical fact. The question at stake was not whether the mentally ill whose disorder in no way affected their ability to consent to marriage invalidated the contract or not; that it would *not* invalidate was agreed upon by all. The question, rather, was whether those whose mental disorder seemed to be restricted to a certain line of thought and behavior that ostensibly did not affect one's ability to consent, in reality could be judged thereby to retain unimpaired their due discretion for valid marriage. The answer belongs to the psychiatrists, not to the canon lawyers. Ravá, therefore, cannot see why the question deserves the prominence which it is wont to receive. [59] Klemme observes that "in later jurisprudence this distinction lost its importance since it was replaced by other divisions." [60] Certainly, it can no longer be said with Van Ommeren that "the only distinction of legal import,

[58] C. Mattioli (Bononien.), Nov. 6, 1958.

[59] RAVÀ, "Il *defectus discretionis iudicii* come causa di nullità del matrimonio nella giurisprudenza rotale," *Il Diritto Ecclesiastico*, LXVIII (1957), II, p. 440.

[60] KLEMME, *Lucid Intervals and Matrimonial Consent*, p. 36.

therefore, in cases of mental illness or insanity is the time-honored distinction of the law between *amentia* and *dementia.*" [61]

D'Avack, claiming to take into account the modern tendency within Rotal jurisprudence, lists four directive criteria which ecclesiastical judges might employ in ascertaining the effective marriage capacity of monomaniacs:

1) Having established the existence of mental alienation in an individual case, the afflicted person is presumed, until contrary proof, to be totally insane or *amens... insanire circa omnia et non circa unam tantum vel alteram rem.*

2) Having established the existence of a truly restricted *dementia,* the principle holds that monomaniacs "*in his quae ad eorum dementiam pertinent, amentibus aequiparantur*", and that, therefore, if their monomania reflects directly or indirectly the field of matrimony, this *dementia* has the same invalidating force as total insanity.

3) In case of doubt whether this partial insanity (*dementia*) extends to the field of matrimony, it is presumed to exist *in ordine ad matrimonium;* hence, the burden of proof rests with him who asserts the contrary, that is, he must prove certainly that the *dementia* does *not* embrace this specific field.

4) Even if the *dementia* is demonstrated as limited to fields other than that of matrimony, this cannot be considered as sufficient to show that the subject was actually in possession of due discretion for marriage and hence capable of valid marriage; such capacity must be positively clarified in court in the sense that, until contrary proof be produced, the demented person is presumed to have contracted without due discretion, hence, invalidly. [62]

Practically speaking the above-stated presumptions, in effect, abolish the distinction between *amentia* and *dementia.* Although d'Avack states that there should be no doubt about their accuracy and legitimacy since they reflect the legal presumption of penal law (canon 2201, §2), [63] yet the very format of these criteria is in counter-current

---

[61] VAN OMMEREN, *Mental Illness Affecting Matrimonial Consent*, p. 168.

[62] D'AVACK, *op. cit.*, pp. 175-176.

[63] *Ibid.* Concerning the legitimacy of borrowing criteria from penal law, cf. *supra*, "Some Irrelevant Norms," p. 9.

with modern Rotal jurisprudence. D'Avack's extrinsic construct of directive presumptions, whose application according to varying external qualities of a given mental aberration generates a conclusion of psychic competence or incompetence of the contractant, is formalistic and unrealistic as an evaluative method. The Rota, on the other hand, wary of applying pat rules of thumb and axioms, seeks more and more to gauge psychic ability to marry from the subjective starting point of due discretion, its nature and positive requirements. Exactly in what this consists might be delineated in an examination of psychic capacity *circa rem uxoriam.*

It is clear from the general principles of jurisprudence that if a mental disease or disorder invalidates marriage, it is because it includes at least "*insania circa rem uxoriam.*" Thus, amentia has invalidating force only because as *insania quoad omnia* it includes, as a part within the whole, *insania circa rem uxoriam;* abnormality outside of this nucleus has no bearing on the possible invalidity of the bond. It seems clear, therefore, that the notion of due discretion for valid marriage lies in the concept of psychic ability *circa rem uxoriam.* The question is: what is *res uxoria?*

Rotal jurisprudence and canonical writers have used various phrases to describe it:

— "quando fertur in ipsum matrimonium." (c. Quattrocolo, Nov. 17, 1932: Vol. XXIV, 455).

— "si respicit rem matrimonialem." (c. Wynen, Dec. 21, 1937: Vol. XXIX, 757).

— "si vertatur circa obiectum contractus." (c. Morano, April 30, 1935: Vol. XXVII, 282).

— "si restricta est ad rem eroticam et uxoriam." (c. Sebastianelli, April, 9, 1910: Vol. II, 145).

— "si consensus matrimonialis pathologicis impulsibus per se afficitur." (c. Filipiak, Feb. 14, 1958: Davenportensis).

— "nisi respiciant ipsam rem sexualem et matrimonialem." (c. Felici, May 22, 1956: Florentina).

— "si obiectum formale dementiae appareat ipsa res uxoria, seu matrimonialis." (c. Mannucci, Aug. 8, 1931: Vol. XXIII, 373).

— "si eorum insania pro obiecto habeat ipsum matrimonium aut res sexuales." (Conte a Coronata, *Institutiones*, III, *De matrimonio*, n. 438).

— "when his abnormality concerns precisely the matter of marriage, its religious, ethical, juridical, or social aspects." (Mans-Bernárdez, *Derecho matrimonial canónico*, I, p. 324).

— "qui insaniunt circa aliquod genus rerum (e.g. religiosarum, sexualium) ad officia coniugalia pertinentium." (Vlaming-Bender, *Praelectiones iuris matrimonii*, p. 380).

The terms "*rex uxoria, res matrimonialis, res sexualis, res erotica, etc.*" are vague terms at best, and the authors' efforts to specify further with the concepts of "the religious, juridical, ethical, and social aspects of marriage" not only do not clarify the issue but actually lead to inaccuracies. A pair of more recent Rotal decisions made a point to narrow the general phrase "*res uxoria*" to its essential meaning:

> Coram Quattrocolo, March 10, 1944: "Ubi tamen animadvertendum, quod non omnes perturbationes vel morbidae affectiones, quae in genere feriunt intellectum et voluntatem, attendendae heic veniunt ad validitatem vel nullitatem decernendam coniugii; sed illae dumtaxat, quae *specifice obiectum et naturam spectant matrimonialis contractus, ac influunt ad nuptialem ponendum consensum.* Affectiones propterea, quae se habent ad aliud obiectum et exulant a sacramentali contractu, matrimonii valori obstare nequeunt." [64]

> Coram Pasquazi, May 12, 1949: 'Ad dementiam autem quod attinet sub forma zelotypiae coniugalis, animadvertendum est eam irritare matrimonium tantummodo si versetur *circa ipsum obiectum contractus matrimonialis, id est circa naturam, finem et proprietates essentiales matrimonii.* at non autem circa omnes res quae ad matrimonium referuntur, quaeque verbo nimis generali dicuntur res uxoriae vel matrimoniales." [65]

It seems not out of place to state here a conclusion, the validity of which we shall attempt to demonstrate in the following chapter, namely, *insania circa rem uxoriam* means psychic disorder or defect which invalidates marriage for one of two reasons: (1) it prevents the subject

[64] *S.R.R.Dec.*, Vol. XXXVI, 151.
[65] *S.R.R.Dec.*, Vol. XXXXI, 219.

from constructing sufficient internal consent to generate the contract of matrimony, precluding an indispensable cognitional or volitional element necessary in the determination of the will towards the essential formal object of the contract; or (2) prescinding from the power to elicit naturally sufficient internal consent, it renders the subject naturally unfit for the state of marriage, naturally incapable of assuming the essential rights and obligations of the contract, *subiectum incapax iurium et obligationum contractus maritalis,* because psychically incapable of sustaining and honoring the aforementioned rights and obligations.

Conversely, "due discretion" — the minimum psychic aptitude required for validly entering the contract — includes a twofold aspect in the concept of mental competence *circa rem uxoriam*: (1) the psychic ability to elicit internal consent naturally sufficient to initiate the contract (*causa efficiens matrimonii*); (2) the psychic aptitude to assume the essential rights and obligations of the contract, to be a *subiectum capax iurium et obligationum matrimonialium* (*causa materialis matrimonii*).

Article 3. Amentia Perfecta seu Plena.

The third and, by far, the most important condition which must be verified in establishing the invalidating force of mental illness is that the disorder be what Rotal jurisprudence has traditionally called "*perfecta seu plena.*"[66]

---

[66] "Iurisprudentia tam doctrinalis quam iudiciaria una voce affirmat tunc tantum insaniam matrimonium prohibere contractumque dirimere cum perfecta et plena sit." — c. Teodori, June 9, 1942 (Vol. XXXIV, 467-468). Cf. also c. Prior, May 15, 1915 (Vol. VII, 217); c. Rossetti, May 10, 1921 (Vol. XIII, 87); c. Rossetti, July 1, 1922 (Vol. XIV, 210); c. Wynen, Mar. 1, 1930 (Vol. XXII, 130); c. Wynen, June 3, 1939 (Vol. XXXI, 373). That this principle has been traditional is affirmed in a decision c. Parrillo, Feb. 16, 1928: "Auctores et iurisprudentia, praesertim nostri fori, interpretationes cap. *Dilectus,* 24, *De spons. et matrim.,* quo Innocentius III declarat: 'Propter alienationem furoris, legitimus non potuit intervenire consensus' (legitimus nempe, iuxta naturae legem, prout ait Gonzalez in *Comm.* ad huiusmodi caput), unanimes docent, tunc tantum insaniam matrimonium prohibere, contractumque dirimere, cum perfecta et plena sit, nam si semiplena, a valide contrahendo coniugio non arcet." — *S.R.R.Dec.,* Vol. XX, 59.

It is well known that mental derangement extends in its gravity and damaging effect over countless degrees from normality to utter insanity. It is likewise clear, at least in theory, that mental illness or impairment incapacitates for valid marriage only when it has reached such gravity as to deprive the subject of the minimum degree of discretion required for entering the marriage contract. Immediately, however, a point must be made in order to understand the background of the many conflicting axioms about *amentia perfecta* and *imperfecta* that we find among the *motiva in iure* of early Rotal sentences and among canonical commentaries even today.

The terms "*perfecta, imperfecta, plena, semiplena*" can be taken in three distinct senses: (1) *juridically*: a mental disorder is "*perfecta seu plena*" if it effectively deprives the subject of due discretion for marriage; it is "*imperfecta seu semiplena*" if it leaves the minimum degree of due discretion intact.[67] In this sense, then, there are two certain principles, namely, "*amentia perfecta*" invalidates marriage; "*amentia imperfecta*" does not. (2) *medically*: a given mental disorder is "*perfecta*" if it is, in its etiological course, full-blown, terminal, fully developed, or, as Rotal sentences are wont to say in Italian, "*conclamata*". The disorder might be called "*imperfecta seu semiplena*" if it is still in its initial stage of development, or at least has not yet reached its term of gravity. In this sense, a certain mental disorder or defect might be medically perfect (v.g. certain psychoneuroses and nervous disorders) and yet be juridically "*imperfecta*". On the other hand, a disease might be medically "*semiplena*" and yet be juridically "*perfecta seu plena*".[68] (3) *Psychologically*: a mental disorder is perfect if it fully deprives the subject of the use of reason, imperfect if it partially deprives him of the use of reason.

---

[67] Cf. FÄSSLER, *Die Schizophrenie als Ehenichtigkeitsgrund im kanonischen Recht*, p. 120.

[68] "Quibus intelligitur quare scite notaverat R.P.D. Pericles Felici in una d. 26 februarii 1952 mentis discretionem insufficientem esse, non modo in terminali seu conclusiva phasi dementiae praecocis, sed etiam in phase initiali, dummodo tamen revera constiterit, auxilio peritorum, actu iam tunc exstitisse dissociationem, qua constituitur istud malum." — c. Lefebvre (Quebecen.), Apr. 7, 1960.

Understood in the juridical sense, there can be no objection to such Rotal axioms as:

> Non omnis habitualis infirmitas mentis arcet a valido consensu ponendo, sed ea tantum, quae ad gradum plenae et perfectae insaniae pervenit.[69]
> Matrimonium non invalidat amentia imperfecta...[70]
> Qui laborant insania semiplena contrahere valent matrimonium.[71]

Cappello, however, places the question whether *amentia imperfecta* invalidates marriage and answers that it does, since due discretion for marriage can be destroyed not only if the use of reason is completely eliminated, but also if it is seriously impaired.[72] Regatillo states that *amentia imperfecta* invalidates if it leaves the afflicted person closer to a state of insanity than to the state of sanity.[73] Noting this discrepancy among authors, d'Avack states that the Rota, although adhering to the "old" opinion in principle, is nevertheless swinging its position in practice to the principle that *amentia imperfecta* also invalidates marriage.[74]

It seems, however, that neither the principles nor the practice of the Rota has changed in this regard, at least in the last forty-five years. The apparent controversy rests on the confusion between the juridical and psychological understanding of the terms "*perfecta*" and "*imperfecta*". Already at the time of the Code the Rota recognized that "*usus rationis non sufficit*" as a criterion of psychic ability to marry validly; a person might well be endowed with

---

[69] C. Wynen, June 3, 1939 (Vol. XXXI, 373).

[70] C. Morano, Dec. 21, 1935 (Vol. XXVII, 695).

[71] C. Rossetti, July 1, 1922 (Vol. XIV, 210); c. Rossetti, July 3, 1922 (Vol. XIV, 223).

[72] "Alii censent amentiam semiplenam sive imperfectam impedire actum humanum ideoque obesse validae celebrationi matrimonii. Quae sententia, perspectis gravissimis officiis matrimonialis contractus eiusque perpetuitate et indissolubilitate, certa videtur." — *De matrimonio*, n. 579.

[73] "*Plene amentes* sunt incapaces ad matrimonium. *Semiamentes*, ut capaces iudicentur, debent magis de sana quam de insana mente participare; in quo discernendo est maxima difficultas, quia ab insana ad sanam mentem multi sunt gradus semiamentiae. Unde non solum amentia plena et furor, qui omnino usum rationis adimit, matrimonium dirimit; sed et ea quae infra semiamentiam vel semifurorem plus minus posita est." — *Ius sacramentarium*, n. 1316.

[74] *Cause di nullità e di divorzio*, p. 183.

the simple use of reason, be able to manage his affairs prudently, and yet be devoid of due discretion for marriage. Rotal jurisprudence is unanimous, both in principle and in practice, that a person need not be fully deprived of reason before he be considered devoid of due discretion for marriage. In this psychological sense which considers the invalidating force of mental illness solely on the premise of "use of reason", certainly "*amentia imperfecta*" can invalidate marriage. If Rotal jurisprudence is changing its position, it is in the direction of abandoning the terms "*perfecta*" and "*imperfecta*" because they have not only caused this apparent confusion and doctrinal controversy, but also because they are not especially relevant, since the whole question of the invalidating force of mental illness is resolved in the simple question of due discretion, which can easily prescind from the bearing of psychic disorder on the "use of reason." On this theme a recent Rotal decision stated:

> Consequenter aptius expungi debet conceptus juridico-contractualis amentiae semiplenae seu imperfectae relate ad consensum matrimonialem.
>
> A) Imprimis *nomen istud* --- amentia semiplena --- *sat aequivocum perhibetur.* Nam ansam dedit decisionibus et opinionibus omnino contradictoriis... Distinctio, ideo, inter plenam et semiplenam amentiam instrumentum sat inidoneum apparet, si fovet talem confusionem et contradictionem.
>
> B) Reapse, si acceptatur definitio supra tradita (n. 2, a), evidenter *locus amplius non est amentiae sic dictae "semiplenae"*, quia vel adest illa sufficiens discretio iudicii, vel non adest. Si prius, habetur sanitas; si alterum *amentia* simpliciter.
>
> C) Amentia sic dicta "*plena*" sensum, *non iuridicum*, sed tantum *medicum* habere potest, et designat statum subiecti, in quo perturbationes mentem ita invaserint, ut quamlibet facultatem sive intellectivam sive volitivam penitus pessumdederint.
>
> Unde ulterius quoque confirmatur medicinae nomina et species non posse simpliciter transferri in provinciam iuris, sed debere per iuridica principia quodammodo colari et iuridico ordini aptari.
>
> D) Intra traditum conceptum amentiae contractualis simpliciter talis, evidenter comprehenditur etiam monomania seu *insania circa rem uxoriam.*
>
> E) Ad valedicendum huic distinctioni inter plenam et semiplenam amentiam, *Nos impellere videntur quaedam deci-*

siones N.S.O. (*S.R.R. Dec.*, XXXV-87-2)... Conferatur quoque *S.R.R. Dec.*, Vol. XXX, dec 2, n. 2, coram E.mo Heard, ubi quoque tota quaestio reducitur ad discretionem iudicii. [75]

This evaluation of the distinction between *amentia perfecta* and *amentia imperfecta* should be kept in mind for a proper consideration of what follows.

I. *Amentia Habitualis.*

In the line of axiomatic principles in both jurisprudence and canonical doctrine, we find contradictions. On the one hand, early writers and court decisions declared that only he who is completely devoid of the use of reason is incapable of marriage, [76] while other writers and decisions, equally prominent, declare that the full use of reason, liberty, and deliberation must be retained for valid entry into matrimony. [77] If we substitute the words "minimum degree of discretion" in place of the words "use of reason", both sides are equally correct, but left in the psychological sense, both sides are equally incorrect. An attempt to detach the norm from the ambiguous "use of reason" gauge brought about the adoption of a formula familiar in civil law... the ability to manage one's affairs. Thus *amentia perfecta* was defined as mental disorder which renders the afflicted person incapable of managing his own affairs.[78] That this was not an accurate or safe

[75] C. Sabattani (Januen.), Feb. 24, 1961. Published in *Monitor Ecclesiasticus,* LXXXVI 1961), pp. 633-634.

[76] Cf. CASTAÑEDA, *La locura y el matrimonio,* pp. 44-45.

[77] CASTAÑEDA, *ibid.* A fairly recent sentence states: "Sapientissime ergo canonica doctrina a contrahendo valide matrimonio arcet eos qui sive deliberata voluntate destituuntur, sive *plena* libertate privantur." — c. Caiazzo, July 30, 1940 (Vol. XXXII, 612). Cappello seems to lean to this side too when he states: "Nuptiae ineuntur per consensum matrimonialem, qui natura sua est *actus humanus* vere et proprie dictus, ideoque necessario exigit sufficientem mentis discretionem seu *perfectum usum rationis.*" — *De matrimonio,* n. 383.

[78] "Insania mentis admittit diversos gradus; est enim maior vel minor pro diversitate casuum. Hoc sub respectu est valde communis. Ea tamen usum rationis non tollit nisi attingat gradum qui hominem incapacem faciat apte providendi suis negotiis. Ideo insania distingui solet inter insaniam perfectam et insaniam imperfectam. Perfecta dicitur quae hominem incapacem facit apte providendi suis negotiis; imperfecta quae hanc capacitatem tantummodo attenuat. Illa censetur auferre usum rationis; ista rationis usum tantummodo debilitat. An vero mentis infirmitas attigerit gradum insaniae perfectae, quae nempe hominem incapacem faciat

criterion was obvious, and the classical phrase of Mannucci is still cited in Rotal sentences: "*Unde nil mirum, si quis appareat adhuc sua posse apte agere et ordinare negocia, qui tamen ad matrimonium censeri incapax debeat*".[79] As is so often the case in the matter of marriage and insanity, the dictum of Cardinal Gasparri remains the most accurate:

> Tandem illi, quos *fatuos* vel *stupidos* appellamus, si sufficientem habeant discretionem, possunt utique matrimonium inire, sicuti alios contractus.[80]

Here again the tendency is away from extrinsic distinctions and towards resolution of the entire problem in the universal intrinsic criterion of due discretion.

Particularly difficult is the judicial evaluation of psychic competence in cases of so-called *progressive* mental diseases.[81] Generally mental derangement does not strike suddenly[82] but gradually develops in gravity over a span of months or perhaps years.[83] Precisely at what point in the person's mental deterioration he loses due discretion for valid marriage is often nebulous and sometimes complicated by the fact that the degenerative process is latent beneath equivocal or, at best, inconclusive signs prior to the marriage.[84]

---

apte providendi suis negotiis, id remissum est existimationi ac prudentiae iudicis." — c. Morano, Apr. 30, 1935 (Vol. XXVII, 281-282). "Amentia invalidat matrimonium, si sit perfecta et concomitans. Perfecta autem ea dicitur quae tollit usum rationis, ita ut hominem incapacem faciat providendi suis negotiis. Propterea matrimonium non invalidat amentia imperfecta, quae nempe usum rationis tantummodo minuit, ita ut hominem non faciat incapacem providendi suis negotiis." — c. Morano, Dec. 21, 1935 (Vol. XXVII, 695-696).

[79] C. Mannucci, Aug. 8, 1931 (Vol. XXIII, 373).

[80] GASPARRI, *De matrimonio*, n. 785.

[81] "Tandem amentia potest esse *subitanea*, ut si quis veluti uno ictu usum rationis amittat, vel alio ex morbo, aut *progressiva*, quam vocant." — c. Sincero, Dec. 23, 1918 (Vol. X, 143).

[82] "Nam regulariter ad eam pervenitur sensim sine sensu." — D'ANNIBALE, *Summula theologiae moralis*, I, n. 31.

[83] "Morbi mentis enim cum morbis corporis id commune habent, quod generatim neque exoriantur ex abrupto neque statim appareant plene evoluti, sed potius initium capiant ex certis dispositionibus et saepe per annos sensim et pedetentim se evolvant, usque dum infirmi ad statum plenae et perfectae amentiae perveniant." — c. Wynen, Mar. 1, 1930 (Vol. XXII, 130).

[84] "Non raro valde difficile est scire cum certitudine, quo tempore morbus amentiae inceptus sit, et ad quam gradum evolutionis pervenerit

It is clear, then, that the judge must distinguish carefully between the effective damage upon the psychic faculties at a given stage of the disease's development and its external manifestation at that time.[85] Symptoms of mental aberration prior to the wedding, often equivocal in themselves, can often be reduced to a certain diagnosis by the experts in light of the subsequent course of the illness so that at least the existence of the same illness can be established at the time of the wedding. However, as one Rotal decision pointed out: "For some doctors, proof of the existence of mental illness suffices to prove a defect of liberty; this is not enough; it is necessary, moreover, to prove that, given its gravity, he could not give consent."[86]

It is again the presumption of continuity which is the indispensable instrument in ascertaining the existing degree of mental competence for marriage at the moment when the contract was entered. Regarding the question of concomitant gravity of mental illness, d'Avack makes three hypotheses:

1) Antecedent and subsequent *amentia* present the identical degree of gravity and there is neither direct nor indirect proof of the degree of gravity of concomitant *amentia*. In this case, which presents little difficulty, concomitant insanity is presumed to have retained the same degree of gravity of antecedent and subsequent insanity. Thus, if it is clear that the person, both before and after the wedding, was deprived of due discretion, it is presumed that at the very moment of contracting he was mentally incompetent for marriage. Conversely, if it is not clear that he was deprived of due discretion either before or after the wedding, it is presumed that he possessed due discretion during the ceremony.

---

die quo matrimonium contractum est, cum non omnes sint furiosi et 'saepe sint constituti in conspectu umbratae quietis, nec tamen sint mentis sanae, licet videantur.' " — c. Heard, July 19, 1941 (Vol. XXXIII, 653).

[85] "Dein in ipsa amentia progressiva, quae gradatim evolvitur, distingendum est inter gradum evolutionis amentiae, et eiusdem manifestationem per signa et indicia." — c. Sincero, Dec. 23, 1918 (vol. X, 143).

[86] C. Massimi, Nov. 20, 1931 (Vol. XXIII, 464): "Neque ad excludendam libertatem satis est ostendere hominem infirmitate aliqua mentis laborare, sed probare oportet consensum, attenta gravitate morbi, praestari haud potuisse."

[87] *Cause di nullità e di divorzio*, pp. 179-184.

2) Antecedent and subsequent *amentia* present the identical degree of gravity, but there is evidence that concomitant *amentia* was probably less than the two extremes. This is often the case with cyclic diseases like manic-depressive psychosis. Referring to the doctrine on lucid intervals, d'Avack states that until it is proved that the person effectively regained due discretion at the time of the wedding, one may presume that, in doubt, the person lacked due discretion. [88]

3) Antecedent and subsequent *amentia* present different degrees of gravity and there are not sufficient elements of proof to establish the degree of concomitant gravity. This is the usual situation in progressive diseases: at a certain point after the wedding it is certain that the person is psychically incompetent for valid marriage although before the marriage the mental illness was probably not serious enough to preclude due discretion. As a result the condition of the contractant on the wedding day is doubtful. Should the judge presume that concomitant insanity approaches more the antecedent condition (*amentia imperfecta*) or rather the subsequent condition (*amentia perfecta*)? D'Avack and Ravà answer simply that concomitant *amentia* is to be presumed to have already reached the graver subsequent stage and hence it is presumed that the afflicted person contracted invalidly. [89]

---

[88] *Ibid.*, p. 180. RAVÀ, "Il *defectus discretionis iudicii* come causa di nullità del matrimonio nella giurisprudenza rotale," *Il Diritto Ecclesiastico*, LXVIII (1957), II, p. 466: "Così, in caso di alienazione mentale periodica con cicli susseguentisi di accessi morbosi o di soste più o meno lunghe e complete, si presumerà, fino a prova in contrario, che il matrimonio sia stato contratto dall'infermo in periodo di accesso morboso dell'infermità stessa." It should be noted that the Rota does not apply the presumption only on the basis of the two extremes having been established; this leads only to a founded possibility of concomitant insanity. Rather, the legitimacy of the presumption in cases of manic-depressive psychosis must be supported by evidence of mental derangement surrounding the wedding day. cf. *supra*, footnote 27.

[89] "...si è giustamente concordi nel ritenere... che l'*amentia* concomitans debba presumersi assurta già al grado di un'*amentia plena seu perfecta* e che pertanto il contraente abbia invalidamente contratto il suo matrimonio *ex defectu debitae discretionis judicii.*" — D'AVACK, *op. cit.*, pp. 182-183.

"Così, in caso di alienazione mentale progressiva, dove il grado di gravità della malattia aumenta col trascorrere del tempo, si presumerà, fino a prova in contrario, che l'*amentia concomitans* abbia già raggiunto il grado dell'*amentia plena seu perfecta,* intendendosi, per tale, quella

Castañeda repeats this principle but qualifies it in the sense that such a presumption is legitimate only if the subsequent term of *amentia perfecta* has been established as existing within a few months after the wedding.[90] That in case of doubt, writes d'Avack, concomitant insanity is to be presumed as having reached the more acute stage of true *amentia perfecta* is recognized without difficulty in all canonical doctrine and jurisprudence.[91]

It seems, however, that the bald presumption, as enunciated by d'Avack, is of doubtful validity even in the abstract. He states that it is to be employed when the judge has not attained moral certitude either of the fact of due discretion at the time of the marriage ceremony or of its defect.[92] In the last analysis, then, it is this presumption which would decide the case. The *favor matrimonii,* which normally should be operative so long as the judge has not attained to moral certitude of the existence of a cause of nullity, is in direct antithesis to this personal presumption and, according to d'Avack, cedes to it since "once the existence of any *amentia habitualis* has been positively established, the presumption of the *favor matrimonii* becomes inoperative and the *amentia* is presumed *a priori* to constitute an *amentia in actu matrimonii, in ordine ad matrimonium et in gradu proportionato matrimonio,* that is, precisely of such a nature as to constitute an impediment and correlative cause of nullity of the marriage bond."[93] That this is an inaccurate conception of the nature of both personal presumptions and the legal

---

che toglie nell'individuo la *capacitas ad matrimonium intelligendum et eligendum,* nel senso a suo tempo delineato." — RAVÀ, *op. cit.*, p. 466.

[90] "Si la enfermedad aparece en dicho período *conclamato* mucho tiempo después de celebrado el matrimonio, creemos más bien debe presumirse celebrado aquél en un estado de amencia semiplena, en el período de incubación de le enfermedad, debiendo, por el contrario, presumirse la amencia concomitante plena y perfecta cuando aquel período de *estado* de la enfermedad aparece claramente manifiesto pocos meses después de celebrado aquél." — CASTAÑEDA, *La locura y el matrimonio,* p. 106.

[91] "Ora che in caso di dubbio l'*amentia concomitans* debba essere presunta come già assurta allo stadio più acuto della vera *amentia perfecta* appare evidente dalle osservazioni fatte e tutta la dottrina e giurisprudenza lo riconoscono senza difficoltà". — D'AVACK, *Corso di diritto canonico: Il matrimonio,* I (Milano: Giuffrè, 1961), p. 149.

[92] D'AVACK, *Cause di nullità e di divorzio,* p. 182.

[93] *Ibid.*, p. 184.

presumption of the *favor matrimonii* has been indicated elsewhere.[94]

Furthermore, the Rota itself has never enunciated such a presumption as a general principle. Current jurisprudence, in fact, is tending away more and more from axiomatic principles and presumptions in ascertainig the *quaestio facti,* insisting rather on constructing presumptions only on the facts of a given case. This is a far more realistic approach and more in accord with the nature of personal presumptions, for the legitimacy, strength, and ultimate value of a personal presumption in the formation of moral certitude depend entirely on the "certain and determinate" facts from which it is conjectured in a given case.[95]

II. *Mentis Debilitas* and *Defectus Sensuum.*

In general the phrase *mentis debilitas* in ecclesiastical law indicates a mental illness or disease which *partially* deprives a person of the use of reason, whether the disorder is congenital or acquired, permanent or temporary.[96]

---

[94] Cf. *supra, "Praesumptiones Hominis* and the *Favor Matrimonii,"* pp. 46-50.

[95] Canon 1828: "Praesumptiones, quae non statuuntur a iure, iudex ne coniiciat, nisi ex facto certo et determinato, quod cum eo, de quo controversia est, directe cohaereat."

An excellent example of building a practical judgment concerning the gravity of concomitant *amentia* based on the particular nature of a given case is had in the recent Rotal decision *coram* Sabattani (Januen.), Feb. 24, 1961. The crucial point of the case was to ascertain whether or not in the defendant, afflicted by a progressive alcoholic psychosis, due discretion had already been destroyed at the time of the wedding:

"C) Implexior est *quaestio de gradu hujus debilitatis mentis determinando relate ad tempus matrimonii.*

Oportet enim quod, in casu particulari alicujus alcoholismi chronici, Iudex elementa habeat ad discernendum quando requisita maturitas iudicii ad contrahendum servata dici debeat, quando vero amissa.

En elementa, ex quibus Iudex iudicium suum practicum haurire forsan poterit:

a) *Antiquitas processus toxici...* b) *Gravitas processus toxici...* c) *Detrusiones in amentium valetudinaria...* d) *Stigmata qualificata amentiae...* utpote deliria, alucinationes et huiusmodi. e) *Effectus iam deductus,* vel minus, *anaesthesiae moralis.*

D) Haec criteria perpendendo, difficile non erit Iudici ex circumstantiis casus particularis sufficientia elementa haurire ad determinandum gradum huius mentalis infirmitatis, ac proinde sufficientis vel minus discretionis iudicii ad contrahendum." — *Monitor Ecclesiasticus,* LXXXVI (1961), pp. 639-640.

[96] Noval defines it as: "Imperfectus usus rationis aut voluntatis ob

Although the Code recognizes criminal responsibility in the *mente debiles* [97] and denies them full juridical capacity to stand in court by themselves, [98] it says nothing of their capacity to marry. Nevertheless, the terms *mente debiles mentis debilitas, mentis infirmitas,* etc., are commonly used by canonical doctrine and jurisprudence in regard to marriage capacity.

If *mentis debilitas* is taken in the sense of *amentia iuridice imperfecta,* that is, mental illness which does not deprive one of due discretion for marriage, then it is clear that *mentis debilitas* has no relevance in the matrimonial forum. If it is taken in the psychological sense of early doctrine and jurisprudence, that is, simply as a mental illness which partially handicaps the use of reason without destroying it, then *mentis debilitas* might invalidate the bond or not, depending on whether, *per accidens,* it also deprived the subject of minimal due discretion. Again it is seen how an axiom such as "*Ii qui amentia tantum semiplena laborant valide possunt inire matrimonium*" [99] is true in one sense and false in another.

In matrimonial jurisprudence the phrase has taken on a peculiar sense, referring to that category of mental illnesses which psychiatrists have traditionally labeled "mental deficiency." Although the phrase is used in a wide sense denoting an intermediate stage in progressively deteriorating psychoses towards terminal maturation, [100] when

---

defectum sive congenitum, sive acquisitum, vel perpetuum vel temporaneum sed aequaliter stabilem, in organis perceptionis vel appetitus sensibilis, qui tamen non impedit omnino usum rationis et libertatem." — "De semi-amentibus et semi-imputabilitati obnoxiis," *Jus Pontificium,* IV (1924), p. 82. MICHIELS, *Principia generalia de personis in Ecclesia,* p. 84: "Praeter amentes et dementes sive habitualiter sive incidenter usu rationis penitus carentes, de quibus hucusque egimus, a legislatore ecclesiastico speciatim attenduntur personae quae usu rationis gaudent, sed gradu plus minusve incompleto aut imperfecto, ita ut iis desit *sufficiens discretio mentis* ad plenam responsabilitatem moralem aut criminalem suorum actuum vel ad certos actus juridicos valide ponendos requisita (can. 2201, § 3 et § 4)."

[97] Canon 2201, § 4.

[98] Canon 1650.

[99] C. Many, Aug. 11, 1913 (Vol. V, 564).

[100] C. Sabattani (Januen.), Feb. 24, 1961: "*Duae sunt praecipuae formae* hujus infirmitatis: (a) *mentis debilitas sensu lato.* Haec est status morbi mentalis ingravescentis, *momentum in itinere ad amentiam,* et complectitur illas morbidas condiciones *ex se capaces gradatim confluendi in*

a marriage is attacked on the grounds of *mentis debilitas,* it usually means the defendant is alleged to have contracted while suffering from oligophrenia, mental retardation, feeble-mindedness, etc. — and this, usually, as a borderline mental defective.

Noyes and Kolb describe mental deficiency as a "defect in mental competency, resulting either from an innate fault in developmental potentiality or from an arrest in developmental progress, that it is impossible for the patient to make an adequate and independent social adjustment. According to this definition the mental capacity possessed by the average person has not been attained by the feeble-minded person, either because an innate relative poverty in his capacity for mental development has retarded his mental growth *ab initio,* or, as is now believed to be more frequently the case, disease or injury of the brain has caused a retardation in mental development." [101]

The classifications of mental defectives are usually made according to psychometric tests which evaluate the deficiency in terms of the individual's mental age and intelligence quotient. The common categories are:

Above 135	— Genius
125-135	— Very superior
115-125	— Superior
105-115	— High normal
95-105	— Normal
80-95	— Dull normal
70-80	— Borderline
50-70	— Moron or feeble-minded
30-50	— Imbecile
0-30	— Idiot

---

amentiam, quaeque tamen in casu specifico videntur exstitisse in gradu intermedio, in phasi haud certo terminali.

Ad hanc speciem pertinent: insania progressiva in stadiis intermediis, insania alterna quoad stadia dubia, alcoholismus chronicus, toxicomania, etc.

(b) *mentis debilitas sensu stricto.* Haec est permanens condicio morbida, usque ad mortem duratura, incapax se evolvendi usque ad totalem defectum usus rationis, neque in stadiis gravioribus." — *Monitor Ecclesiasticus,* LXXXVI (1961), p. 636. Cf. also D'Avack, *Cause di nullità e di divorzio,* p. 218; Ravà, *op. cit.,* pp. 469-470.

[101] Arthur P. Noyes and Lawrence C. Kolb, *Modern Clinical Psychiatry* (5th ed.; Philadelphia and London, W. B. Saunders Co., 1961), p. 324.

There can be little doubt about the marriage capacity of those with extreme cases of mental deficiency, like idiots and high grade imbeciles. The question of the marriage capacity of the *mente debilis* is centered about cases involving low grade imbecility, feeble-mindedness, and high grade borderline deficiency.

A recent Rotal decision made it clear that although Canon Law judges the feeble-minded to be capable of mortal sin and delicts, nevertheless, since due discretion for marriage involves more than penal imputability, there is at law no general presumption either of capacity or incapacity for marriage regarding the *mente debiles.* The entire question is remitted to an investigation in each individual case of the presence of absence of due descretion.[102] The same decision, however, pointed out that given the particular situation of a certain case, the judge might have two distinct starting points:

1) In cases of mental debility in the wide sense, i. e., as an intermediary stage in a steadily deteriorating condition which terminally deprived the individual of due discretion: *"mentis debilitas sensu lato praestat grave indicium deficientis discretionis iudicii".*[103]

2) In cases of mental debility in the strict sense, i. e., a stable condition partially depriving the person of the use of reason: *"mentis debilitas, stricto sensu accepta, praesumitur, e contra, imperfecta, ita ut relinquat discretionem iudicii".*[104]

Not uncommon in Rotal jurisprudence are nullity cases involving a mental defective pleaded on the grounds of relatively grave fear or force. It can happen that a person suffering from a low grade mental deficiency or from other mental disorders which do not deprive him

---

[102] C. Sabattani (Januen.), Feb. 24, 1961: "Qui *mente debilis est, in iure poenali* iudicatur habilis ad lethaliter peccandum et ad crimen patrandum. At, quia discretio iudicii matrimonio proportionata plus importat quam poenalis imputabilitas, *ex mentis debilitate non habetur generalis praesumptio neque habilitatis neque inhabilitatis* ad matrimonium contrahendum: in singulis casibus, omnibus circumstantiis attente cribratis, statuendum erit utrum hujusmodi habilitas permaneat, an non." — *Monitor Ecclesiasticus,* LXXXVI (1961), pp. 635-636.

[103] *Ibid.,* p. 636.

[104] *Ibid.* This presumption supposes that we are not speaking of extreme cases of mental deficiency (e.g., idiots), but of moderate cases.

of due discretion be rendered thereby easy prey to undue extrinsic duress.[105] A recent Rotal decision, answering affirmatively on the grounds of relatively grave fear in a man suffering from a depressive psychoneurosis, made the observation among the motives *in iure*:

> In aestimanda proinde gravitate metus perpendere debet iudex non modo *naturam* mali quod timetur, necnon *indolem* incutientis, sed etiam qualitates subiectivas patientis. Facilius enim trepidant puellae quam viri, aegroti quam sani, adolescentes quam aetate maturi, mente debiles quam homines constantes.[106]

A problem closely aligned with that of mental debility and frequently discussed by the medieval canonists is that of the marriage capacity of the deaf, dumb, and blind from birth. It is not, of course, that these defects constitute immediately a cause of nullity, but they might arrest intellectual development to such an extent that the afflicted person never attains to the minimal degree of psychic aptitude basic to true marital consent or, even allowing such development, the person can easily be the victim of actual ignorance or error *de re matrimoniali.* D'Annibale called it a "*quaestio delicatior quam vulgo existimetur, obscura et difficilior*".[107]

Canonical doctrine sees no difficulty regarding the capacity of those who are either deaf or dumb or blind

---

105 "Contingere autem potest alicui minus firmae mentis ut, servata quidem discretione rationis sufficiente ad valide contrahendum, facilius tamen ob mentis debilitatem subiaceat auctoritati alterius, cui iniuste imperanti resistere non valeat, trepidans ubi aliquis sanae mentis non timeret aut leviter timeret. Verum ut talis metus dicatur invalidans matrimonium, comprobentur oportet conditiones iure ad hoc requisitae, nempe: sit metus gravis pro illa persona, ab extrinseco et iniuste incussus, a quo contrahens ut se liberet, eligere cogatur matrimonium, cfr. can. 1087." — c. Jullien, Feb. 23, 1935 (Vol. XXVII, 80).

106 C. Pinna (Romana), Nov. 30, 1961. The same *ponens* elsewhere states: "Ipse metus mali *supernaturalis* boni, seu privationis *supernaturalis* boni, qui per se *ab intrinseco* procedit, et ideo impar est ad vitiandum consensum, evadere potest gravis et irritans matrimonium, si quis eodem utatur ad impellendum nupturientem quem novit facile trepidaturum... Perpendenda praeterea sunt psychica adiuncta personae metuentis, quae firma manente capacitate intelligendi ac volendi et ideo praestandi validum consensum, ita extenuatas habeat facultates ut impulsui de se haud gravi resistere non valeat... quia ob mentis debilitatem inhabilis est." — c. Pinna (Burdigalen.), Feb. 16, 1960.

107 D'ANNIBALE, *Summula theologiae moralis*, I, n. 30.

from birth, or regarding the incapacity of those who are simultaneously deaf, dumb, and blind from birth or early infancy.[108] The problem is restricted to combinations of two of the three defects:

1) Deaf-blind: Medieval canonists were divided on the question. The authoritative Sanchez held them incompetent on the grounds that: "*Mutus solis signis edoceri potest, quid sit matrimonium; caecus autem signa haec percipere nequit; nec etiam verba cum simul surdus sit.*"[109] Although recent canonical doctrine overlooks the question, d'Avack sees no reason to dismiss the opinion of Sanchez, and holds for a presumption of incompetence which yields only to positive proof that the afflicted person certainly possessed due discretion.[110]

2) Deaf-mute: The decretal *Cum apud* of Innocent III treated of this problem *ex professo*, holding for the capacity of the deaf-mute to contract matrimony since there was no prohibitive prescription and, as far as the manifestation of consent was concerned: "*Quod verbis non potest signis valeat declarare*".[111] Innocent's reply gave impetus to the opinion favoring the capacity of deaf-mutes, but a reaction was not long in coming. First of all it was not clear whether Innocent had been referring to those afflicted from birth; secondly, it was question-

---

[108] GASPARRI, *Tractatus de matrimonio*, II, n. 786: "*Surdi-muti-caeci* simul a nativitate, quos *idiotas* vocant, accensentur infantibus, ideoque matrimonii sunt incapaces... Qui autem sunt tantum vel *caeci* vel *muti* vel *surdi*, etsi a nativitate, ratione pollent sufficienti ad matrimonium." Cappello repeats the common opinion on the incapacity of those deaf, dumb, and blind conjunctively from birth but observes: "At pro casibus extraordinariis, praesertim iuxta recentiora experimenta et progressus nostra aetate factos in iisdem instruendi, *absolute* inhabiles dici nequeunt." — *De matrimonio*, n. 87. For the doctrine of the early canonists, cf. D'AVACK, *op. cit.*, pp. 202-205.

[109] SANCHEZ, *De sancto matrimonii sacramento*, Lib. I, Disp. VIII, n. 13.

[110] Cf. D'AVACK, *op. cit.*, p. 204; idem, *Corso di diritto canonico*: *Il matrimonio*, I, p. 160.

[111] C. 23, X, IV, 1: "Sane, consuluisti nos per nuncios et literas tuas, utrum mutus et surdus alicui possint matrimonialiter copulare. Ad quod fraternitati tuae taliter respondemus, quod, quum prohibitorium sit edictum de matrimonio contrahendo, ut, quicunque non prohibetur, per consequentiam admittatur, et sufficiat ad matrimonium solus consensus illorum, de quorum quarumque coniunctionibus agitur, videtur, quod, si talis velit contrahere, sibi non possit vel debeat denegari, quum quod verbis non potest signis valeat declarare." (Innocent III to the Bishop of Arles, 1198).

able whether the Pope was speaking of the deaf and dumb conjunctively or disjunctively. Thus, later canonical doctrine swung to the other side, not however excluding the possibility of due discretion in certain cases. Modern doctrine, tending away as always from extrinsic axioms, banks the question on the training and education of the individual in a particular case.[112]

As might be expected, marriage tribunals will not encounter many cases of *defectus sensuum*, since the defect, being manifest at the time of marriage, will prompt closer investigation into the person's due discretion and knowledge *de re matrimoniali* as he prepares to enter the contract. A case, however, was brought before the Rota recently, pleaded on the grounds of ignorance of the nature of marriage and marital rights and duties in the man, who was deaf and dumb from infancy. The court, in handing down an affirmative decision, stated:

> In limine necesse est subiectum perpendere quod nescivisse praedicatur formale matrimonii obiectum. Surdus et mutus erat actor ab infantia, et huic defectui peculiaris conditio pathologica accedebat consequens trauma grave seu fracturam calvariae quae a biennio aetatis suae normalem praepedivit evolutionem psychophysicam. Hinc insufficiens educatio quae causam endogenam habuit in mentis debilitate, causam vero exogenam in surditate et absentia eloquii, quibus praepedita fuit debita institutio... Hisce accessit negligentia parentum in suppeditanda proportionata et congrua educatione puero, qui post nativitatem alius filii "était negligé et livré à lui même".
>
> Hinc nemo ipsi res sexuales collustravit; imo praeceptor monitus fuit a parentibus de tali argumento non explicando. Ceteras res externas ex visu percepit, id neque ex visu neque theoretica illustratione attingere potuit ab externo, dum debilitas mentis haud permisit rem a seipso suspicari.
>
> In casu tamen, attenta deficiente discretione et evolutione psychophysica, instinctus docere nequivit essentiale matrimonii obiectum.[113]

---

[112] GASPARRI, *op. cit.*, II, n. 786: "*Surdi-muti* simul a nativitate, si instituti sunt, et peccandi et delinquendi et contrahendi capaces habentur; et de hoc nullum potest esse dubium." Cf. REGATILLO, *Ius sacramentarium*, n. 1318; CAPPELLO, *op. cit.*, n. 579; MANS-BERNÁRDEZ, *Derecho matrimonial canónico*, I, pp. 324, 325, 331.

[113] C. Pinna (Parisien.), Oct. 30, 1958. This affirmative decision was subsequently reversed in appeal, c. Pasquazi, July 20, 1961.

III. *Mentis Exturbatio.*

In the category of mental disturbance (*mentis exturbatio*) are included all those causes of marital nullity arising from a *temporary* state of mental incompetence for placing valid consent in an otherwise habitually competent person. For example, a marriage might be null because consent is expressed by one in a state of alcoholic intoxication, narcotic euphoria or depression, somnambulation, hypnotic trance, epileptic seizure, febrile delirium, etc. Both canonical commentaries and jurisprudence group these causes of nullity together with insanity under the same *caput nullitatis.* The supposition is that both *amentia habitualis* and *mentis exturbatio* invalidate the contract in identically the same way, the only difference being that in the first case the incompetence is habitual while in the second case it is temporary — an incidental difference at best, since antecedent and subsequent incompetence have no direct bearing on the possible invalidity of the bond. [114] Thus, Rotal jurisprudence seems to assign to both an identical *caput nullitatis;* in each case the marriage is null because the contractant was " *incapax valide praestandi consensum* ".

It seems to us, however, that the phrase "*incapacitas valide praestandi consensum*" includes two distinct sources of nullity and that, *salvo meliori judicio,* habitual insanity and passing mental disturbance have two distinctive *capita nullitatis.* From the very nature of the situation, supported by not a few clear indications in Rotal jurisprudence itself, a marriage null because of schizophrenia, for example, and

---

[114] Writes D'AVACK: "...è intuitivo come anche il semplice *exturbatus mentalis,* durante questa sua transitoria *perturbatio usus rationis,* debba riconoscersi incapace *ad contrahendum* allo stesso identico modo dell'amens... » — *Cause di nullità e di divorzio,* pp. 208-209. "A parte però tale caso particolare, in sostanza poi la *mentis exturbatio,* per quanto riguarda la sua portata e i suoi effetti nel campo del diritto matrimoniale canonico, non solo non presenta alcuna effettiva differenza dall'*amentia,* ma, per lo meno nella sua formulazione e determinazione astratte e teoriche, finisce addirittura per identificarsi con essa, nel senso che, precisamente come l'*amentia,* viene a configurare un *impedimentum* e una *causa nullitatis matrimonii* appunto e soltanto quando presenti i tre distinti e concorrenti caratteri di una *mentis exturbatio concomitans seu in actu matrimonii, matrimonialis seu in ordine ad matrimonium, perfecta seu in gradu proportionato matrimonio...*" — *Ibid.,* pp. 210-211.

a marriage null because of drunkenness are not null for the same intrinsic reason.

As Del Giudice has pointed out, marital consent means an accord or agreement of two wills in the marriage contract. Although "consent" cannot be conceived except in this sense of concord of *two* distinct wills, yet the Code and canonical doctrine, for the sake mainly of juridical investigation of nullity, usually speak of consent as existing in only one of the parties, considering it by itself.[115]

But even considering consent as inherent in only one party, marital consent is not consent which is merely the internal will of the party, not manifested exteriorly; the internal will must, by the law of nature itself, be sufficiently manifested externally in order to constitute marriage, for "*intentio mente retenta nihil in humanis contractibus operatur*".[116] Thus, marital consent is constituted essentially by the internal will and its sensible declaration, or, as some put it, by internal consent and external consent.[117]

Although its external manifestation or declaration is an act which is accomplished momentarily, internal consent must not be conceived as something which is formed or constructed on the spur of the moment when the party says "I will" before the priest, as though prior to this instant the party had not determined his will to marry. Rather, it is usually the case that the will of the contractant has already been determined to marry for days, weeks, months, even years previous during the period of engagement. The internal determination of the will does not effect the contract unless it be manifested externally in accord with the other party.

Canon Law speaks of internal consent as something persevering. Cardinal Gasparri calls it an "*animi disposi-*

[115] Del Giudice, *Nozioni di diritto canonico*, n. 104, p. 256.

[116] 1. 6, Dig., *Locati conducti*, XIX, 2. St. Thomas defines the efficient cause of marriage: "Causa efficiens matrimonii est consensus per verba de praesenti *expressus.*" — IV Sent., D. 28, q. unic., art. 3.

[117] "Consensus debet esse *externe*, etquidem sensibili signo, *manifestatus.* Seu praeter consensum *internum* requiritur consensus validus *externus* quoque, cuius validitas non tantum iure naturae, sed etiam iure positivo regitur." — Bánk, *Connubia canonica*, pp. 328-329. "Ad validum matrimonium contrahendum non sufficit consensus internus, sed requiritur externus, signo aliquo sensibili (verbis, nutu etc.) manifestatus; idque tum ratione contractus tum ratione sacramenti quod essentialiter in signo sensibili consistit." — Cappello, *De matrimonio, n.* 576, 4°.

tio" that resides within until revoked.[118] In this sense the institutes of marriage by proxy and "*sanatio in radice*" are rendered possible, for this attitude or disposition of the will *virtualiter perseverans* is naturally sufficient to constitute valid marriage. It is clear that internal consent or "*voluntas*" need not be actual at the very moment the contract is negotiated; virtual intention certainly suffices.[119] That internal consent is not destroyed or extinguished by mental disturbance (e.g., drunkenness, narcotic stupor, sleep, etc.) is only too clear; were it otherwise the Church could never grant a *sanatio in radice* and proxy marriages contracted while the principal is asleep, drunk, or otherwise temporarily incompetent could not be valid. Canonical doctrine is unanimous, however, in upholding their validity.[120] Furthermore, with regard to the simple convalidation of marriage null by reason of a diriment impediment, the law of *renewal* of consent is purely of ecclesiastical law.[121] And in the simple convalidation of marriages null by reason of a defect of consent, Canon Law recognizes a twofold source of defective consent, prescribing one method of convalidation if the internal

---

[118] "Exinde apparet consensum actualem, qui matrimonium efficit, et consensum virtualem seu habitualem post matrimonium esse unum eumdemque numero consensum seu indicare unam eamdemque animi dispositionem tradendi-acceptandi ius coniugale; consensu actuali haec animi dispositio enascitur et foris exprimitur; virtuali seu habituali continuat, intus in mente reposita, donec revocetur; quae revocatio, utpote factum, non praesumitur, sed claris probanda est argumentis." — GASPARRI, *Tractatus de matrimonio*, II, n. 781.

[119] "Sicut autem ab una parte non sufficit voluntas mere *interpretativa* seu hypothetica — quae scilicet in certa hypothesi *exstitisset* sed de facto non exstitit ideoque voluntatis nomen nequaquam meretur — ita ab altera parte non requiritur voluntas *actualis* sed sufficit *virtualis.* Quod e tractatu de Sacramentis in genere sat notum est et intelligibile. Unde e.g. virtute voluntatis actualis qua ad maritum sibi ducendum procuratorem quondam constituit, puella vere et sufficienter consentit eo adhuc tempore quo procurator mandatum exsequitur, licet ipsa tunc de matrimonio quod contrahitur nihil plane cogitet et hinc nihil *actu* velit. Quare nemo verum matrimonium contrahit nisi vero actu voluntatis hoc nunc vult aut semel actu voluit et nunc virtualiter adhuc vult." — VLAMING-BENDER, *Praelectiones iuris matrimonii*, pp. 375-376. Cf. also MANS-BERNÁRDEZ, *Derecho matrimonial canónico*, I, p. 310; GASPARRI, *op. cit.*, II, n. 781.

[120] "Matrimonium valet quia consensus virtualiter perseverat." — GASPARRI, *op. cit.*, II, n. 874.

[121] Canon 1133, § 2: "Haec renovatio iure ecclesiastico requiritur ad validitatem, etiamsi initio utraque pars consensum praestiterit nec postea revocaverit."

will was defective, another if the external manifestation was defective.[122]

That the manifestation or declaration of internal will must itself be a truly human act is evident. The declaration of marital consent is a juridical act, by its very definition a human act.[123] It is inconceivable that a contract of such proportions could arise from an act which was not within the power of the party. Add to this that Christian marriage is a sacrament and that to administer a sacrament the minister must place a sensible human act.[124] In either case, an external declaration of internal will, which declaration is not a truly human act, cannot be said to effectively signify the internal will.

Let us take the case of the man who has determined to marry a certain girl but, "to carry him through the ordeal" gets drunk and expresses consent in such a state. The marriage, if it is null, is null not because of insufficient internal will, but because the act of manifestation was not a human act, a juridical act, an act capable of juridically signifying a virtually persevering internal will. As one Rotal sentence put it, the act of manifestation of the drunk is merely a set of material sounds which cannot adequately signify the human mind:

> Quapropter invalide contraheret qui in actu celebrationis perfecte ebrius foret, etiamsi antea habuerit nec revocaverit animum contrahendi; verba enim tum prolata, seu soni materialiter emissi ab ebrio, non habent modum humanum manifestandi mentem.[125]

Nearly all the Rotal decisions dealing with cases of drunkenness and hypnosis speak in the same tone. They suppose that passing mental disturbance does not extinguish

---

[122] Canon 1136. Del Giudice writes that among other conditions, there is needed for valid marriage "esistenza del consenso matrimoniale, il quale, oltre che presente, non dev'essere viziato *nè nella sua determinazione, nè nella sua manifestazione.*" — *Nozioni di diritto canonico*, n. 99, p. 234.

[123] Cf. MICHIELS, *Principia generalia de personis in Ecclesia*, pp. 572, 586; MARCONE, "An matrimonium consummetur actione tantum hominis," *Monitor Ecclesiasticus*, LXXXII (1957), pp. 643-645.

[124] C. Mannucci, Jan. 28, 1929 (Vol. XXI, 60): "Contrahens autem, cum sit ipse sacramenti minister, debet ponere actum humanum, qui nempe procedat humano modo, ab humana intentione."

[125] C. FLORCZAK, Jan. 31, 1929 (Vol. XXI, 83).

internal consent, but whatever be the sufficiency of the internal will perduring through the wedding, the act of manifestation, if it is not a human act, simply is not an adequate mode of declaration of whatever internal will:

> Ebrietate vero ligatur potentia humana, et verba prolata ab ebrio non possunt mentem humanam, ne praeteritam quidem (voluntatem scilicet virtualem), significare.[126]
>
> In celebratione enim inanes soni ab eo emitterentur ad instar vocis brutorum, nec quidquam deliberatum exprimerent, quaecumque fuisset intentio antea habita.[127]
>
> Hoc loco... agitur de verbis, seu melius de sonis, quos quis haud sui compos, in actu celebrationis protulit. Verum quae ita more brutorum animalium ponuntur, absque ullo rationis motu nec per consequens voluntatis, non habent naturam actus humani, qui ex voluntate procedit (Div. Thomae, I, II, q. 1, art. 1), nec igitur possunt significare mentem humanam vel voluntatem etiam praeteritam. Ergo qui tales sonos ore, non ex animo, emisit, nil egit, quamvis antea habuisset voluntatem contrahendi.[128]

In cases of true insanity, Rotal jurisprudence delves into the question of psychic ability to construct internal consent. The problem centers about due mental development, habitual psychic aptitude, due knowledge and ability to grasp the rudimentary nature of marriage, habitual power of discretion, etc. In cases of mental disturbance, on the other hand, the question is entirely about *actual* deliberation, advertence, discernment, consciousness, etc., in expressing consent.[129] The crucial point in cases of mental disturbance is not about sufficient internal will but about sufficient actual advertence, deliberation, and discernment in the act of expressing consent.[130] Mans points out

---

[126] C. Mannucci, Jan. 28, 1929 (Vol. XXI, 60).

[127] C. Jullien, Dec. 11, 1937 (Vol. XXIX, 734).

[128] C. Jullien, Feb. 23, 1935 (Vol. XXVII, 78-79).

[129] "Oportunamente se indicó que es preciso distinguir entre la madurez o discreción de juicio proporcionada al negocio matrimonial, como estado *habitual* determinante de la capacidad del sujeto para que pueda prestar verdadero consentimiento, y la advertencia o discernimiento *actuales*, esto es, la deliberación acerca del acto que se celebra, como cualidad esencial del mismo consentimiento." — MANS, *El consentimiento matrimonial*, p. 55.

[130] This distinction has been recognized by canonical writers and applied in the construction of the "twofold" legal test of minimum essential psychic competence for valid marriage. Cf. *infra*, "The Tests Suggested by Canonical Writers."

that it is therefore erroneous to equate the *mente exturbati* to the insane or to infants, for these latter lack habitual discretion and are incapable of constructing sufficient internal will, a condition not at all verified in cases of *mentis exturbatio* in normal persons.[131] If, perchance, sufficient internal will is lacking, it is not because of the alcoholic intoxication, for example, but because of a defect which is verified in normal people, a defect of consent listed in Caput V of the matrimonial law of the Code, like simulation, error, fear, etc. The defect of internal will is not the defect of due discretion which is verified in the insane. Thus, perhaps, a man who does not wish to marry a certain woman but is forced to do so, takes to drink to carry him through the ceremony. If his act of manifested consent was not a human act, the marriage is at least null because of invalid declaration; if this cannot be proved, then the court might investigate the existence of grave fear or a contrary intention, defects which were not, however, induced by the intoxicating beverages.[132]

The manifestation of consent must be qualified by that advertence, discernment and deliberation which assure that it be a human act. In this sense, the "mortal sin" rule of Sanchez can rightly be applied, i.e., he can validly marry who can commit a mortal sin.[133] This norm has been both

---

[131] *Derecho matrimonial canónico,* I, p. 321. Mans concludes, therefore: "...la consideración de la embriaguez, hipnotismo, sonambulismo, etc., tiene su lugar aducuado dentro del estudio de la imposibilidad de la necesaria deliberación acerca del acto, pues todos estos estados consisten en anormalidades psiquicas transitorias que *accidental* y *actualmente* obstan a la advertencia o discernimiento del acto como requisito esencial del mismo consentimiento." — *Ibid.,* pp. 321-322.

[132] C. Jullien. Dec. 11, 1937 (Vol. XXIX, 735): "Contingere autem potest ut quis valde repugnans a matrimonio quodam contrahendo, immo ad celebrandum compulsus, potum alcoholicum sumpserit ut celebrationem sibi tam odiosam facilius expleverit. Tum circa validitatem matrimonii ita celebrati, quaerendum est in primis an constet de plena ebrietate: qua probata exsulat a causa nullitas ex capite simulationis aut nullitas ob metum. Sunt enim humanae actiones quas ponere nequit ebrius, sive consensus, utut datus ob metum, sive positiva exclusio consensus seu simulatio totalis. Deficiente autem probatione plenae ebrietatis, is qui matrimonium celebravit potest rursus contendere se *aut* dedisse consensum, sed vitiatum metu gravi, *aut* non dedisse consensum, quia ob repugnantiam simulavit."

[133] MANS-BERNÁRDEZ, *op. cit.,* p. 319; "En conclusión, en cuanto a la capacidad de los sujetos para prestar verdadero consentimiento matrimonial, no basta el grado de desarrollo mental requerido para pecar

defended and rejected vigorously in canonical doctrine and jurisprudence precisely because it can be interpreted in two distinct ways: (1) With regard to the ability to construct sufficient internal consent... in which case the rule is obviously wrong, for a child of seven can commit a mortal sin but certainly lacks due discretion required for the formation of internal marital consent; (2) With regard to the measure of deliberation, advertence, actual discernment which assures that the manifestation of consent be a truly human act, a juridical act, adequately signifying the internal will of the contractant. Although it seems that in certain passages Sanchez was applying his rule only to this latter situation, [134] it is clear that he extended it also to the first category. [135] In this sense the Rota has correctly rejected his rule repeatedly during the last forty-five years.

At precisely what point the act of declaring consent ceases to be a truly responsible human act when placed during a state of mental disturbance is a difficult problem. [136] One thing is clear, however: the sufficiency of internal will and the sufficiency of its external declaration must be gauged according to two distinct norms.

---

letalmente, sino que se requiere mayor discreción o madurez de juicio para consentir en la creación de un vínculo exclusivo y perpetuo sujeto a tan graves cargas como es el del matrimonio; mas presupuesta dicha capacidad, o sea, *la habitual* madurez o discreción de juicio proporcionada a la gravedad del negocio matrimonial, de parte del consentimiento mismo, es decir, en quanto a la advertencia o discernimiento del acto que se celebra, entonces sí que es suficiente el grado de deliberación *actual* que se requiere y basta para pecar mortalmente, para que también la persona previamente dotada de la necesaria discreción de la mente pueda otorgar verdadero consentimiento matrimonial."

[134] Cf. MANS, *El consentimiento matrimonial*, pp. 55-56. Writes BIDAGOR: "Quis potest dubitare Sanchez agere de advertentia mentis necessaria ut deliberatio habeatur non defectuosa, et non agere de scientia requisita ad lethaliter peccandum vel ad sponsalia contrahenda? Et quis potest doctrinam a Sanchezio pronuntiatam improbare?" — RAYMUNDUS BIDAGOR, S. J., "Circa ignorantiam naturae matrimonii," *Periodica*, XXIX (1940), pp. 269-289 at p. 273.

[135] Cf. *infra*, "A Critique of the Mortal Sin Norm."

[136] Concerning drunkenness, see especially A. SZENTIRMAI, "De consensu matrimoniali ob ebrietatem nullo," *Periodica*, XLIV (1955), pp. 369-384; and concerning hypnosis, cf. BENEDICTUS OJETTI, S. J., *Commentarium in Codicem Juris Canonici*, II, *De personis* (Romae: apud Aedes Univ. Gregorianae, 1928), pp. 161 ff.

In conclusion, then, it seems that the lunatic and the drunk are incapable of validly entering the marriage contract for different reasons. Although both are incapable of placing valid consent, there are two distinct *capita nullitatis* contained in the "*incapacitas valide praestandi consensum*:" (1) inability to construct sufficient internal consent, the proper *caput nullitatis* in insanity cases; (2) inability to manifest validly the internal will, the proper *caput nullitatis* in cases of *mentis exturbatio*.

CHAPTER THREE

THE LEGAL TEST OF DUE DISCRETION FOR VALID MARRIAGE

Understanding "due discretion" in its present-day acceptance as the minimum positive psychic aptitude necessary that a person be able to marry validly, we come to the "subjective" legal test of due discretion for valid marriage. From indications already made in Chapter I and to be made further on, it seems that due discretion comprises two distinct mental capacities: (1) the traditionally acknowledged requisite of psychic ability to place *sufficient consent* for matrimony; (2) the recently recognized requisite of mental maturity necessary to sustain *sub gravi* the essential obligations of the marriage contract.

Part I: PSYCHIC CAPACITY TO ELICIT SUFFICIENT CONSENT

If the mental incapacity to elicit an act of marital consent psychologically sufficient in itself to generate the contract of marriage has been recognized as a *caput nullitatis matrimonii* in ecclesiastical jurisprudence for centuries, its concept has not been fixed, but has evolved and is, in fact, still evolving in Rotal jurisprudence. One can well expect such development, for the notion of what constitutes true and sufficient consent is not immediately self-evident, nor, consequently, is the correlative personal capacity to place such an act very clear. The question is: what positive powers must a person retain in the face of mental illness so that he be considered still capable of eliciting the internal psychological act of marital consent sufficient to initiate the bond?

Article 1. A Survey of Rotal Jurisprudence.

The rule of Sanchez, already traditional in Catholic theology,[1] easily entered ecclesiastical jurisprudence and was, at the turn of the last century, a fixed norm in the adjudication of insanity cases in the tribunals of the Holy See. He who enjoyed the simple use of reason, who could place human acts, who could commit a mortal sin, was deemed capable of eliciting sufficient marital consent.[2] Juridicial investigation, therefore, concerned itself with the requisite components of a truly human act and, perhaps ironically, recourse was frequently made to the principles of human acts as enunciated by St. Thomas.[3]

When the Sacred Roman Rota was re-instituted in 1909 by Pope St. Pius X, it inherited, naturally enough, the already established norms of jurisprudence from the Congregation of the Council, which at the time had been the competent marriage tribunal of the Holy See. The legal test of the times, if we may speak of it in those terms, was no more than the "simple use of reason" criterion, or "human act" test, and this, as a *positive* norm of minimum psychic competence required for consent. In the early Rotal decisions, the authority of Sanchez was bolstered by frequent citations from Cardinal D'Annibale,[4] Wernz,[5] and Carriè-

---

1 A. Amanieu, "Aliénation mentale en matière de nullité de mariage," *DDC*, Tom. I, col. 436.

2 Taken in this wide sense of a general gauge of minimum psychic capacity to elicit sufficient consent, it would follow that according to the mortal sin norm, a person should be judged capable of sufficient consent if he enjoys the simple use of reason of a seven-year-old child.

3 *Summa theologica*, I-II, qq. 1, 6, 21, 74 *passim*. We say "ironically" because, as we shall see later on, St. Thomas was being cited to support a theory which he opposed.

4 *Summula theologiae moralis*, Tom. I, n. 31, nota 15: "In periodo autem incubationis, uti aiunt, latentis, quamdiu tanta in eis superest vis intelligentiae, quanta pollent hi qui infantiam vix egressi sunt, sanis, non amentibus, sunt accensendi." *Ibid.*, Tom. I, n. 141: "Sufficit aptitudo ad ponendam actionem, seu actum humanum quae procedat nempe a principio intrinseco scienter et libere."

5 *Ius decretalium*, IV, *Ius matrimoniale* (1904), n. 41: "Quare a matrimonio contrahendo arcentur, qui laborant habituali plenaque amentia et fatuitate eoque mentis defectu, qui verum consensum in ipsa celebratione matrimonii non admittit velut infantes septennio minores."

re.[6] Thus, in a decision *coram* Many, Aug. 11, 1913, the Rota could state that the doctrine of Sanchez is admitted by everyone:

> Praedicta non valent nisi quando amentia (seu respective dementia) est plena et perfecta, non vero quando amentia est tantum semiplena, ita ut ii qui amentia tantum semiplena laborant, valide possint inire matrimonium. Ratio est quia, in matrimonio contrahendo, non alia requiritur voluntatis deliberatio, quam quae requiritur ad peccandum lethaliter, uti dicunt theologi; quae profecto deliberatio adesse potest in iis, qui dicuntur semifatui. Et haec est doctrina ab omnibus admissa.[7]

The critical point of judicial investigation was the question whether, from the weight of evidence furnished by witnesses, expert examinations, and relevant circumstances, the person had lost at the time of the wedding sufficient use of reason to place a human act,[8] since only that *intellectus cognitio, voluntatis deliberatio, ratiocinandi facultas, iudicium,* and *libertas* are required which suffice for a formal mortal sin.[9]

The pure "human act" test became subject to modification. It was soon after the re-inauguration of the Rota that the question of *due knowledge* for marriage became a central point in insanity cases. Not only is the simple

---

[6] *De matrimonio*, Tom. II, n. 827: "Illi quorum amentia non est absoluta, sed qui sat rationis habent ad peccandum lethaliter, possunt valide contrahere."

[7] *S.R.R.Dec.*, Vol. V, p. 564.

[8] C. Sincero, Dec. 23 1918 (Vol. X, 144): "Circumspecte igitur hac in re procedendum est, atque videndum an ex factis, ex depositionibus testium, ex peritorum iudiciis in examine amentis et facti circumstantiis fundatis, concludendum sit amentem iam caruisse usu rationis sufficienti ad actum humanum, quum matrimonium celebravit."

[9] C. Rossetti, July 1, 1922 (Vol. XIV, 210): "Qui laborant insania semiplena contrahere valent matrimonium; ad hoc enim non alia requiritur intellectus cognitio, et voluntatis deliberatio, quam quae requiritur ad lethaliter peccandum: semi-fatui huius rei sunt capaces."

C. Rossetti, July 3, 1922 (Vol. XIV, 223-224): "Nam in matrimonio contrahendo non alia requiritur intellectus cognitio et voluntatis deliberatio quam quae requiritur ad lethaliter peccandum: semi-fatui, qui ratiocinandi facultate non privantur, huius rei sunt capaces... nisi satis fundata appareant, ut concludi possit, amentem caruisse rationis usu, sufficienti ad actum humanum, quum contraxit matrimonium.

C. Massimi, Oct. 29, 1924 (Vol. XVI, 372): "Itaque amentia, vel dementia, semiplena seu imperfecta, matrimonium irritum non facit, dummodo contrahens tantum iudicii et libertatis habeat, quantum requiritur, subiective seu formaliter, ad peccatum mortale."

use of reason necessary (i.e., the general power of placing simple human acts and committing mortal sin), but one must, of course, also have the requisite knowledge content for this particular act. *Nil volitum nisi praecognitum.* The decision *coram* Sincero, Aug. 28, 1911, citing his *Tractatus canonicus de matrimonio,*[10] employed Gasparri's terminology of "*debita discretio seu maturitas iudicii*" to describe this essential rudimentary knowledge, "*ita ut contrahens naturam et vim contractus, seu, in casu nostro, quit sit matrimonium, eiusdemque essentiales proprietates, sat intelligere valeat, saltem in confuso.*"[11] This same decision, apparently, did not see any contradiction between the latter addition concerning due knowledge and the "mortal sin" norm, which it proposed as a positive test.

The element of requisite knowledge soon was seen as the critical point in insanity cases,[12] and the mortal sin norm was adjusted to read:

> Qui igitur semi-fatui sunt, seu semi-amentes, matrimonium valide contrahere possunt, dummodo deliberatione uti possint, quae sufficit ad lethaliter peccandum, et nuptialis contractus substantialia cognoscant.[13]

A turning point in Rotal jurisprudence came in the decision *coram* Prior, Nov. 14, 1919. For the first time the rule of Sanchez is expressely rejected as false; for the first time, likewise, St. Thomas is quoted on "due discretion" and found in opposition to Sanchez.[14] The decision

---

[10] Ed. 1904, n. 881.

[11] *S.R.R.Dec.,* Vol. III, p. 450.

[12] C. Prior, May 15, 1915 (Vol. VII, 217): "Cum amentes incapaces sint eiusmodi cognitionis rationalis consensum liberum praestare nequeunt, ac proinde a matrimonio contrahendo arcentur."

[13] *Ibid.,* pp. 217-218.

[14] "Regula simplex ad omnes casus diiudicandos dari nequit, nec certe approbari potest regula a Sanchesio indicata (Lib. I, Disp. VIII, n. 15) quod nempe satis est ut contrahens 'deliberationem sufficientem habeat ad lethaliter delinquendum,' cum ad lethaliter delinquendum sufficit simpliciter usus rationis, dum, ut supra retulimus, maturius iudicium requirunt Doctores ad contractum matrimonii faciendum. Imo ipse Divus Thomas id requirit pro contractu sponsalium, ac proinde a fortiori requiri debet pro graviori et irrescindibili contractu matrimonii. Scribit in IV Dist. 27, qu. 2, art. 2 ad 2: 'Ad peccandum mortaliter sufficit etiam consensus in praesens; sed in sponsalibus est consensus in futurum; maior autem rationis discretio requiritur ad providendum in futurum, quam ad consentiendum in actum unum praesentem; et ideo, ante potest homo

strongly favors the "more than mortal sin" test of the Angelic Doctor and interprets his "*maior rationis discretio*" in the sense of Gasparri's "*debita discretio*", i.e., due knowledge of the substance of the marriage contract. [15] Banking on canon 1082, § 2, of the newly promulgated Code of Canon Law, the decision drew a connection between " due discretion" and puberty:

> Praesumitur quidem omnibus inesse huiusmodi discretionem iudicii post pubertatem adeptam: haec praesumptio tamen est tantummodo iuris, non iuris et de iure, et probationem in contrarium admittit. [16]

The following insanity decision, also *coram* Prior, again rejected the rule of Sanchez explicitly and reduced the entire question of psychic capacity to due knowledge of the nature of marriage. [17] The traditional "human act" test (*capacitas ad actum humanum ponendum*) was giving way to the "qualified human act" test (*capacitas ad matrimonium intelligendum et volendum*). Although the norm of Sanchez is often stated thereafter merely as a negative norm, [18] there continued to be some instances where it was still proposed as a positive norm. [19] The 1920's, a pe-

peccare mortaliter, quam possit, se obligare ad aliquid in futurum.'" — *S.R.R. Dec.*, Vol. XI, p. 174.

[15] *Ibid.*, p. 172: "Ad contractum ineundum, vero, non sufficit simpliciter usus rationis, sed necessaria est etiam discretio iudicii contractui ineundo proportionata qua semper natura eiusdem confuso saltem modo intelligitur, necnon essentiales proprietates." This discretion is understood as knowledge: "...discretionem seu maturitatem iudicii ad obligationes essentiales matrimonii intelligendas." (p. 173) "...Videndum est... praesertim an essentialia matrimonii iura et obligationes confuse saltem in eodem ineundo intellexerit." (p. 174).

[16] *Ibid.*, p. 173.

[17] C. Prior, July 27, 1920 (Vol. XII, 204-205). Ignorance of the nature of marriage seemed to be the *quid probandum* in insanity cases: "Ad irritandum matrimonium ex capite amentiae, nempe, requiritur et sufficit ut, momento quo contractum est, nupturiens mente captus fuerit, seu rationis usum non habuerit ad substantiam matrimonialis contractus intelligendam." — c. Prior, Aug. 17, 1922 (Vol. XIV, 314).

[18] The element of *sufficiency* is omitted: "...seu, ut Sanchez (*De matrim.*, Lib. I, Disp. VIII, n. 5), aliique opinantur Doctores, illam requiri mentis considerationem et advertentiam, necnon voluntatis deliberationem, quae necessaria est ad conficiendum testamentum, et ad mortaliter peccandum." — c. Rossetti, Mar. 16, 1921 (Vol. XIII, 48). As a negative norm, the mortal sin test, or "human act" test, is certainly self-evident, and is proposed in almost all Rotal decisions.

[19] Cf. *supra*, footnote n. 9.

riod of rich jurisprudence for the variety of cases handled (e.g., drunkenness, narcotic intoxication, hypnosis, paranoia, etc.), was marked, nevertheless, by a certain unsettled tension between the two norms.

The decision *coram* Parrillo of February 16, 1928, tackled the problem *ex professo* and proposed an ingenious reconciliation. We must, said the sentence, distinguish the question of the intellect from the question of the will, that is, the question of due knowledge from the question of due deliberation. St. Thomas was speaking only of due knowledge, while Sanchez was speaking of due deliberation. The norm of St. Thomas should be applied in cases involving congenital mental disease, while that of Sanchez should be employed in cases involving accidental mental disease, that is, mental disease which strikes the adult. [20] The decision *coram* Wynen of March 1, 1930, repeated the conciliatory theory. [21] But the reconciliation was seen as a strained and artificial attempt in a brief period of transition that saw the final rejection of Sanchez and the acceptance of the Thomistic axiom. The "twofold" norm, as it is called, was never repeated. Instead, the norm of Sanchez is seen in direct opposition to that of St. Thomas, and it is the long traditional "simple use of reason" norm which gives way:

> Ad quem commensurandum, quaestio est inter Doctores, utrum sufficiat quae vulgo dici solet capacitas ad peccandum lethaliter: et hodie plures sunt qui calculum adiiciant sententiae Angelici Doctoris explicite dicentis: "Maior descretio rationis exigitur ad providendum in futurum, quam ad consentiendum in actum praesentem; et ideo *ante* potest homo peccare mortaliter, quam sese possit obligare ad aliquid." (S. Thomas, Dist. XXVII, qu. 2, art. 2, ad II), multo quod omnes consentiunt ad matrimonium rite ineundum, seu ad obligationem quae est *servitus* totius vitae, maiorem requiri quam in ceteris negociis consilii et arbitrii *libertatem*. Unde nil mirum, si quis appareat adhuc sua posse apte agere et ordinare negocia, qui tamen ad matrimonium censeri incapax debeat. [22]
>
> Disputatur, an simplex rationis usus, qualis septennio expleto unumquemque habere praesumitur, sufficiat ad valide matrimonium ineundum, prouti sufficit ad lethaliter pec-

---

[20] *S.R.R.Dec.*, Vol. XX, pp. 59-67.
[21] *S.R.R.Dec.*, Vol. XXII, pp. 128-129.
[22] C. Mannucci, Aug. 8, 1931 (Vol. XXIII, 372-373).

> candum. Cui quidem quaestioni esse negative respondendum iure merito censuerunt appellati Patres... Hinc praestantiores inter Doctores docent ad valide matrimonium contrahendum requiri rationis usum proportionatum contractus naturae.[23]

The use of reason proportionate to the contract of marriage, if it had previously been pegged at the level of the average seven-year-old child, now approached the level of the adolescent at puberty. The so-called "puberty" norm, at least as a negative norm, was proposed thus:

> Tunc enim ad matrimonii nullitatem evincendam satis erit ostendere coniuges aut unum ex ipsis quo tempore matrimonium fuit celebratum, nec eo quidem rationis usu fuisse praeditum quo puberes in genere fruuntur.[24]

Practically speaking, the legal test of psychic capacity came to be a test of due knowledge. But cases were coming to the Rota in which it was obvious the person enjoyed at least the use of reason of the average adolescent at puberty and knew the rudimentary nature of marriage. The marriages were attacked on the grounds of a defect of internal liberty which coexisted with due knowledge. Could it be that there be a defect merely in the will power of the individual, and not in the intellect? One Rotal sentence declared the admissibility of such grounds but added:

> Animadvertendum quoque est minime sufficere ad excludendam libertatem probare in certa persona adfuisse internos impulsus, sed requiri ut simul probetur eisdem resisti non potuisse.[25]

It was not long that a doctrine common in some civil law systems regarding criminal imputability was offered also in the ecclesiastical matrimonial forum, viz., the doctrine of the "irresistible impulse".

Not only scholastic philosophy, but the doctrine of the Council of Trent seemed to rule out any acceptance of the "irresistible impulse". Since both the intellect and the will are spiritual faculties and cannot, therefore, be direct-

---

[23] C. Grazioli, July 1, 1933 (Vol. XXV, 406-407). Cf. also c. Grazioli, Nov. 3, 1934 (Vol. XXVI, 709); c. Teodori, Jan. 19, 1940 (Vol. XXXII, 83).

[24] C. Grazioli, June 25, 1926 (Vol. XVIII, 216).

[25] C. Massimi, July 28, 1928 (Vol. XX, 318).

ly affected by disease or malfunction in themselves, the damaging factors must lie in the material or sense faculties on which the spiritual faculties depend extrinsically. But since the will is blind and its nature is to follow what is proposed by the intellect, the conclusion seems to be that there can be no psychic malady rooted strictly in the will while the intellect remains whole:

> Pariter non exsistunt morbi, quibus voluntas eaque sola *directe* afficitur, ita ut liberum arbitrium tollatur. Quare admitti nequeunt placita quorundam psychiatrorum modernorum, dari casus, in quibus homo, utcumque gaudeat pleno usu rationis, ob quendam morbum voluntatis perdat libertatem suorum actuum et trahatur irresistibiliter ad certos actus ponendos, v.g. ad crimina patranda... Nam voluntas tunc tantum deficere potest, si intellectus morbo afficiatur; sed ne intellectus quidem directis morbis laborare potest, cum defectus rectae cognitionis proveniant ex perturbatione sensuum, phantasiae, etc. quibus intellectus, per se potentia spiritualis, ad agendum indiget.[26]

The response of the Rota to the doctrine of the irresistible impulse was simply "*Ubi intellectus, ibi voluntas*",[27] and "*Quoties habetur usus rationis, libera permanet voluntas.*"[28] If such a position would reduce the question of criminal imputability logically to a "right and wrong" test, it reaffirmed that the test of the sufficiency of marital consent had to be a test of due knowledge.[29]

The effort to find a successful avenue towards the annulment of the unhappy marriages of the psychopathic personality led to the so-called "doctrine of values". The psychopath, often described as a person with no moral sense or conscience, who never learns from experience or

---

26 C. Wynen, Feb. 27, 1937 (Vol. XXIX, 171-173).

27 *Ibid.*, p. 172. Cf. D'ANNIBALE, *Summula theologiae moralis*, Tom. I, n. 31, nota 18; MICHIELS, *De delictis et poenis*, I (2. ed., 1961), pp. 200-202.

28 C. Quattrocolo, June 16, 1943 (Vol. XXXV, 434). The same decision continues: "In homine... sanae mentis separari nequit intellectus a libertate arbitrii, homo siquidem utens ratione libertate simul carere nequit iuxta Conc. Trid. sess. VI, cap. X, nam in homine sanae mentis voluntas necessario adesse debet."

29 "Ex adverso semiamentes et semifurore correpti, prouti etiam qui pathologicis subiacent morbis, vel passionibus pertrahuntur, si de sana mente ita ipsi participant ut dignoscant matrimonium consistere in perpetua societate inter virum et mulierem ad filios procreandos, sufficienti liberaque deliberatione perfrui dicuntur ad matrimonium ineundum." — *Ibid.*, p. 436.

suffers remorse for the cruelty he inflicts on others by his anti-social behavior, apparently was psychically capable of marriage because he could well apprehend the substance of the marriage contract and freely intend to enter it.

Thus it was that a new theory of "due knowledge" was proposed in a case presented to the Rota, the celebrated "constitutional immorality" case adjudicated *coram* Wynen on February 25, 1941.[30] It was proposed that in order to place a human act, the simple use of reason, or rather, simple conceptual knowledge is not sufficient; there is required also an appreciation, an appraisal of the very object of the act, an appreciation and evaluation which, containing both the cognoscitive element and the volitional element, would explain together, as a third integrating faculty, the function of the intellect and the will.

Carried over to the field of matrimonial consent, a person would have to be able to estimate and ponder the esthetic, social, ethical, and juridical values of the object of marital consent. Unable to do this, he would be incapable of placing an act of consent naturally sufficient to generate the bond. It was alleged in the above-mentioned Rotal case, that Titus, a professional man who well knew conceptually what marriage is, did not and could not, however, have adequate evaluative knowledge of the import and consequences of his act, especially in its ethical aspect, since he was afflicted by "moral" insanity at the time of the wedding. It was alleged that since such a defect renders moral acts unimputable, it also renders civil acts null. Therefore, Titus's act of consent was invalid.[31]

The Rotal decision treated the doctrine of values at great length, stating that this doctrine, in a certain sense, has long been a tenet of scholastic philosophy and theology as regards moral imputability. But its application to marital consent, not as a moral act, but as a valid or invalid act, was rejected, mainly on two counts: (1) the question of marital consent is not about its moral imputability as good or evil, but about its natural sufficiency. And who is to say that this evaluative knowledge is necessary for

---

[30] *S.R.R.Dec.*, Vol. XXXIII, pp. 144-168.
[31] *Ibid.*, pp. 146-147.

the psychological sufficiency of consent? It is a nebulous area to delineate with certainty and the greatest minds of the world, from Aristotle to the present have been trying to elucidate the spiritual workings of the human mind.[32] (2) Even if such evaluation were necessary in the act of placing marital consent, how could it be judicially verified and made the clear criterion to declare the nullity or validity of a marriage?[33]

Succeeding Rotal sentences repeated the rejection of the doctrine of values, insisting only on a vague notion of the nature of marriage as enunciated in canons 1081 and 1082.[34] The concept of "due discretion" and "mature judgment" did not include an insight into the importance of marriage or its ethical and social values:

---

32 *Ibid.*, p. 152.

33 "Sed quomodo scire possumus, talem defectum esse adeo gravem, ut aestimare nequeant *substantialem* valorem matrimonii, si ipse Tanzi fatetur difficulter statui posse fines certos inter normam et anomaliam?" — *ibid.*, p. 156. The court is wary of those who would try to reduce a behavioral disorder to a necessary psychic incapacity to elicit sufficient consent: "Ex omnibus rationibus adductis apparet, quam caute perpendere oporteat peritias asseclarum doctrinae expositae, iuxta quam certus quidam homo, qui se maculavit repetitis delictis iisque gravibus, incapax declaratur ad validum consensum matrimonialem eliciendum." — *Ibid.*

34 C. Wynen, Apr. 13, 1943 (Vol. XXXV, 272): "Contrahentes igitur de natura matrimonii nonnisi scire debent, illud esse societatem permanentem (non autem, illud esse societatem indissolubilem, uti directe eruitur ex can. 1084) inter virum et mulierem ad filios procreandos (quin necessaria sit, nedum scientia obiective sumpta, cognitio seu scientia subiective sumpta de modo quo filii procreantur). Qui hanc cognitionem habet, eo ipso praeditus est illa iudicii maturitate et discretione, quam auctores, praeeunte S. Thoma, sub nomine 'maturius iudicium' postulare solent." Cf. also c. Canestri, July 16, 1943 (Vol. XXXV, 432 ff); c. Felici (Florentina), Apr. 6, 1954, *Monitor Ecclesiasticus* LXXIX (1954), pp. 585-586.

Some very recent decisions rebuked the conclusions of the expert because they rested on the doctrine of values. Approving the stand of the preceding Rotal turnus (c. Pasquazi, July 8, 1958), the decision *coram* De Jorio stated: "Itaque quoad hoc punctum improbarunt judicium peritioris, quia is falso nititur fundamento, nempe 'che per la validità del contratto matrimoniale si richieda la valutazione meditata delle conseguenze future.'... Etenim fere omnes homines sunt ad matrimonium ineundum destinati, dum paucissimi capaces providendi atque perpendendi quae propria vita matrimonialis secumferat." C. Lamas (Mediolanen.), May 28, 1958: "Tandem, praecipua ratio ob quam reiicienda est sententia peritioris, est falsa notio quam ipse habet de obiecto consensus matrimonialis, quae praetergreditur illum gradum discretionis et maturitatis qui requiritur, inspecto can. 1082, ad validum consensum praestandum.

"Sufficiat, ad praecedentem assertionem probandam, recolere quasdam affirmationes a doctore C. factas: 'Non basta — ipse ait — la semplice

> Pressius circa discretionem, censuerunt quidam non valere matrimonium nisi contrahens percipiat momentum matrimonii, id est eius valorem ethicum, socialem, religiosum. Hoc quidem esse peroptabile nemo sane neget; at esse prorsus necessarium, ita ut secus matrimonium non valeat, non una iam Rotalis decisio explosit: conferatur notissima decisio c. Wynen (dec. XV, anno 1941) et, praxim quod spectat, recolantur praesertim quae habentur in una c. Canestri, d. 16 iulii, 1943.[35]

Lest the *caput nullitatis* in insanity cases seem to be reduced, at least in the line of principle, to that of ignorance, the decision *coram* Wynen of December 7, 1946, offered an explanation, not altogether satisfying, of the difference between the two *capita nullitatis*:

> Cum defectu tamen cognitionis, qui ex impedito usu rationis habetur, non est confundendus ambitus necessariae cognitionis de quo can. 1082, § 1. Etsi enim ignorantia naturae matrimonii post pubertatem non praesumitur (can. 1082, § 2), nihilominus haec ignorantia aliquando habetur in hominibus mentis omnino sanae; et tunc nullitas matrimonii non provenit ex deficiente seu impedito usu rationis, sed ex defectu necessariae cognitionis de natura matrimonii. Quare unum caput non est confundendum cum altero capite.[36]

Although the mortal sin norm is today considered obsolete both as a general gauge of minimum psychic competence for true consent, and as restricted merely to volitional or deliberative capacity,[37] recent Rotal decisions have stressed the fact that a mentally ill person might have all the necessary knowledge for true consent, and yet lack "due discretion" because deprived of due internal liberty. The defect of due internal liberty is not conceived in the order of the "irresistible impulse" or as some sort of "but for" test.[38] Rather, the court recognizes that, as

---

cognizione, per così dire, definitoria della cosa; occorre, da parte del contraente, la capacità di valutarla, che è quanto dire una sufficienza mentale 'proporzionata', idonea a *comprendere* il significato, la natura e la portata giuridica e morale del matrimonio."

[35] C. Felici (Florentina), May 22, 1956, *Monitor Ecclesiasticus*, LXXXI (1956), p. 264.

[36] C. Wynen, Dec. 7, 1946 (Vol. XXXVIII, 572).

[37] Cf. *infra*, art 3, "A Critique of the Mortal Sin Norm."

[38] In one case it was alleged by the expert that "but for" the injection of morphine, the woman would never have consented. The Rota decision answered: "Iam dictum est peritiorem errasse, quia ad valide

the function of the intellect can be disrupted by a disordered imagination, for example, so the function of the will can be disturbed by emotional factors, by pathological phobias and obsessions, etc.[39]

The most recent jurisprudence of the Rota, contained in the unpublished decisions of the last ten years, commonly includes within the essential notion of *"debita discretio"* or *"maturius iudicium"* a certain psychic power that is something more than the sheer power to grasp the elemental notions of canon 1082 and to freely intend them. Building upon its original enunciation in a sentence *coram* Quattrocolo of June 16, 1943,[40] the decisions *coram* Felici

---

contrahendum quoad *intellectum* asserit usum rationis non sufficere, sed insuper requiri sanam criticam, prudentiam, consilium, iudicium, etc. Etiam *quoad voluntatem* plus postulat quam necessarium est. Dato siquidem, non concesso, quod actrix sine iniectione morphinae consensum suum non dedisset, id in casu non obstaret valido matrimonio. Nam indifferens est, *quomodo* quis ad volendum perveniat, utrum nempe tantum ab intrinseco, an etiam ab incitamento extrinseco: requiritur scilicet et sufficit ad valide contrahendum, ut contrahens ponat positivum actum voluntatis, legitime manifestatum." — c. Wynen, Feb. 27, 1937 (Vol. XXIX, 195).

Dr. Henry A. Davidson writes: "This 'but-for' formula is very popular with psychiatrists. It has one great weakness. Nobody does anything except as a manifestation of his mental processes, so that if a person has any mental disorder at all, it can be said that, *but for* that disorder, he would not have behaved thus." — "The Psychiatrist's Role in the Administration of Criminal Justice," *Criminal Psychology*, p. 20.

[39] C. Canestri (Neo-Eboracen.), May 6, 1954: "Sufficiat hic sistere in statu nolentis et volentis a cuius fluctuatione animus sese districare nequit, ut facile intelligatur Barbaram absolute incapacem fuisse ex ipsa sua physica conditione emittendi actum validum in ordine ad rem circa quam perturbabatur. Etiamsi in actu affirmandi suum consensum in matrimonium coram sacerdote, habuisset voluntatem capacem committendi peccatum mortale, relate ad matrimonium ipsum, actum humanum aptum ad valorem tanti et *illius* determinati negotii, elicere nequibat... Voluntas Barbarae per pathologicum statum continuo nutans inter affirmationem et negationem, impotens facta fuerat ad se protendendum valide ad speciale matrimonii obiectum... nubendo eo in statu, Barbara promisisset quod promittere nequivisset."

C. Heard (Oranen.), May 17, 1958: "Sicut non sequitur nullitas matrimonii ex eo quod contrahens non undequaque totam essentiam contractus comprehendat, dummodo illum minimum et vagum gradum scientiae habet de quo can. 1081, ita non necessario sequitur ejus validitas ex eo, quod contrahens habet perfectam notionem contractus, nam haec notio potest esse pure conceptualis; quando autem agitur de hoc determinato matrimonio ineundo, judicium practicum sibi formare idem nequit ob obsessionem vel phobiam pathologicam. De statu autem pathologico audiendi sunt periti. Nimis propere scribit defensor vinculi in casu: 'Era conscio di ciò che faceva e quindi agì in piena volontà e libertà.'"

[40] *S.R.R.Dec.*, Vol. XXXV, p. 433: "Et ratio est quia in iis abest usus

have outlined what is called the "*facultas critica*" or the "*facultas discretiva*" — indispensable in the formation of of true marital consent.[41]

Even the old "use of reason" norm seemed to suppose that a person, besides having the power of simple apprehension of the nature of the marriage contract, must also be endowed with the power to "reason", that is, to be able to form judgments and to draw inferences from various judgments. The *facultas critica* seems to consist in the power of balanced judgment and logical deduction:

> Cum causa efficiens matrimonii sit consensus, qui procedit ab intellectu et voluntate, evidens est ad matrimonium contrahendum inhabiles esse quotquot judicii discretionem matrimoniali contractui ineundo proportionatam non habent. Ad talem discretionem habendam non sufficit facultas cognoscitiva, quae sistit in simplici apprehensione veri, sed requiritur facultas critica, quae est vis judicandi ac ratiocinandi et judicia una componendi ut novum judicium substantialiter objectivum inde logice deducatur.[42]

If a person is deprived of this faculty through mental illness, he is incapable of eliciting sufficient marital consent:

> Matrimonium tunc tantum valet, quando per hanc criticam facultatem homo potuit deliberationes efformare et liberae voluntatis excitare actus.[43]

The *facultas critica* is not merely the simple use of reason. For a child of seven might have the simple use of reason, but the "critical faculty" does not normally appear in the growing child before puberty. How does it differ?

Although mentioned briefly in two sentences *coram* Felici, the *facultas critica* is not examined at length until the decision *coram* Felici of Dec. 3, 1957. The observations

---

rationis; unde incapaces redduntur aliquid humani agere, consensumque praestare. Usus autem rationis tum ipsam rationem supponit, tum facultatem reflectendi super se ipso, quam psychiatri vulgo nuncupant 'potere critico', quaeque dominatur quandoque a sensibus internis, seu a concupiscentia et a passionibus influxum exercentibus in illam, et praepedientibus rationis exercitium."

[41] C. Felici (Florentina), Apr. 6, 1954; c. Felici (Romana), July 12, 1955; c. Felici (Quebecen.), Dec. 3, 1957.

[42] C. Anné (Campifontis in Mass.), Nov. 25, 1961, *in iure.*

[43] C. Sabattani (Januen.), Feb. 24, 1961, *in iure.* — *Monitor Ecclesiasticus*, LXXXVI (1961), p. 632.

made in this remarkable decision have been repeated in many subsequent ones: [44]

1) We must distinguish the cognoscitive faculty of man from his critical or discretionary faculty. The latter power arrives later in a person's mental development:

> In intelligentia hominum rite distinguas facultatem cognoscitivam quae sistit in operatione abstractiva rei universalis ex particulari, seu in apprehensione simplici veri: et facultatem criticam, quae est vis judicandi et ratiocinandi seu affirmandi vel negandi aliquid de aliqua re, et iudicia una componendi ut novum iudicium inde logice deducatur.
> Facultas critica serius in homine apparet quam facultas cognoscitiva. [45]

2) The discretionary power is not the ability to *know* the obligations of the marriage contract (*cognoscere*), but the power to *undertake* these obligations (*suscipere*):

> Sed dum ad peccandum lethaliter sufficit discretio pueri qui septennium egressus est, quatenus hic communiter potest voluntatem divinam cognoscere et rimari pro modulo suo quam probrum sit voluntatem Dei offendere: non sufficit neque potest sufficere huiusmodi discretio pro suscipiendis peculiaribus officiis matrimonio inhaerentibus et totam vitam, aliquando usque ad sacrificium, urgentibus. Id docent communiter doctores praeeunte Angelico (cfr. IV, Dist. 24, q. 2, art. 2, ad II). [46]

3) Although a person at puberty might be presumed to possess the rudimentary knowledge of the nature of marriage (canon 1082, §2), yet, at puberty, due discretion is easily demonstrated as missing, as the legislator supposed in establishing canon 1067 on the impediment of nonage:

> Prout appellati Patres recolunt, fundamentum et ratio huius canonis non est tam immaturitas corporis contrahentium et facultatis generativae acerbitas (quae caeterum matrimonii essentiam non vitiaret, licet retardandus esset matrimonii usus), quam potius facile demonstrabilis defectus discretionis necessariae (cfr. Gasparri, *De matrim.*, I, n. 492-493). Neque ita vulnus infligitur praesumptioni enuntiatae

[44] C. Lamas (Neo-Eboracen.), Oct. 21, 1959; c. Sabattani (Januen.), Feb. 24, 1961; c. Sabattani (Tridentina), Mar. 24, 1961; c. Anné (Campifontis in Mass.), Nov. 25, 1961.

[45] *Monitor Ecclesiasticus*, LXXXIII (1958), p. 47.

[46] *Ibid.*

in can. 1082: nam si post pubertatem non praesumitur partes ignorare matrimonium esse societatem permanentem inter virum et mulierem ad filios procreandos (quod iure naturae sufficit ad matrimonialem consensum praestandum): talis mentis discretio debilis, ante aetatem per can. 1067 constitutam, esse solet: et propter hanc causam Ecclesia maiorem aetatem pro matrimonii valore exigit.[47]

IN FACTO: --- Itaque quando matrimonium contractum est conventus, etsi amens adhuc dici nequiret, ea erat in mentali aetate constitutus ut obligationes matrimoniales valide suscipere non posset... In hanc propterea conclusionem deveniunt Patres, ut licet tempore contracti coniugii Andreas conventus demens, uti forte hodie, dici non posset, eam tamen non haberet mentis discretionem, quae iuxta ius naturale, positivis praescriptis firmatum, satis esse ad valide promendum matrimonialem consensum.[48]

The conclusion of our survey of Rotal jurisprudence must be that it is extremely difficult to formulate exactly what the essential psychological components of the act of marital consent are, and that it is difficult, therefore, to formulate the positive psychic powers which a person must possess in order to elicit this psychological act. If not stated explicitly among the *motiva in iure*, it is a tone running through all the decisions *in facto* that no concise judicial norm can be formulated, or if formulated, scientifically applied. The watchword seems to be "*...modo humano!*"

Article 2. THE TESTS SUGGESTED BY CANONICAL WRITERS

Nearly all the canonical writers who have dealt at some length with the problem of a legal test of minimum psychic competence for valid marriage have proposed a twofold test. Claiming authority from some early Rotal decisions of the transition period in which both the norm of Sanchez and the view of St. Thomas were mentioned among the *motiva in iure*, these authors separate the various powers of the human psyche, assigning the "mortal sin" norm of Sanchez to gauge one power and the "more than mortal sin" norm of St. Thomas to gauge another.

---

[47] *Ibid.*, p. 48.
[48] *Ibid.*, p. 55.

They state that the two views, although generally thought to be contrary, are, in reality, complementary to one another if we interpret them correctly. The repeated repudiation of the norm of Sanchez in later Rotal jurisprudence, it is said, is unjust and due to a lamentable misinterpretation of the mind of Sanchez and to a failure on the part of the Rota to keep distinct the various powers of the human psyche.

Perhaps the original impetus to this thesis in canonical writings came from the article of A. Amanieu, "Aliénation mentale en matière de nullité de mariage", published in the *Dictionnaire de Droit Canonique.*[49] Writing at an early date, the author had at his disposal only the Rotal decisions handed down prior to 1920, the very time of the beginning of the transition from the "human act" test to the "qualified human act" test. Amanieu made a theoretical reconciliation of the two:

> En quoi consiste le degré d'intelligence et de volonté requis pour que le mariage soit valide? D'après la jurisprudence, il est caractérisé par deux choses: l'intelligence et la volonté suffisantes pour pécher mortellement, et en même temps la connaissance, au moins générale, de la nature et de la portée du contrat matrimonial. Si la première de ces conditions se réalise vers l'âge de sept ans, la seconde n'apparaît qu'à l'époque de la puberté.[50]

Hence, it is not true, of course, that anyone who is capable of committing a mortal sin is thereby to be judged capable of valid marriage. But the mortal sin norm of Sanchez, which Amanieu calls "traditional in Catholic theology",[51] is saved from rejection if we distinguish between intelligence and knowledge. Thus, a person should be judged capable of valid marriage if he has the capacity of intelligence and will of a seven-year-old child plus the actual knowledge of the nature and import of marriage (*ad normam can.* 1082, §1) attained by the normal child at the onset of puberty.[52] Hence, the seven-year-old child, capa-

---

[49] Tom. I, coll. 417-440.

[50] *Ibid.*, col. 436.

[51] *Ibid.*

[52] Therefore, the norm of Sanchez is not absolute, but has a restricted application: "Mais à elle seule, elle ne suffit pas. Elle détermine uniquement l'etat de l'intelligence et de la volonté. C'est sans doute ce qu'a

ble of mortal sin, is incapable of valid marriage because of ignorance of the nature and import of marriage.

In a doctoral dissertation published in 1950 at the Catholic University of America, Smith separates the notions of deliberation and discretion:

> As a general principle, it may be stated that one who is capable of the degree of deliberation postulated for the commission of mortal sin is likewise endowed with the requisite mental capacity for the contracting of marriage.[53]

This does not mean, however, that anyone who is capable of committing a mortal sin is thereby capable of valid marriage, for besides the requisite degree of deliberation, there is also needed for valid marriage consent a grasp of the "complex concept of marriage", which requires a greater maturity of judgment (discretion) than does the commission of a simple mortal sin:

> Therefore, according to the norm given, if the state of the mind allows of a deliberation which is founded on a discretion proportionate to the concept of marriage, in the same degree that is required for the commission of a mortal sin, when the deliberation is founded on a discretion proportionate to the possible commission of the sin, then the mentally afflicted person must be deemed capable of eliciting a valid matrimonial consent.[54]

Therefore, the seven-year-old child who has the power of deliberation sufficient to commit a mortal sin, is incapable of valid marriage because he lacks the mental maturity or discretion to grasp the concept of marriage, ignorance of which necessarily renders consent invalid.

In his doctoral dissertation, *Die Schizophrenie als Ehenichtigkeitsgrund im kanonischen Recht*, published in 1951 at the University of Freiburg in Switzerland, Hans Fässler argues that Sanchez never held the mortal sin

---

voulu dire dans la sentence du 14 nov. 1919. Il ne suffit pas, en effet, de considérer l'intelligence uniquement dans sa capacité, pas plus du reste que cela ne suffirait pour estimer s'il y a eu, dans un cas donné, péché mortel. Il est nécessaire de plus que cette intelligence ait réellement exercé ses facultés et ait acquis le degré de connaissance voulu pour l'acte dont il s'agit dans une espèce." — *Ibid.*

[53] VINCENT M. SMITH, *Ignorance Affecting Matrimonial Consent* (Washington, D.C.: Catholic University of America Press, 1950), p. 51.

[54] *Ibid.*, p. 52.

norm as a general gauge of minimum psychic development necessary to contract marriage. Citing passages from "*De malitia supplente aetatem*" of Sanchez's *De sancto matrimonii sacramento,*[55] Fässler concludes that Sanchez actually held with St. Thomas that a greater degree of discretion is necessary for marriage than that required to commit a mortal sin.[56] The so-called mortal sin norm attributed to Sanchez merely refers to the requirement of actual deliberation and advertence at the time of placing consent to assure that the consent be a human act.. Thus, maturity of judgment or discretion is the inner natural capacity comprising the two concurrent, separate, and dependent elements of understanding and willing: 1) die Fahigkeit des Verstandes... 2) die Fahigkeit des Willens (*potestas sui actus ad opposita*). Sanchez's mortal sin norm applies only to the question of the will; as regards the question of the intellect, Sanchez held with St. Thomas that a greater capacity is required for valid marriage than that required to commit a mortal sin.[57] The seven-year-old, then, is incapable of valid marriage because, though volitional capacity be sufficiently developed, the intellectual capacity is as yet insufficiently developed to grasp the elemental knowledge of canon 1082, § 1. Consequently, the marriage attempted by the insane is ultimately null because of ignorance.

Also in 1951 Fazzari published his monograph, *Valutazione etica e consenso matrimoniale,* in which he proposed that Sanchez held the mortal sin norm of mental development for the engagement contract, but certainly not for the marriage contract. For valid marriage, Sanchez demanded that a child be "*doli capax*" no matter what his age be.[58] Fazzari claims that although for many authors "*doli capaces*" means the power to commit mortal sin, in Sanchez it means "*close to puberty*". For in another dispu-

[55] Lib. VII, Disp. CIV, nn. 20-23.

[56] *Die Schizophrenie...*, pp. 35-36.

[57] *Ibid.*, pp. 26, 32, 35, 36.

[58] "Caeterum verissima sententia est solo jure ecclesiastico eam aetatem praescriptam esse: ac proinde, attento solo jure naturae, valere matrimonium initum a pueris cujuscumque aetatis, dummodo doli capaces sint." — SANCHEZ, *De sancto matrimonii sacramento*, Lib. VII, Disp. CIV, n. 9.

tation Sanchez says: "*Doli autem capax dicitur, qui est pubertati proximus.*"[59] On the other hand, the same degree of *deliberation* which is required for mortal sin is required likewise for marital consent. Hence, it seems that for Fazzari the twofold norm would read: (a) mortal sin norm as regards the requisite degree of deliberation; (b) puberty norm as concerns the degree of discretion. Discretion is a certain knowledge of marriage, not merely the conceptual knowledge of marriage as demanded by canon 1082, § 1, but also an indispensable evaluative knowledge of the ethical aspect of marriage which spontaneously arises from the conceptual knowledge in the normal individual. For true matrimonial consent there is required not merely the elemental conceptual knowledge of canon 1082, § 1, but also the power of spontaneous transformation of this knowledge into a rational evaluation and appreciation of all the substantial aspects of marriage, especially the ethical aspect.[60]

Although he does not go into the problem at great length, Pickett in his dissertation, *Mental Affliction and Church Law*, published in 1952 at the University of Ottawa, repeats the double norm of Amanieu. Hard pressed by the fact that the norm of Sanchez had been traditional in Rotal jurisprudence, and yet is currently repudiated by the same Rota, he concludes:

> It would seem to be necessary, therefore, to make a subtle distinction between *intelligence* and *knowledge* in the matter at hand. The power of intelligence which is peculiar to a normal child at seven years of age is sufficient for the validity of a marriage contract. The law of nature, however, and that of the Code (Canon 1082) demand the knowledge (*in materia matrimoniali*) normally present only at the age of puberty for the validity of the same.[61]

---

[59] *Ibid.*, Lib. VI, Disp. XXXVIII, n. 2.

[60] "...per la capacità di prestare un valido consenso matrimoniale non basta l'uso di ragione necessario per non ignorare quanto il can. 1082 dichiara non potersi ignorare senza sostanziale deficienza del consenso matrimoniale, ma è necessaria la maturità e la normalità di collegamenti psichici che permettano la spontanea trasformazione della conoscenza del matrimonio in valutazione razionale, almeno confusa e implicita, di tutti i suoi lati sostanziali, particolarmente di quello etico." — FAZZARI, *Valutazione etica e consenso matrimoniale*, p. 77.

[61] *Mental Affliction and Church Law*, pp. 146-147.

The question, then, of due discretion is reduced to a question of ignorance *de materia matrimoniali.* If a child of seven is incapable of valid marriage it is because, although his spiritual faculties are developed enough for mortal sin and marriage, yet he is *de facto* ignorant of the nature of marriage. This necessary knowledge usually comes with the advent of puberty. The mentally ill are incapable of valid marriage if they lack the intelligence of a seven-year-old or the knowledge of marriage usually possessed by the adolescent at puberty.

The dissertation of Eudoxio Castañeda, submitted to the University of Salamanca in 1955, was reprinted as a book under the title *La locura y el matrimonio.* In it he states that Sanchez has been misinterpreted by the Rota which has failed to see that the problem of due discretion is divided into two completely distinct questions, that pertaining to the capacity or maturity of the intellect, and that pertaining to the capacity or maturity of the will.[62] When Sanchez speaks of the mortal sin norm, he is speaking only of requisite deliberation (the question of capacity of the will); St. Thomas, on the other hand, was speaking of intellectual capacity. A close reading of Sanchez, especially in "*De malitia supplente aetatem*" will reveal that, as regards the question of intellectual capacity, Sanchez and St. Thomas held the same opinion, viz., a greater degree of intellectual maturity is required for valid marriage than that required to commit a mortal sin. Thus, a child of seven can have the deliberative (volitional) power sufficient for marital consent, but he lacks the intellectual power to acquire the degree of knowledge that canon 1082 demands. Since canon 1082 presumes this knowledge to arrive at puberty, it also presumes this intellectual capacity to arrive at puberty. Hence, that the mentally ill person be judged capable of valid marriage, he must be endowed

[62] De aquí que el problema del grado de madurez del juicio necesario en orden a la capacidad para contraer matrimonio, se excinde en dos cuestiones netamente distintas, a saber: en una cuestión de *entendimiento,* dirigida a determinar cuál sea el grado de capacidad intelectiva o de madurez de razón para poder contraer y en una cuestión de *voluntad* en orden a determinar el grado de deliberación volitiva o de madurez de voluntad relativo al mismo vínculo matrimonial." — *La locura y el matrimonio,* p. 53.

with the volitional capacity of a seven-year-old and the intellectual capacity of the normal adolescent at puberty.[63]

Jaime Mans, professor of Canon Law at the University of Barcelona, published his *El consentimiento matrimonial* in 1956 in which he makes the same distinction between deliberation and discretion, based on the distinction of intellect and will. Sanchez, according to Mans, spoke only of actual deliberation, advertence, and discernment (the question of the will), and not of habitual discretion (the question of the intellect) as St. Thomas did.[64] The important distinction is between actual requirements and habitual requirements:

> En conclusión, en cuanto a la capacidad de los sujetos para prestar verdadero consentimiento matrimonial, no basta el grado de desarrollo mental requerido para pecar letalmente, sino que se requiere mayor discreción o madurez de juicio para consentir en la creación de un vínculo exclusivo y perpetuo sujeto a tan graves cargas como es el del matrimonio; mas presupuesta dicha capacidad, o sea, la *habitual* madurez o discreción de juicio proporcionada a la gravedad del negocio matrimonial, de parte del consentimiento mismo, es decir, en cuanto a la advertencia o discernimiento del acto que se celebra, entonces sí que es suficiente el grado de deliberación *actual* que se requiere y basta para pecar mortalmente, para que también la persona previamente dotada de la necesaria discreción de la mente pueda otorgar verdadero consentimiento matrimonial.[65]

The failure to make this important distinction has caused, according to Mans, serious confusion and a poor interpretation of Sanchez. Discretion is the habitual intellectual capacity to acquire the elemental knowledge of canon 1082, §1; this capacity comes with the approach of puber-

---

[63] *Ibid.*, pp. 46-55, 174-177, 198-202, 224. Castañeda concludes: "...un niño de siete años puede tener potencia deliberativa para pecar mortalmente y esa deliberación de que es capaz sería suficiente para el consentimiento matrimonial, suponiendo que la conociera, pero ese niño carece de potencia intelectiva para adquirir el grado de conocimiento que del matrimonio exige el c. 1082; es decir, el desarrollo mental y volitivo que posee normalmente un niño de siete años es capaz de una deliberación suficiente para pecar mortalmente, pero su razón no es capaz de adquirir aquel grado de conocimiento exigido para el matrimonio por el derecho natural." — *Ibid.*, pp. 174-175.

[64] *El consentimiento matrimonial*, p. 29.

[65] *Ibid.*, pp. 29-30.

ty.[66] The power of deliberation of the seven-year-old is necessary and suffices for marital consent as far as the actual volitional requirement is concerned; therefore, the seven-year-old child is capable of the actual deliberation required for valid marital consent (and this is all Sanchez was referring to with his mortal sin norm) but lacks the habitual intellectual capacity to comprehend the elemental notions of the nature of marriage as stated in canon 1082, §1. Thus, lack of due discretion means ignorance.[67]

Finally, perhaps the fullest treatment of the problem was done recently by Van Ommeren in his doctoral dissertation published in 1961 by the Catholic University of America.[68] His conclusions are much in accord with the conclusions of those cited above. The norm of Sanchez is saved by applying it merely to the power of deliberation, so that a person enjoying the power of deliberation of the normal seven-year-old has sufficient deliberation to place valid marital consent. However, one must also have the requisite conceptual knowledge demanded by canon 1082, §1. But this is not what is meant by discretion; rather, discretion is what the author means by an evaluative knowledge or appreciation of the nature, import, consequences, purpose, etc. of marriage.[69] This evaluative knowledge or insight into the nature, purpose, and import of marriage is essential to true marital consent and may not be lacking without invalidating the marriage.[70] This evaluative know-

---

66 *Ibid.*, p. 30.

67 *Ibid.*, p. 29. Cf. also MANS-BERNÁRDEZ, *Derecho matrimonial canónico*, I, pp. 319 ff.

68 WILLIAM M. VAN OMMEREN, *Mental Illness Affecting Matrimonial Consent*, Washington, D.C., 1961.

69 "By discretion, on the other hand, is meant what the writer would like to call the 'content' or insight of the deliberation. It is the knowledge and appreciation of the object about which the mind deliberates before giving or not giving consent to a certain act. It is precisely here that different requirements are made for different acts. Discretion, therefore, concerns the question: How much does a person have to know about the nature, purpose, import, consequences, etc., of an act to make such an act imputable to him if he deliberately chooses to place the act?... Discretion, therefore, is the degree of evaluative knowledge necessary for a specific act." — *Ibid.*, pp. 124-125.

70 It is rather surprising that Van Ommeren resumes the doctrine of values without any attempt to distinguish it from the doctrine so unanimously condemned by Rotal jurisprudence. Cf. *supra*, "A Survey of Rotal Jurisprudence."

ledge is attained normally at the time of puberty. Thus we arrive at a puberty norm for due discretion:

> Consequently, if a person has psychical capacity in the same degree as the average adolescent at puberty, that person is to be considered as being able to give valid matrimonial consent. Such a person must be considered capable of matrimony even if, by medical standards, he is regarded as being mentally ill or disturbed. On the other hand, if a person by reason of mental illness does not meet this same norm, he must be judged incapable of giving valid consent.[71]

Hence, the seven-year-old may have the power of deliberation sufficient to commit a mortal sin and to give marital consent, but he lacks not only the conceptual knowledge demanded by canon 1082, §1, but also due discretion, i.e., that evaluative knowledge or insight to realize what marriage is and what it implies. The maturity of judgment by which the necessary conceptual and evaluative knowledge of matrimony is attained is that maturity of judgment which is, by virtue of general human experience, normally, i.e., usually, found in young people when they have reached actual physical maturity or puberty.[72]

For the sake of clarity it might be well at this point to make some general observations on the twofold legal test, stating the basic positions common to all the proposed versions of the double test.

1) All these authors place the criterion of psychic ability to contract marriage squarely on the psychological integrity of the act of marital consent by proposing to delineate exactly what the cognitional and volitional components are of the psychological act of consent, naturally sufficient in itself to effect this specific contract. Hence, the invalidating force of mental illness is seen restricted to its effect of precluding this psychological act of consent; the twofold test does not consider possible invalidity stemming from another source distinct from the material act of consent.

---

[71] *Op. cit.*, p. 177.
[72] *Ibid.*, p. 225.

2) These authors uniformly attempt to save the classical mortal sin norm of Sanchez from oblivion by stating that Sanchez never held the mortal sin norm as a general gauge of psychic competence for valid marriage. In proposing his mortal sin norm, either he was speaking only of the psychic ability to enter the engagement contract, or else, if applying it also to the marriage contract, he was speaking only of a restricted power of the human psyche, such as the power of deliberation as opposed to the power of discretion, or the maturity of the will as opposed to the maturity of the intellect, or the power of intelligence as opposed to its actual knowledge content, etc.

3) Hence, by so dividing the human psyche into its various component powers, a way is found to reconcile the mortal sin norm of Sanchez and the "more than mortal sin" norm of St. Thomas. Each applies to a different power. The end result is the twofold test composed of a mortal sin norm for one power and a puberty norm for another. There are several, although isolated, Rotal decisions which seem to make such a reconciliatory twofold norm.[73]

4) This twofold norm is offered not merely as negative norm but as a truly positive norm. Hence, for example, a person found to possess the minimum degree of deliberation necessary for the commission of a mortal sin and the degree of mental maturity of the average adolescent at the onset of puberty, is judged to be psychically capable of marriage. Or, another way one might say it: He who has the volitional capacity of a seven-year-old and the intellectual capacity of the adolescent at puberty, is mentally competent for valid marriage. Were the twofold norm proposed only as a negative norm, then all we could say is: He who lacks the above-mentioned capacities is incapable of marriage; but he who possesses them is not therefore mentally competent for marriage. A negative norm therefore, does not draw a definite line between the psychically competent and the psychically incompetent.

5) Due discretion, or the question of the intellect, is ultimately a question of the essential knowledge for valid consent, either the conceptual knowledge of canon 1082, §1, or the necessary evaluative knowledge of the nature,

---

[73] Cf. *supra*, p. 114.

import, consequences, etc., of marriage. Due discretion practically means due knowledge; defect of due discretion means ignorance. *Nil volitum nisi praecognitum.* Thus it would seem that this *caput nullitatis* is essentially the *caput ignorantiae de materia matrimoniali.* If it is distinct from ignorance, it is only as *de posse* is distinct from *de facto;* the ignorant man is simply *de facto* ignorant while the mentally ill is incapable of knowing the essential notions required for valid consent. *A non posse ad non esse valet illatio;* hence even if theoretically distinct, the *caput nullitatis* in insanity cases is practically reducible to an ignorance case.

As primary observations regarding the validity of the twofold legal test of minimum psychic capacity for valid marriage, we might make the following points:

1) It is rather clear that the whole question of the invalidating force of mental illness on the marriage contract is not resolved exclusively in the integrity of the psychological act of consent or its defect. Hence, even from this aspect alone, it is quite inaccurate to offer the twofold test as a *positive* norm, for a person might very well be able to meet the requirements of the twofold test and yet be psychically incapable of marriage for another reason which lies outside of the question of integral consent.

2) The overwhelming weight of canonical authority, both from jurisprudence and doctrine, interprets Sanchez as having held his mortal sin norm as a general gauge of mental competence for valid marriage in the sense that if a person is capable of mortal sin, no matter what age he is, he is psychically capable of validly marrying. Hence, the norm attributed to Sanchez has been overwhelmingly rejected. One wonders why recent writers are trying to recive it in the face of such opposition when its restoration would not bring any special utility to the matrimonial forum.

3) The authority claimed from some early isolated Rotal decisions is quite weak. For one thing, these decisions numerically do not exceed four and even in these four decisions, no attempt was made to apply such a twofold norm. And, as far as a reconciliation of the mind of St. Thomas with that of Sanchez is concerned, it is startling to find that Sanchez himself, who probably understood his own

opinion better than any of the recent commentators, thought his opinion contrary to that of St. Thomas and listed St. Thomas as an adversary.[74]

4) The critical point in Sanchez's norm is that it be not merely a negative norm, but a positive norm. That is, it is held that the power of deliberation which is necessary for the commission of a mortal sin is also *sufficient* for valid consent. That such deliberation is necessary is obvious (negative norm), for otherwise the act of marital consent would not even be a human act. But that this degree of deliberation is *sufficient* (positive norm) was never proved by Sanchez. He offered several reasons why it is necessary but no reason why it is sufficient. Nor do the authors who seek to revive his norm provide any arguments for the element of sufficiency, but only for necessity.

5) If discretion is reduced to knowledge then we cannot speak of a silence of the Code regarding the cause of nullity by reason of insanity, for it is contained in the canon on ignorance (canon 1082). But Rotal sentences have spoken of such silence repeatedly. Moreover, many, if not the majority, are the cases wherein a decision for nullity is granted by reason of defect of due discretion in which there is no question whatever of ignorance in the defendant.

The possibility of applying the twofold test in judicial practice is quite problematical. For example, the test proposed by Van Ommeren would seem to run into insuperable difficulties if it were ever applied in court with the hope of gaining morally certain results. The judge, with the help of the court experts, would have to ascertain the following points in order to decide on the psychical ability of the defendant to marry validly. Remembering that the scope of the investigation is to ascertain the integrity of a past internal act, it must be shown to the judges with moral certainty that the person was deficient in one of the following categories:

a) Conceptual knowledge: Did the person at the time of giving consent possess the basic knowledge of the na-

---

[74] *De sancto matrimonii sacramento,* Lib. I, Disp. VIII, n. 15.

ture and object of matrimony, the ends and properties of marriage?

b) Evaluative knowledge: Did the person at the time of giving consent possess the requisite degree of discretion, i.e., the insight into, the appreciation of, the nature, import, implications, and consequences of marriage to the same degree that would be in the power of the normal adolescent at the onset of puberty?

c) Power of deliberation: Did the person when giving consent exercise that degree of deliberation which is the minimum necessary for the commission of a mortal sin?

d) Psychological freedom: Did the person at the time of giving consent enjoy that degree of psychological freedom which is necessary and sufficient to insure his basic power of choice (i.e., philosophical freedom)? [75]

The harried expert might well ask the judge how he might measure such degrees of deliberation, evaluative knowledge, psychological freedom, etc., in an act that took place years previous. Even if the expert were standing next to the defendant at the moment of giving marital consent, this might be a formidable, if not, in fact, an impossible task. For how can the intellect and will be separated as though in a schoolman's syllogism and their acts and powers measured in isolation?

Professor d'Avack, professor of Canon Law at the University of Rome and a lawyer of the Sacred Roman Rota, once observed that a twofold norm is incapable of concrete application:

> As every student of medicine knows, it is a plain fact that it is impossible to succeed in isolating completely the "*quaestio intellectus*" from the "*quaestio voluntatis*" in mental illness, much less to weigh and determine distinctly the "*defectus cognitionis*" and the "*defectus voluntatis*" which it generates... In reality, every intellectual disturbance automatically redounds to a volitional disturbance and vice versa, such that in mental diseases there is always an inseparable and reciprocal influence of the one on the other; it is precisely from their necessary interplay and amalgamation that there results the automatic unwittingness and unreasoning compulsion of acts done by the sick person. [76]

---

[75] *Mental Illness Affecting Matrimonial Consent*, pp. 139, 140, 158.
[76] *Cause di nullità e di divorzio*, p. 135.

Hence, the twofold norm appears more as a purely academic construction than as a reasonable judicial norm. But even in the theoretical sphere alone the twofold norm is inaccurate and inadequately founded. For the sake of clarity in its appraisal, we will treat separately the two prongs of the twofold norm, the mortal sin norm and the puberty norm.

Article 3. A Critique of the Mortal Sin Norm

The mortal sin norm of Sanchez has usually been understood as a general test of mental competence for valid marriage. Stated thus, a person who is mentally capable of committing mortal sin is judged mentally capable of valid marriage. The jurisprudence of the Holy See has understood it thus, both in early times when it accepted the norm and presently when it has staunchly rejected it. Understood in this general sense, the mortal sin norm is the same as a human act test, or the use of reason test. He who has the mental capacity of the average seven-year-old child has sufficient mental capacity to marry.

Sanchez never really offered proof for this rule. That the psychic ability to commit a mortal sin is required for entry into marriage is obvious, for if a person cannot commit a mortal sin, he cannot (if we except the extraordinary prerogatives of Christ and the Blessed Mother) place a human act. Such a person cannot place the human act of marital consent for he cannot assume gravely binding obligations by an act which was not even a responsible human act within his rational powers.

The key to Sanchez's norm and its challengeable aspect is the all-important element of sufficiency. D'Avack states that the reason generally offered for the sufficiency of such deliberation for valid consent was a moral argument: If a person mentally capable of committing a mortal sin be barred from marriage because mentally incapable of valid marriage, he would be in danger of losing his immortal soul, forced to fornication. [77] Such a reason was obviously shallow; but what was lacking to this argument in intrin-

---

[77] *Ibid.*, pp. 128-129.

sic force was filled by the unquestioned authority of the name of Thomas Sanchez.

Authors who repeat the mortal sin norm of Sanchez, even in a restricted sense within a twofold legal test, do not attempt to prove the element of sufficiency but simply take it for granted. Van Ommeren offers a justification for introducing the mortal sin norm on the grounds that both marriage and mortal sin are serious matters:

> The writer holds that, because of the gravity and seriousness of matrimony, the necessary deliberation in making the choice and the philosophical freedom in the actual choosing, can and must be compared with the requirements for mortal sin. [78]

His argument why the degree of deliberation required to commit mortal sin is sufficient for valid marital consent is somewhat obscure:

> The act of committing a mortal sin and the act of giving matrimonial consent both require that the act be free and deliberate. Consequently, the norm attributed to Sanchez, which equates the deliberation necessary for matrimonial consent with the deliberation necessary for the commission of mortal sin, is perfectly sound and acceptable. [79]

The conclusion seems to exceed the premises. The conclusion should read: "Consequently, *at least* that deliberation necessary to commit a mortal sin is necessary for a valid act of marital consent; otherwise consent would not be a free and deliberate human act." But his conclusion that this degree is also sufficient ("equated") is a gratuitous assertion.

Some authors have proposed that Sanchez offered the mortal sin norm only as a gauge of actual advertence, deliberation, or discernment in the very act of expressing consent. And, indeed, if we restrict ourselves to certain passages of *De sancto matrimonii sacramento* it may appear that Sanchez did just that. If a person, while giving consent, is overcome with passion or anger to such an extent that his reason is clouded and it renders him incapable

---

[78] *Mental Illness Affecting Matrimonial Consent,* p. 152.
[79] *Ibid.,* p. 124.

of a human act, certainly his act of consent is deficient. For no one can be considered to bind himself to grave obligations by an act which was not even a human act. In this sense, such a mortal sin norm is applicable to everone, the mentally sound and the mentally ill. Speaking specifically of the engagement contract Sanchez writes:

> Nihilominus dicendum est, eam deliberationem sufficere, et exigi, quae in materia lethalis culpae sufficeret, ut consensus esset culpa mortalis, unde si quis ira, aut alio passionis motu subito percitus sponsalia contrahat, si tanta fit passio, ut rationis iudicium obtenebrarit, et deliberationem ad peccatum mortale requisitam impedierit, ut si illo subito motu hominem interimeret, non esset mortale; tunc sponsalia non erunt valida defectu deliberationis; si autem non ita impedit deliberationem, quin homicidium illud tunc admissum esset culpa lethalis, sponsalia erunt valida. Probatur id requiri, quia sponsalia suapte natura obligant ad mortale, ergo petunt deliberationem ad mortale requisitam: et confirmatur quia minor deliberatio non est sufficiens ad violandam fidem sponsalium nec ut actus sit simpliciter voluntarius. [80]

If Sanchez actually intended his mortal sin norm only for this, namely, the actual advertence and deliberation to assure that the act of consent be a human act, then we admit that the Rota has misinterpreted and unduly repudiated him. For no one can deny this position, at least in the sense that such deliberation is *necessary;* otherwise consent would not be " *simpliciter voluntarius* ". However, it is clear that Sanchez extended his mortal sin norm to the marriage contract, and this, as a general test of psychic competence.

In speaking specifically of the mentally ill, Sanchez writes:

> Hoc tamen unum adverto, judicari sanae mentis, ut valide contrahat sponsalia, quando eam deliberationem habet, quae in materia gravi sufficeret ad culpam mortalem. [81]

---

[80] *De sancto matrimonii sacramento,* Lib. I, Disp. VIII, n. 5. Here Sanchez speaks of the obstacle to valid engagement "*ex defectu praemeditationis*" in normal people. He speaks of the mentally ill in numbers 12-14 (*destituti sensibus*) and 14-24 (*amentes*).

[81] *Ibid.,* Lib. I, Disp. VIII, n. 17.

He certainly extended this doctrine from its application to the contract of betrothal to an application to the contract of marriage:

> Ex quibus constat, a furioso fieri nihil posse consensum liberum exigens, qualem petunt sponsalia. et matrimonium. Et idem dicendum est de mente capto... qui omnino rationis usu destituitur; secus est, si non caret omnino intellectu, quem vulgo *tonto*, o *atondado* appellamus, vel dicimus, *no tiene tanta sabiduria como Salomone,* ironice: hic enim sponsalia, et matrimonium inire potest... et ratio est manifesta, quia deliberationem sufficientem habet ad lethaliter delinquendum. [82]

Those who propose to save the Sanchez norm hold that he actually taught the same opinion as St. Thomas, i.e., a greater degree of discretion is required for marriage than that required to commit a mortal sin. Thus Fazzari makes the citation:

> Caeterum verissima sententia est, solo iure Ecclesiastico eam aetatem praescriptam esse: ac proinde attento solo naturae iure valere matrimonium initum a pueris cuiuscumque aetatis dummodo doli capaces sint. Ratio est aperta. Quia impotentia temporalis non dirimit matrimonium. [83]

Although this passage would seem to clearly make the simple use of reason (mortal sin norm) a general test of psychic aptitude, nevertheless, according to Fazzari, Sanchez meant by "*doli capaces*" not the sheer ability to commit mortal sin which accompanies the simple use of reason in the normal seven-year-old child, but rather he meant the age approaching puberty. Fazzari argues from the meaning which Sanchez attaches to the phrase "*doli capaces*" in Books I and VI:

> Approximare autem pubertati in hac materia dicitur puer decimum annum cum dimidio excedens, et foemina cum excedit nonum et dimidium. Ante hanc autem aetatem dicitur puer infantiae proximus, et puella infantiae proxima... Doli autem capax dicitur, qui est pubertati proximus. [84]
>
> Sed dicendum est... quoad hunc effectum dici doli capaces, quando ita proximi pubertati sunt, ut intellectum ac discre-

---

[82] *Ibid.*, n. 18.

[83] *Ibid.*, Lib. VII, Disp. CIV, n. 9. FAZZARI, *Valutazione etica e consenso matrimoniale*, p. 48 ff.

[84] SANCHEZ, *op. cit.*, Lib. VI, Disp. XXXVIII, n. 2.

> tionem habeant, ad firma omnino et irrevocabilia reddenda sponsalia, non tamen amplius explicant, quando dicantur pubertati proximi: at generaliter ad contractus docent aliqui tunc esse, quando masculus excedit decimum et dimidium annum, foemina vero nonum et dimidium. [85]

If we consider the context of these passages quoted by Fazzari, we see that Sanchez is speaking of something besides an engagement or marriage contract. In Book I he is discussing the juridical capacity required to solemnize the engagement contract by an oath. Hence, his *capacitas doli* seems to refer properly to the oath, for Sanchez has already determined quite clearly that one with the capacity to commit a mortal sin can make an engagement contract. It should be noted, therefore, that Sanchez qualifies carefully in both passages and says "*quoad hunc effectum* dici doli capaces, quando... " In the other passage he says "approximare autem pubertati *in hac materia*" and merely states that a child approaching puberty is capable of deceit, without denying that a child just out of infancy is also capable of deceit. As Klemme has pointed out:

> The final question, then, is: can the status of making a solemn oath and the natural law requirements for the capacity to marry be compared?
>
> It is doubtful whether a direct analogy can be drawn between the two citations, and hence whether *a priori* the same age bracket or age of discretion is intended in both instances. [86]

Another argument that Sanchez really held the puberty norm with St. Thomas is offered by Bidagor and repeated by Castañeda, Fässler and Van Ommeren. [87] It is taken from a parallel section in "*De malitia supplente aetatem*" in Book VII, Disputation 104, where Sanchez is treating of the impediments to marriage. The ecclesiastical impediment of nonage provided an exception. A boy less than fourteen years of age or a girl less than

---

[85] *Ibid.*, Lib. I, Disp. LI, n. 24.

[86] *Lucid Intervals and Matrimonial Consent*, p. 21.

[87] BIDAGOR, "Circa ignorantiam naturae matrimonii," *Periodica*, XXIX (1940), p. 274; CASTAÑEDA, *La locura y el matrimonio*, p. 54; FÄSSLER, *Die Schizophrenie als Ehenichtigkeitsgrund im kanonischen Recht*, pp. 35-36; VAN OMMEREN, *Mental Illness Affecting Matrimonial Consent*, pp. 110-112.

twelve years of age could marry validly "*si malitia suppleat aetatem*" or "*si prudentia suppleat aetatem*".[88] That is, they could validly marry if they possessed in spite of deficient age, *both* the power of generation (physical puberty) and sufficient mental discretion. Thus *malitia* was a suppletory norm by which those who had prematurely developed this twofold capacity were exempt from the ecclesiastical law prohibiting marriage before fourteen and twelve years of age.

In his discussion Sanchez maintains that the mere power of generation, without the relative discretion, does not warrant the exception, nor, vice versa, discretion alone without the actual power of generation. The possession of both faculties simultaneously is required, a situation inconceivable in a child of seven years of age:

> Nam in tam tenera aetate nequit reperiri discretio sufficiens ad perpetuum consensus coniugalis vinculum.[89]

> Secundo deducitur, nec prudentia sola suppleri aetatem matrimonio necessariam: nisi simul adsit generandi potentia. Nec obstat sponsalia ante septennium valere, modo tunc rationis usus adsit. Quia cum sponsalia advenienti pubertate solo puberis consensu cessari valeant, non tantam discretionem ad sui valorem desiderant, quantam matrimonium, quod est vinculum perpetuum.[90]

> At multo probabilius est, nomine malitiae supplentis aetatem ad matrimonium petitam, comprehendi potentiam ad copulam, ac prudentiam et discretionem ad intelligendam consensus coniugalis vim. Quae cum sit res gravissima et perpetua, exigit majorem discretionem ea, quae in tenera aetate reperitur: quare non sufficit ad matrimonii impuberis valorem sola generandi potentia aetatem praeveniens, nisi ea quoque prudentia adsit.[91]

This discussion on *malitia* is no real indication of the thought of Sanchez concerning the basic requirements of discretion necessary for marriage according to the natural law since it can well be argued (and is, in fact, more probable) that *malitia* was determined by the ecclesiastical legislator as a norm which supplanted the im-

---

[88] C. 9, X, *De desponsatione impuberum*, IV, 2.

[89] SANCHEZ, *De sancto matrimonii sacramento*, Lib. VII, Disp. CIV, n. 22.

[90] *Ibid.*, n. 23.

[91] *Ibid.*, n. 21.

pediment of nonage which had been established by positive ecclesiastical law. The lawmaker required both *prudentia* and *potentia ad copulam* to allow the exception. Certainly this was not remitting the question to the requirements of the natural law, for actual physical puberty is not required for valid marriage by the natural law. Furthermore, Sanchez states that the reason why most children are ineligible for the exception before fourteen and twelve years of age is not that they lack discretion, but that they lack the power to generate:

> Et e contra, quando puer pubertati proximus est, solet discretione sufficienti àd hoc praeditus esse: cum tamen raro potentiam generandi tunc habeat. [92]

These oblique arguments from other sections of Sanchez's work can hardly offset the stated and clear assertions in the sections wherein he is treating specifically of the natural law requirements for valid marriage. If there is any doubt that Sanchez held that, according only to the natural law, a person, at whatever age, could validly marry provided he had the use of reason, it is dispelled in the passages where Sanchez is clearly speaking only of the natural law requirements:

> Hinc deducitur primo, infideles valide contrahere in quacumque aetate, dummodo rationis usu sint praediti. [93]
>
> Secundo deducitur, integrum est summo Pontifici dispensare, ut in quacumque aetate matrimonium initum valeat, modo pueri rationis usus participes sint. Sicut potest in quolibet alio iure humano dispensare. [94]

In the final analysis, then, the norm of Sanchez either refers to actual advertence and deliberation and is, therefore, a pure truism and unworthy of note; or it refers to the entire psychic requirement for valid marriage and is, therefore, evidently erroneous. In this latter sense the Rota has commonly interpreted the mind of Sanchez. And whatever be the mind of Sanchez, certainly the mortal sin norm itself is untenable and has, in fact, been rejected

---

[92] *Ibid.*, n. 27.
[93] *Ibid.*, n. 10.
[94] *Ibid.*, n. 11.

by most canonists.[95] So foreign is it to Rotal jurisprudence today that a recent decision could say of it:

> Igitur, derelicta hodie in Nostra iurisprudentia communiter fuit thesis Sanchezii de sufficientia, pro contrahendo coniugio, illius gradus discretionis iudicii quae sufficiens reputatur ad lethaliter peccandum, adhaerendo e contra thesi Angelici qui superiorem gradum discretionis exigit, nempe illum qui sit proportionatus gravitati vinculi contrahendi, quod, utpote indissolubile, perpetuam secumfert et gignit servitutem.[96]

Not only in Rotal jurisprudence, but generally everywhere the thesis is abandoned:

> Sive in prima, sive in altera, ex huius causae sententiis, aliquid sustinetur, quod cum recenti doctrina ac jurisprudentia satis componi non potest.
>
> Verbigr. in sententia Philadelphien. citatur decisio quaedam Rotalis quae se refert ad doctrinam veterum nonnullorum juristarum, juxta quos "ea deliberatio, sive ea libertas, cum ea consideratione, necessaria est ad contractum matrimonii, et ad sponsalia, quae necessaria est ad peccatum mortale."
>
> Quod autem hodie a nemine sustinetur.[97]

The application of the mortal sin norm to a separate power of the human psyche has, as seen above, neither the authority of Sanchez, nor is it acceptable for intrinsic reasons:

> Si enim voluntas et intellectus pari gressu procedant oportet, immo una simul profunde operentur, uno exigito pro mentis capacitate, plus vel minus exigi pro capacitate voluntatis absonum esset.[98]

---

[95] Cf. GASPARRI, *De matrimonio,* II, n. 783; WERNZ-VIDAL, *Ius canonicum,* V (3. ed., 1946), *Ius matrimoniale,* nn. 456-457; CAPPELLO, *De matrimonio,* nn. 579, 582; D'AVACK, *Cause di nullità e di divorzio,* p. 130; JEMOLO, *Il matrimonio nel diritto canonico,* p. 124; GIACCHI, *Il consenso nel matrimonio canonico,* pp. 37-38; TRIEBS, *Praktisches Handbuch,* III, p. 443; DOHENY, *Canonical Procedure in Matrimonial Cases,* I, p. 512; BÁNK, *Connubia canonica,* pp. 345-346; OESTERLE, "Amentia," *Ephemerides Iuris Canonici,* XI (1955), p. 292.

[96] C. Lamas (Neo-Eboracen.), Oct. 21, 1959, *in iure.*

[97] C. Doheny (Philadelphien.), Dec. 10, 1956, *in iure.*

[98] C. Fiore (Romana), May 16, 1961, *in iure.*

Article 4. A Critique of the Puberty Norm.

The puberty norm might be stated thus:

> Proportionata autem ad matrimonium dici potest maturitas judicii hominis, qui illas facultates psychicas assecutus est iisque fruitur, quae in omnibus generatim reperiuntur tempore naturalis pubertatis advenientis. Id quod probatur tum ex jure naturae, tum ex jure positivo, antiquo simul et recenti.[99]

For those who understand "discretion" in a general sense as synonymous with "psychical competence", this norm would be contrary to the mortal sin norm or use of reason norm understood in a general sense. Thus, Bensch continues:

> Quo principio statuto, refutatur opinio plurimorum, qui in matrimonium valide ineundum eam sufficere mentis discretionem dicunt, quae requiritur ad lethaliter peccandum, quaeque, saltem ex sententia eorum, in infantibus septennio expleto invenitur.[100]

In this general sense, according to the proponents of the puberty norm, those who are endowed with the psychic aptitude of a normal adolescent at puberty are to be judged psychically competent to contract marriage.

On the other hand, those who take a limited view on the notion of discretion as a certain knowledge or power of knowledge of marriage leave room for the complementary mortal sin norm for another required psychic power, e.g., the power of deliberation. Used in conjunction with the mortal sin norm for deliberation, the puberty norm for discretion reads much the same as that given above, but we must remember that discretion here has a restricted meaning:

> The norm to determine the minimum degree of knowledge and of maturity of judgment necessary for a valid matrimonial consent, as required by canon 1082, is the fol-

---

[99] T. Bensch, *Wplyw Chorob Umslowych na Waznosc Umowy Malvenskiej* (*Influxus amentiae in validitatem consensus matrimonialis*), (Lublin: Universitas Catholica, 1936), p. 294, quoted by Pickett, *Mental Affliction and Church Law*, p. 147.

[100] *Loc. cit.*

lowing: The degree of knowledge and maturity of judgment necessary for matrimony is that degree of knowledge and maturity of judgment which is, by virtue of general human experience, normally, i.e., usually, found in young people when they have reached actual physical maturity or puberty.[101]

The chief argument concluding to the puberty norm comes from canon 1082 which states that ignorance of the nature of marriage may not be presumed after puberty.[102] Hence, if the law presumes the requisite knowledge present at puberty, and if discretion is conceived as the requisite knowledge, then the analogy is only too evident that the law supposes due discretion at puberty:

> Canon Law rightly presumes that sufficient maturity of judgment, discretion, and prudence to contract marriage are present at the age of puberty. However, since this is a presumption it must of necessity yield to facts in individual cases.[103]

> It does not seem rash to add that, at the time when puberty is reached, the absence of these psychical requirements cannot be presumed; in fact, the law presumes their presence... If the Code holds that the knowledge for matrimony is to be presumed present when puberty is reached, it must also accept the proposition that the deliberation and maturity of judgment necessary for matrimony is to be presumed upon the presence of puberty.[104]

Thus, if the law presumes that due discretion is attained when the adolescent reaches physical puberty, the application of this to the mentally ill is quite easy, even though they be far beyond adolescence and the advent of puberty:

> Consequently, if a person has psychical capacity in the same degree as the average adolescent at puberty, that person is to be considered as being able to give valid matrimonial consent. Such a person must be considered capable of matrimony even if, by medical standards, he is regarded as being mentally ill or disturbed. On the other hand, if a person by reason of mental illness does not meet this same norm, he must be judged incapable of giving valid consent.

---

[101] VAN OMMEREN, *Mental Illness Affecting Matrimonial Consent*, p. 225.
[102] § 2: Haec ignorantia post pubertatem non praesumitur.
[103] DOHENY, *Canonical Procedure in Matrimonial Cases*, I, *Formal Judicial Procedure*, p. 784.
[104] VAN OMMEREN, *op. cit.*, p. 138.

> Mental illness, or any other mental disturbance or defect, can, and often does, affect a person's knowing, willing and judging to such an extent that the mentally ill or defective person lacks the psychical requirements for matrimony and fails to measure up to the psychical standard or norm, i.e., the mental capacity normally and usually present at puberty.[105]

The puberty norm seems to rest on false support claimed from the Code in canon 1082 and from Rotal jurisprudence. Not only does the law not presume the attainment of due discretion at the onset of puberty, but actually supposes it absent at that time. Secondly, Rotal jurisprudence has definitely rejected the puberty norm. Thirdly, Cardinal Gasparri, who is cited as the authoritative doctrinal source for the puberty norm, probably did not hold it.

First, if we examine canon 1082 closely, it appears that no legal presumption is established therein:

> § 1. Ut matrimonialis consensus haberi possit, necesse est ut contrahentes saltem non ignorent matrimonium esse societatem permanentem inter virum et mulierem ad filios procreandos.
>
> § 2. Haec ignorantia post pubertatem non praesumitur.

Paragraph 2 does not establish a presumption, but merely denies one, namely, we may not presume ignorance after puberty. But to deny a presumption is not to establish its contrary, i.e., the presumption of knowledge. *Datur tertium*: There is no legal presumption at all, either of ignorance or of knowledge. Hence, although it be a legitimate "*praesumptio hominis*" to conjecture in the majority of cases that the adolescent at fourteen and twelve years of age has attained these elemental notions of the nature of marriage, nevertheless, we cannot say that this is a legal presumption. In other words, it seems inaccurate to say that "the law presumes" the attainment of due knowledge at puberty.

Much less does canon 1082, § 2, establish a presumption of ignorance prior to puberty. It says nothing whatever of pre-puberty knowledge or ignorance and simply pre-

---

[105] *Ibid.*, p. 177.

scinds from it. However, this is a necessary supposition to the formation of the puberty norm on the authority of canon 1082. It is alleged that canon 1082 presumes ignorance before puberty, knowledge after puberty, so that it equivalently presumes the actual attainment of due knowledge to coincide with the attainment of puberty. Thus, it is at this time in the gradual development of discretion in the growing child that the minimal degree of discretion necessary and sufficient for valid marital consent is attained.

It may be objected that the puberty norm does not purport to maintain that before puberty due discretion is lacking, but only that, at puberty at least, due discretion is present. To hold this, however, would be to destroy the puberty norm as a norm. Unless it be supposed that due discretion is lacking before puberty, the puberty norm does not offer any criterion of minimum mental aptitude for valid marriage.

Thus, to say that the law presumes due discretion to arrive at puberty seems inaccurate. If we can speak of "presumptions" of the law in this wide sense, then it is precisely the contrary presumption which is true. That is, the "law presumes" that due discretion for marriage is not present at puberty.

First of all, as St. Thomas pointed out, actions involving the assumption of obligations require a geater degree of discretion than those actions which do not involve the incurrence of abiding obligations. Hence, the law seems quite anxious about the discretion and responsibility of adolescents until the age of twenty-one.[106] Regarding marriage itself, canon 1034 bids pastors to discourage minors from marrying except with the caution that their parents know of the impending marriage and give their consent.

In canon 1067 the Church prohibits the marriages of adolescents under the age of sixteen and fourteen *ad validitatem.* The canon bids pastors to avert marriages of those who, although of this required minimum age, are younger than the accepted norm and custom of the region.

---

[106] Cf. canons 89, 1456, 1648, § 1, 1655, § 2, 1687, § 1, 2214, 2218, § 2, 2230.

In raising the nonage impediment from fourteen and twelve to sixteen and fourteen years for boys and girls respectively, the purpose of the legislator was to assure not so much the attainment of physical puberty as the attainment of due discretion. After all, physical puberty is not a requisite for valid marriage, but due discretion is. As Gasparri relates the reasons for the change:

> Post pubertatem non praesumitur partes ignorare matrimonium esse societatem permanentem inter virum et mulierem ad filios procreandos, quod iure naturae sufficit ad matrimonialem consensum (can. 1082); sed nihilominus Ecclesia iure meritoque maiorem aetatem exigit pro matrimonii validitate, quia mentis discretio necessaria, si ante hanc aetatem habetur, debilis est... [107]

In a recent case presented to the Sacred Roman Rota, the puberty norm was put to the test. The lower court, relying on the reports of experts who were trying to peg the discretion of the defendant in relation to normal mental development of the adolescent, gave a negative decision on the grounds that expert opinion seemed to give him the intelligence quotient of a lad at the onset of puberty. The court psychiatrist said that he would rate the defendant mentally as a lad of fourteen at the onset of puberty. The Rota reversed the decision and made the following observations on the puberty norm employed by the lower court:

> Ceterum, praeterquamquod legislatio nulla civilis, hodie, parem haberet puerum, completo septennio, ad quemlibet contractum agendum, maxime autem ad matrimonialem valide ineundum, remanet etiam hodiernam Ecclesiae legem nedum cum illorum veterum juristarum sententia pugnare, sed etiam cum aliorum, qui tenent sufficientem esse discretionem juvenis pubertatem tangentis. Constat enim, vi ca. 1082, § 2, Ecclesiam statuisse ignorantiam naturae matrimonii, *post pubertatem* praesumi non debere. Ergo, quoadusque homo pubertatem non adipiscatur, talis ignorantia praesumi saltem potest. Unde, in impuberibus omnibus, consensus deficere, generatim, praesumendus est, saltem ob ignorantiam ipsius contractus naturae.
>
> Nec satis: nam, vi can. 1067, impedimentum aetatis ita in hodierna Ecclesiae legislatione constituitur, ut vir, ante decimum sextum aetatis annum completum, et mulier ante decimum quartum item completum, validum matrimonium

---

[107] *Tractatus canonicus de matrimonio,* I, n. 493.

inire non possint, idest duobus jam annis transactis a superata pubertate. Et, cum in Ecclesiae gremio tot sint populi, corporis et mentis maturitate prorsus diversi, ideo, in praecitato canone, additur monimentum: "curent tamen animarum pastores ab eo (i.e., a matrimonio) avertere juvenes, ante aetatem, qua, secundum regionis receptos mores, matrimonium iniri solet."

Quarum praescriptorum fundamentum — ut praeclari docent AA. — non praecipue ponendum est in dubio quod, ante praedictam aetatem, homo adeptus non fuerit generandi facultatem. Ad hoc. cl. Wernz-Vidal: "...porro, actualis potentia generandi, licet sit maxime conveniens ut jam habeatur tempore quo matrimonium initur, ad validum contractum matrimonialem, ex natura rei, non requiritur, matrimonium enim facit partium consensus, et, licet ad eius valorem requirantur corpora habilia, tamquam obiectum circa quod versatur contractus, illa habilitas ex natura rei, non requiritur actu et proxime, sed satis est ut suo tempore habeatur..." (*Jus Canonicum,* 1928, vol. V, p. 229, n. 207, II).

E contra, in hoc impedimento aetatis statuendo, ac praesertim in eo, jure Codicis, reformando, praecipue prae oculis habuit Legislator ecclesiasticus illam judicii discretionem seu maturitate, quae — ut plurimum — in juvenibus adhuc deest, vel non satis firma exhibetur, etiam post mox superatam pubertatem. Audiatur cl. Gasparri: "Post pubertatem, non praesumitur partes ignorare matrimonium esse societatem permanentem etc. sed nihilominus Ecclesia jure meritoque majorem aetatem exigit pro matrimonii validitate, *quia mentis discretio necessaria, si ante hanc aetatem habetur, debilis est...*" (De Matrim. 1932, p. 291, n. 493).

Quamobrem, concludendo: quoties homo adultus, vel propter morbum, vel propter congenitam mentis formam (imbecillitas, fatuitas, etc.), a scientia medica assimiletur, quoad judicii discretionem impuberi septem annorum, vel adolescenti, qui vix pubertatem adeptus fuerit, is, profecto, inhabilis et impar regulariter praesumi potest, quin imo praesumi debet, ad validum consensum promendum, nisi contrarium cogentibus argumentis evincatur. [108]

Thus, if a mentally ill person is found to have the discretion of an adolescent at puberty, not only is it licit to presume him incapable of valid marital consent, but one must presume this incapacity until convincing arguments to the contrary are brought forth. The positive presumption to the contrary, i.e., of incapacity, was expressly stated in another decision:

---

[108] C. Mattioli (Quebecen.), Nov. 6, 1956.

> Insuper, in Ecclesiae hodierna legislatione, nedum impedimentum aetatis suppressum non est, sed confirmatum ac reformatum: eo sensu, quo, dum in antiquo jure aetas pubertatis sufficiebat pro valida matrimonii celebratione, in novo exigitur aetas sexdecim annorum, pro mare, et quatuordecim pro foemina.
>
> Id, autem, praeter quam ob alia gravia motiva, etiam, imo praecipue, quia necessaria omnino tenetur, pro valido consensu proferendo, major discretio quam ea, quae in multis aliis negotiis requiritur, et in ipsis peccatis committendis. Quae equidem major discretio, ad validitatem actus omnino exigenda, praesumitur a Legislatore non adesse, in genere, prius quam vir et foemina ad aetatem illam pervenerint.[109]

Two other recent decisions, banking on the reformation of the impediment of nonage, state that the Legislator supposes that due discretion is not present at puberty. This does not contradict canon 1082 in any way, for due discretion is not the same as the knowledge of which canon 1082 speaks:

> *a*) ...quae ignorantia non praesumitur post pubertatem. Attamen non quaevis cognitio sed maturius judicium postulare videtur legislator, quod homines vix adipiscuntur aetate puberali, scil., 14 annorum in maribus, 12 in foeminis; enimvero in can. 1067 edicitur virum ante decimum sextum aetatis annum completum, mulierem ante decimum quartum, item completum, *validum* matrimonium inire non posse, idque "quia mentis discretio necessaria, si ante hanc aetatem habetur, debilis est". (Gasparri, *De Matrimonio*, ed. 1932, Vol. I, n. 493).[110]
>
> *b*) Canon 1067: Hoc praescripto prae oculis habito, eruere licet ab Ecclesia, pluribus saltem in regionibus, non censeri ea maturitate mentis et corporis praeditos, quae optanda est pro ineundo coniugio, illos iuvenes qui non fuerint adepti aetatem biennio maiorem pubertate legali. Eos enim destitutos reputat maturi iudicii constantisque animi ad condendam regendamque familiam necessarii.[111]

Finally, a very recent decision considered that the age limit of sixteen and fourteen was quite low for entering the marriage contract as compared to the minimum age requirements set for other serious contracts. But this low age is permitted because, as St. Thomas pointed

---

[109] C. Doheny (Philadelphien.), Dec. 10, 1956.
[110] C. Pinna (Romana), Mar. 21, 1959.
[111] C. Lamas (Neo-Eboracen.), Oct. 21, 1959.

out, not as much discretion is needed for marriage as for other contracts since nature itself inclines us to marriage and hence, outfits us at a younger age:

> Bene Vinculi Tutor cum Doctore Angelico adnotat pro matrimonio non tantum vigorem et acumen mentis requiri, quantum in ceteris contractibus, eo quod ipsa natura docemur de hisce rebus.
>
> Hoc tam verum est, ut Ecclesia validum teneat, in hodierna disciplina, contractum matrimonialem foeminarum quatuordecim annorum et marium sexdecim annorum, quo in ceteris contractibus ne intelligi quidem potest.[112]

One might well ask how it is that the puberty norm, so adamantly repected in Rotal jurisprudence, is yet so commonly proposed in canonical writings. If we are not mistaken, the root difficulty lies in the faulty notion of due discretion, unhappily confused with the notion of due knowledge for valid marriage consent. The authorities cited in support of the puberty norm — the Legislator in canon 1082, Rotal jurisprudence, and distinguished canonists — are inaccurately cited, for they are treating only of *debita scientia,* not of *debita discretio,* when speaking of a puberty norm. Or else, these authorities, if speaking of due discretion, offer only a negative norm, not a positive puberty norm.

That due discretion is not resolved in the question of due knowledge has been treated elsewhere.[113] In current Rotal jurisprudence, the phrase "due discretion" has taken on a clear and unequivocal meaning coextensive with the entire psychic capacity of a person so that the entire question whether a person was psychically competent for valid marriage or not depends simply on the question whether he enjoyed due discretion or not:

> ...quod quaeritur est minimum necessarium ad eliciendum validum consensum matrimonialem... De his omnibus debilibus hoc statui potest principium: quoties infirmitas discretionem subiecti infra discretionem necessariam et sufficientem ad consensum matrimonialem valide eliciendum, deprimit, matrimonium irritum erit: quoties vero deminuta discretio pergit superare vel aequare discretionem illam, matrimonium validum erit.[114]

---

[112] C. Filipiak (S. Francisci in California), Dec. 23, 1960.

[113] Cf. *supra,* Chapter I, Art. 1, Sec. B, "Some Irrelevant Norms."

[114] C. Fiore (Romana), May 16, 1961.

> Unica mensura sufficientis consensus est discretio judicii matrimonio proportionata... vel adest illa sufficiens discretio judicii, vel non adest. Si prius, habetur sanitas; si alterum *amentia* simpliciter.[115]

That the Legislator did not establish a legal presumption of due discretion at the onset of puberty is certain. Furthermore, it is highly doubtful whether canon 1082 even establishes a legal presumption of due knowledge at the onset of puberty. It seems that canon 1082 establishes no legal presumption at all. Certainly it does not establish a presumption of ignorance prior to puberty. Hence, it is doubtful that the Legislator has established a presumption in favor of a puberty norm even for due knowledge. That is, the Legislator does not seem to presume that the attainment of due knowledge coincides with the onset of physical puberty.

The confusion of "due discretion" with "due knowledge" is, we think, due to an unfortunate choice of words by Cardinal Gasparri. He used the phrase "*debita discretio*" in one section of his *Tractatus de matrimonio* to mean simply "*debita scientia*", and used it in another section to mean psychic competence for valid marriage. The end result is that in the former passage due discretion is presumed at puberty and falls only to contrary evidence, while due discretion in the latter passage is presumed lacking at puberty and its presence must be positively proved. Speaking only of ignorance of the elemental notions of canon 1082, Gasparri heads the commentary "*Defectus debitae discretionis*" and says:

> In primis ante pubertatem haec matrimonialis mentis discretio non praesumitur, sed probari debet; e contrario post pubertatem praesumitur, nisi contrarium evincatur, uti docet Codex in rel. can. 1082, § 2. Hinc ante pubertatem ille qui affirmat prudentiam, idest debitam mentis discretionem, praevenisse aetatem, probare debet: de qua re vide quae diximus agentes de impedimento *aetatis*. E contrario post pubertatem ille qui negat debitam mentis discretionem adesse, probare debet." [116]

Not only from the heading "*Defectus debitae discretionis*" is it clear that Gasparri intends due discretion to

[115] C. Sabattani (Januen.), Feb. 24, 1961.
[116] *Tractatus canonicus de matrimonio*, II, n. 784.

mean due knowledge, but also in the commentary itself he shows that by due discretion is here meant the possession of the elemental notions about the nature and force of marriage *ad normam can.* 1082, § 1. He speaks only of normal people in this paragraph; his example is of a twelve-year-old girl. When he speaks of the mentally ill in the following paragraphs he never assigns the puberty norm; in fact, it seems that, though not dealing explicitly with the problem, he assigns a mere use of reason or human act test for the insane.[117] The fact that he treats the insane under canon 1082 is, perhaps, unfortunate, for they are only *per accidens* ignorant *ad normam can.* 1082 and ignorance is not the exclusive or the fundamental cause of nullity in the marriages of the mentally ill.

When Gasparri does speak of due discretion as the psychic ability to enter marriage (under canon 1067 on the impediment of nonage), it is clear that he does not hold, nor does he claim that the law holds, that such discretion is presumed at the onset of puberty. *If* such discretion is present at all at puberty, it is weak; hence, the Legislator was anxious to establish the impediment of nonage at sixteen and fourteen years respectively for boys and girls mainly on this supposition. The above-mentioned Rotal decisions which have explicitly treated of the puberty norm and have rejected it as contrary to the mind of the legislator, appeal to Gasparri's reason:

> ...Ecclesia jure meritoque maiorem aetatem exigit pro matrimonii validitate, quia mentis discretio necessaria, si ante hanc aetatem (scil. 16 et 14) habetur, debilis est...[118]

The confusing use of terminology entered Rotal jurisprudence also, and there are quite a few instances wherein the phrase "*debita discretio*" means merely "*debita scientia*".

Aside from the authority inaccurately claimed for it, the puberty norm is in itself unsupported by intrinsic reasons. The argument from "general human experience" seems devoid of force also. Let us imagine a lad of fourteen and a girl of twelve, both at the onset of physical

---

[117] *Ibid.*, II, n. 785.
[118] *Ibid.*, I, n. 493.

puberty, about to get married. Would the common estimation of men deem that these two children are psychologically responsible enough to bind themselves *sub gravi* for life to the obligations of the marriage contract? It is one thing to say that they have the elemental notions *pro modulo suo* that marriage is between a male and a female, for having children, and for life. But it is quite another thing to say that they are therefore mentally mature enough to assume responsibly the obligations involved. If the laws of civilized nations are any indication of "common human estimation", then these two children are not only deemed incapable of entering the marriage contract, but incapable of negotiating *any* onerous contract.

Summing up, we might say that the puberty norm seems to gain no support either from common human estimation, from the mind of the canonical Legislator, from Rotal jurisprudence, or from the authority of Cardinal Gasparri. In fact, it seems that common human estimation, the canonical Legislator, Rotal jurisprudence, and Cardinal Gasparri are all clearly contrary to the puberty norm. Finally, even if the puberty norm were soundly conceived in theory, it would not be a useful judicial norm in insanity cases, for almost all, if not all, marriage cases that come to the ecclesiastical tribunal for adjudication on the plea of mental incompetence involve mentally ill persons who, however, at the time of their marriage, had at least the mental maturity and intelligence of a fourteen-year-old boy or a twelve-year-old girl.

* * *

Part II: Psychic Capacity to Assume the Essential Rights and Obligations of the Marriage Contract

Rotal jurisprudence until recently, and canonical doctrine to the present day, have considered the invalidating force of mental illness as stemming exclusively from the contractant's inability to elicit an integral, psychologically sufficient act of marital consent, an *actus exsistens* which would be naturally sufficient in itself, as an adequate efficient cause, to generate the marriage bond. The stream of judicial proof, accordingly, is directed solely towards the moment when consent was expressed; the person's mental condition is contrasted exclusively against his actual ability at that moment to bring to bear all the cognitional and volitional elements necessary to emit an integral act of consent, psychologically proportionate and sufficient to the contract it must engender. If it is shown that the person at that time *could* not, then it is clear that he *did* not, elicit sufficient consent (*a non posse ad non esse valet illatio*); and since no human power can supply the act of consent for him, there was no effective cause of the marriage bond. The marriage is null by reason of a defect of consent, for lack of an adequate efficient cause. Within such a framework, it is clear why traditional jurisprudence has given so much attention to the question of lucid intervals, for a true lucid interval or remission could change the entire picture since the crucial point and whole criterion of a valid or invalid marriage depends on the person's actual ability or inability to elicit naturally sufficient consent.

Without denying, of course, that mental illness can invalidate marriage by precluding its efficient cause of naturally sufficient consent, recent Rotal jurisprudence has begun to consider mental illness as founding another distinct source of nullity. For valid marriage there is required not only sufficient consent as its constitutive efficient cause, but also fitness of the parties themselves as the apt material cause of the contract. Regardless of a person's ability to elicit sufficient consent, if he is a naturally unfit subject for these rights and obligations, he cannot contract validly. For instance, the incurably impotent man may well be able to construct and elicit sufficient consent, but his naturally sufficient consent is bound to be inefficacious because *aliunde* his natural disability prevents an effective assumption of the right and obligation to place conjugal copula: *Nemo ad impossible obligari potest... Ius ad impossibile ne concipi quidem potest.* In the same way, even if we grant that a mentally ill person can supply adequate consent for marriage, it might happen that his disability render him *subiectum inhabile iurium et obligationum essentialium matrimonii.* It is one thing to be able to know the nature of marriage and to will it, and quite another thing to be psychically equipped to undertake these same obligations, to honor them, to sustain them, to put them into practice... in a word, to assume them *sub gravi.*

Article 1. A Recent Tendency in Rotal Jurisprudence.

During the last ten years there have been several decisions emanating from the Sacred Roman Rota which consider the invalidating force of mental illness more as a diriment impediment residing in the person than as a defect of sufficient consent. Mental disorder or defect is seen as rendering the person incapable of binding himself to the essential obligations of the marriage contract, regardless of his psychological act of consenting in them. In most of these decisions, the court was so anxious to demonstrate that this personal incapacity to bind oneself is a source of nullity distinct from the inability to elicit sufficient consent, that it granted, either in fact or in hypothesis for the sake of clarity, that the person actually did elicit sufficient consent; nevertheless, the sufficient consent failed to generate the bond because the person was an unfit subject of these rights and obligations:

1. After one year of marriage, Louis deserted his wife and left the country, but he was soon apprehended and put into an insane asylum. Five years previous to his marriage, when he was eighteen years old, he had contracted lethargic encephalitis which, according to subsequent expert examination, left him in a psychopathic state. Both before and after his marriage he showed unmistakable signs: e.g., he would rip clothing off girls, he raped his own sister, exhibited sadistic cruelty towards animals, had an eerie laugh, was quick to violent bursts of anger, etc. After marriage he was insanely jealous of his wife to the point of not allowing her to speak to her father or cousins. He refused to work and would sit all day in the kitchen singing to himself.

The case, after receiving an affirmative decision in the court of first instance and a negative decision on appeal, came to the Rota in third instance. After reviewing the evidence, the court was convinced that Louis was incapable of *any* human act at the time of the wedding, much less that of marital consent. But, as an argument *a fortiori,* the Rotal decision stated:

> ...admisso quod vir in se consensum validum praebere potuerit, in contractu matrimonii consentiebat in rem cuius incapax erat (cfr. Sent. Rot. 1941, n. 73). Conventus incapax erat sese obligandi in contractu traditionis sui corporis exclusive et perpetuo uni coniugi. Post morbum tum nervis tum psyche ipse factus fuerat in suis instinctibus bestia; pro eius impetu libidinis nulla lex frenum poterat imponere.[119]

The Rota seems to be making two points here: (a) even admitting naturally sufficient consent, such was bound to be inefficacious, for Louis was incapable of binding himself to the essential obligations of the marriage contract; (b) he was incapable of such obligations because of his behavioral disorder which prevented him from sustaining or honoring said obligations; he was promising something which was simply beyond his powers.

2. Three years after his wedding Andrew is hopelessly insane and is committed to a mental institution. He is diagnosed as suffering from general paralysis arising from congenital syphilis. The court of first instance handed down a negative decision and the case was appealed to the Rota. In the sentence, which was affirmative, the court speaks of those who appear sane to the layman but who in reality are mentally unbalanced:

> Qui, nihilominus, ad actus vitae graviores, ad obligationes illas sumendas, quae successione temporum implentur, maxime autem ad contractus perpetuos ineundos, certo certius impares judicandi sunt. Nam, ipsa ratio vetat huiusmodi infelices devictos tenere oneribus illis, quae lucido equidem intellectu ac plena deliberatione actuali — remittente ad tempus vi morbi — forte contraxerunt, quae tamen, ob jam incoeptam mentis deordinationem. sensim in pejus progredientem, natura sua jam inhabiles sunt ad implendum.
>
> Unde, in similibus, punctum quaestionis saliens non tam ponendum est in statu mentis contrahentis, qualis apparet dum ille, forma a jure praescripta, consensum matrimonialem ad extra pandit. Etenim, jam a priori concedi debet, vel concedi potest, nupturientem, tempore illo, talibus in adiunctis versari, ut, generatim, ne suspicio quidem exurgat

---

[119] C. Heard (Quebecen.), Jan. 30, 1954, *in facto*

> sive de plena cognitione, in ipso, eorum omnium, quae scitu necessaria sunt, sive de voluntate eius libera atque conscienti determinatione, sive, tandem, de eius ipsius valida occupatione (maxime si de viro agitur) in muneribus et officiis, per quae condenda familia sustentari possit.
>
> Potius, e contra, inspiciendum est, ac sedulo investigandum, num, anteacto tempore, aegritudinis mentis signa comparuerint. Quod ad provinciam medicorum praecipue spectat.[120]

The decision seems to make the following important points:

a) The critical issue is not so much the party's mental state at the moment of expressing consent but his previous mental fitness for marriage.

b) Even if the contractant should enjoy a true lucid interval during the wedding, a clear mind and full deliberation, nevertheless the marriage would be null if, given his mental deterioration, he is judged *a priori* incapable by nature of fulfilling the essential obligations he might have assumed when expressing consent.

c) such a thesis is the dictate of reason itself, i.e., the natural law.

3. Gerard and Mathilda married during World War II. Because Gerard had to return to military duty, married life was broken off a few weeks after the wedding. When he returned to civilian life two years later, Gerard found that Mathilda had been unspeakably immoral during his absence. A civil separation followed, and she went off to live with another man. Mathilda then accused the validity of their marriage on the grounds that she entered marriage under grave force and duress. After the negative decision, Gerard then accused the marriage before another tribunal on the grounds that Mathilda had positively excluded marital fidelity. This decision too was negative.

Upon psychiatric examination it was learned that Mathilda was suffering from a serious case of nymphomania, a psychic disorder whereby a woman is irresistibly drawn to reckless fornication. Appealing to the Rota in second instance, the legal doubts were re-arranged so that it was alleged that the obligation of marital fidelity was excluded from the contract not because Mathilda had deliberately

---

[120] C. Mattioli (Quebecen.), Nov. 6, 1956, *in iure.*

excluded it in her consent, but rather because of her objective ineptitude to honor such an obligation owing to her psychic disorder.[121] These new grounds were considered distinct from simulation and constituted a new *caput nullitatis,* so that the Rota treated it in the first instance; subordinately, in case of a negative decision to this *caput,* the court would examine the grounds of positive exclusion in second instance.

In its decision, which was negative to both *capita,* the Rota described the elements of this sexual psychopathy in the *in iure* section as:

1) sexual stimulus which is irresistible;

2) promiscuous sexual offering to men without selection of persons;

3) insatiability of the stimulus.

When nymphomania reaches this degree and is incurable, the court states, there is no doubt that it invalidates marriage, since the woman so afflicted is incapable *ob ipsam suam complexionem* of assuming the obligation of marital fidelity.[122] The sentence continues:

> Relate vero ad inclusionem huius formae in schematibus juridicis, nymphomania videtur forsan magis accedere ad impotentiam quam ad vitium mentis. Nam, saltem frequenter, nymphomanis — nisi nuptias videat tantum uti medium satiandi suum stimulum haud coercibilem quo in casu necessaria cereret libertate — quoad matrimonium in fieri, ele-

---

[121] C. Sabattani (Neapolitana), June 21, 1957, *species facti*: "...dubium propositum fuerit quod mulier bonum fidei rejecerit, potius quam ex positivo voluntatis actu, ex ipsa ineptitudine ad illud servandum ob quamdam abnormem propensionem in res lascivas et psychicam perturbationem, vir petiit et obtinuit quod Turnus Rotalis videret in prima instantia de alio capite, praecedenti capiti praeponendum, quod ita concordatum fuit: 'An constet de nullitate matrimonii ex defectu discretionis judicii mulieris conventae.' ...Caput 'exclusio boni fidei' subordinatum manet praecedenti, de eoque agi tantum debet, si novum caput negative dimissum fuerit."

[122] "A) Ut eam (scil. nymphomaniam) distinguat a simplici hyperaesthesia et ab aliis morbosis formis, doctrina medica nymphomaniae has tribuit proprietates:

a) stimulus sexualis talis est, cui nulla vi resisti possit;

b) promiscua et inconsiderata mulieris sexualis oblatio erga mares, absque delectu personarum;

c) stimulus qui nullo modo satiari potest.

B) Quando nymphomania huiusmodi gradum attingat, nec eidem mederi possit, non est ambigendum matrimonium irritari, cum mulier ita affecta ad obligationem fidei sumendam incapax dici debeat ob ipsam suam complexionem." — *Ibid., in iure.*

> menta cognitionis et etiam voluntatis ad contractum necessaria afferre potest, cum intelligere valeat et substantiam coniugii et ipsum bonum fidei. Difficultatem experitur magis quoad matrimonium "in facto", seu circa usum coniugii.
>
> Neque dicatur nymphomanis potius "hyperpotenti", quam impotenti accenseri debere. Nam impotentia, uti impedimentum est conceptus juridicus, non species psysiologica. Et, si quidem Bender L. ("Conditio apposita et matrimonii nullitas", in *Ephemerides Juris Canonici*, 1945, p. 67) scripsit: "Impotentia in nulla alia re consistit quam in hoc, quod *usus corporis* inter coniuges fieri non potest", dici etiam potest *nymphomaniam* id tantum praecise adducere, quod *usus exclusivus* (qualis semper esse debet usus matrimonialis) corporis inter eosdem coniuges haberi nequeat.[123]

The important points made by the court seem to be the following:

1) Grave and incurable nymphomania certainly invalidates marriage.

2) The invalidating force need not stem from a defective act of consent (*matrimonium in fieri*), since the nymphomaniac may well possess all the cognitional and volitional elements necessary for making the contract; she may understand the substance of marriage and even the obligation of marital fidelity.

3) The court implies that the invalidating force comes rather from an objective inability to assume the *bonum fidei,* an inability that seems to have the nature of a diriment impediment like impotence. Whereas the impotent person is radically unfit for *matrimonium in facto* because constitutionally unable to effect the *usus corporis,* so the nymphomaniac is radically unfit for *matrimonium in facto* because constitutionally unable to effect the *usus exclusivus corporis.*

4. In a case of schizophrenia that came to the Rota after two concordant negative decisions on the grounds of grave fear in the woman, the Rota, in first instance, granted an affirmative decision on the grounds of mental infirmity in the man at the time of the wedding. Among the *motiva in iure,* i.e., in the line of principle, the court repeats the axiom that even if a person should give sufficient consent with clear mind and full deliberation, yet

---

[123] *Ibid.*

the marriage is null by reason of mental disorder if the contractant, because of his deteriorating condition, is judged *a priori* incompetent by nature to fulfill the essential obligations of the contract.[124]

5. Patricia, eighteen years old, took instructions and became a Catholic to marry James. Although the union lasted materially for nine years and brought several children into the world, the marriage was unhappy nearly from the beginning and was interrupted by Patricia's many desertions and infidelities. Patricia was found to be suffering from nymphomania and was certainly diagnosed as a constitutional psychopathic personality. James accuses the validity of his marriage on the grounds of her positive exclusion of the *bonum sacramenti* and *bonum fidei* before the Rota in first instance. The Rota granted an affirmative decision on the grounds of partial simulation by Patricia, excluding indissolubility. On appeal to another turnus of the Rota, both *capita* were re-examined. The psychopathic disorder was not looked upon as a cause of nullity in itself, but only as a motive for simulating consent. The appellate turnus confirmed the first decision that the marriage was null by reason of defective consent in which indissolubility had been deliberately excluded by Patricia. However, the court speaks of the damaging effect of nymphomania as we have spoken of it above, but without attaching immediately to it the force of invalidating marriage:

> Inter huiusce generis morbos habetur nymphomania seu quaedam genitalis instinctus exaggeratio; propter quam incapax est mulier sexualem vitam subiacendi morum regulis; in ipsa enim adeo vehemens est instinctus, ut illum cohibere nequeat: namque consistit hoc malum in quadam morbosa depravatione naturae, plerumque magnitudine, nonnumquam tamen genere habentur et sensus non voluntarius quoad periphericos stimulos, et difficultas, immo impossibilitas, in hunc non voluntarium modum actionem exercendi inhibitricem sensuum nervosorum superiorum; semper enim adsunt nevropathica constitutio et hyperovarismus plus minusve apertus, quibus annectitur ista forma aut eretismo, aut erotomaniae; unde, non raro, ut videre est in una Nanceien. diei 26 aprilis 1958 coram me, impar est aegra

[124] C. Mattioli (Romana), Nov. 28, 1957, *in iure.*

> ad fidem uni viro serio promittendam, aut impellitur ad plures uniones successive contrahendas.
>
> *In Facto*: P. S. psychopathico implicatur morbo, in quantum ei impossibilis sit socialis vitae normas quoad sexuale commercium servare... eam imparem reddente ad matrimoniales obligationes exsequendas.

The court did not consider this disorder as immediately preventing Patricia from assuming an obligation *sub gravi* to something which was simply impossible for her. Instead, following more the traditional stand of jurisprudence, it demanded proof of defective consent:

> Quodsi certo non probetur positivus voluntatis actus ante matrimonium celebratum, stat unio, quin recurratur ad juris praesumptionem c. 1014... Causa simulationis in aperto est, inveniturque in physico morbo quo afficiebatur conventa ...eam imparem reddente ad matrimoniales obligationes exsequendas.[125]

6. In a case in which it was not clear whether the woman was a victim of schizophrenia or biopathic phrenesthenia, the court of first instance granted an affirmative decision which was confirmed and executed. However, the mother of the girl, apparently prejudiced by a declaration of nullity, asked the Apostolic Signatura that the case be re-examined. The favor was granted and hence the case came to the Rota in third instance. The Rotal decision, also affirmative, noted among the *motiva in iure* that although the Code of Canon Law does not define the marriage capacity of the mentally ill, nevertheless, the Code would perhaps be inaccurate if it seemed to resolve the whole question of psychic ability to enter marriage in the question of due knowledge for valid consent, viz., the elemental knowledge that marriage is a permanent society between a man and a woman for the procreation of offspring (canon 1082, §1). Just what the court meant is clarified later in the section *in facto*:

---

125 C. Lefebvre (Miamien.), Dec. 19, 1959. Cf. C. Lefebvre (Nanceien.), Apr. 26, 1958; C. Heard (Sancti Augustini), June 27, 1959; C. Teodori, Jan. 19, 1940 (Vol. XXXII, 81-92); C. Heard, June 5, 1941 (Vol. XXXIII, 488-496); C. Jullien, Oct. 16, 1942 (Vol. XXXIV, 775-781). Cf. SEBASTIANO VILLEGGIANTE, "Ninfomania e cause di nullità matrimoniale," *Il Diritto Ecclesiastico*, LXXI (1960), II, pp. 162-184; "Ninfomania e difetto di consenso," *ibid.*, pp. 315-322.

> Item animadvertendum censemus ad validum * consensum praestandum non sufficere cognitionem intellectivam, sed insuper requiri capacitatem eam rite ac sponte in praxim deducendi. Nunc autem conventa huiusmodi capacitate caret omnino, uti colligitur ex universis actis et comprobatum est ultima eiusdem depositione coram R.P.D. Ponente.[126]

A survey of the above Rotal decisions makes it clear that mental illness can invalidate marriage not merely by rendering the psychological act of consent impossible, but also by rendering impossible an objective observance of the essential rights and obligations of the marriage contract:

— "...in contractu matrimonii consentiebat in rem cuius incapax erat."

— "... nubendo eo in statu, Barbara promisisset quod promittere nequivisset."

— "... ob jam incoeptam mentis deordinationem, sensim in pejus progredientem, *natura sua* jam inhabiles sunt ad implendum."

— ". . . non est ambigendum matrimonium irritari, cum mulier ita affecta ad obligationem fidei sumendam incapax dici debeat ob ipsam suam complexionem."

— "... *nymphomaniam* id tantum praecise adducere quod *usus exclusivus* (qualis semper esse debet usus matrimonialis) corporis inter eosdem coniuges haberi nequeat."

— "... impar est aegra ad fidem uni viro serio promittendam, aut impellitur ad plures uniones successive contrahendas."

— "Titia psychopathico implicatur morbo, in quantum ei impossibilis sit socialis vitae normas quoad sexuale commercium servare ... eam imparem reddente ad matrimoniales obligationes exsequendas."

— "... sed insuper requiri capacitatem eam rite ac sponte in praxim deducendi."

Apart from these recent decisions of the Rota which seem to demand objective ability to honor the essential marital obligations for the effective assumption of said

* It would seem that the word "valid" here is taken in the sense of "juridically efficacious". Cf. Chapter I, footnote 91.

[126] C. De Jorio (Taurinen.), Dec. 19, 1961, *in facto*.

obligations (hence, for valid marriage), many other decisions implicitly, we think, lean to the same position in their description of the notion of due discretion. This notion has been gradually developing in Rotal jurisprudence. Whereas early jurisprudence described due discretion only in terms of the psychological requisites of the act of marital consent (knowledge and volition), more recent jurisprudence describes due discretion more as the psychic ability to effectively bind oneself, to assume marital rights and obligations. Due discretion in early sentences is the power to: *percipere, apphehendere, cognoscere, suspicere, intelligere, non ignorare, habere notitiam, scire obiectum contractus matrimonialis, quid sit matrimonium eiusdemque essentiales proprietates, etc... et sese libere determinare, deliberate velle, ut actus procedat ab eius voluntatis libera determinatione, etc.* Later jurisprudence explains due discretion rather in terms of ability to assume, undertake, fulfill, put into practice, etc., the obligations, duties, burdens of married life. Due discretion is not knowledge but a quality of the psyche — *integritas, maturitas, vigor, robur* whereby a person is capable of: *assumere, suscipere, amplecti, deducere in praxim, implere onera, obligationes, officia peculiaria matrimonio inhaerentibus per totam vitam, condere et regere familiam etc.* For due discretion a person must have "*id robur voluntatis, quod ad corrivantia iura obligationesque danda et acceptanda par sit,*" which is missing if he is "*impar ad illud servandum, natura sua inhabilis ad implendum, ad obligationem fidei sumendam incapax ob ipsam suam complexionem.*"

Article 2. The Notion of Due Discretion

The notion of due discretion for valid marriage has developed, not so much in canonical writings, as in the jurisprudence of the Sacred Roman Rota. The "human act" test of early jurisprudence, for a long time considered a positive norm on the authority of Thomas Sanchez, came to be recognized as a negative norm at best: he who could *not* place a human act, who did *not* enjoy the actual use of reason, who could *not* commit a mortal sin, was psychically incapable of true marital consent, and hence, of marriage itself. *"At non sufficit usus rationis simpliciter"*, and the rule of Sanchez, at least as a positive norm, passed from its traditional place in Rotal jurisprudence, only to be recalled in later sentences for the purpose of repudiation.

When the "qualified human act" test was proposed — *capacitas ad matrimonium intelligendum et volendum* — it, too, was sometimes stated as a positive norm: he who could understand the force and nature of the marriage contract and thus intend it was to be considered psychically competent for valid marriage. But this test too, which again looked only to a person's psychic ability to place a genuine act of marital consent, passed from the status of a positive test to that of a merely negative norm. Certainly, if a person could *not* understand the nature and properties of marriage, he was incapable of eliciting true consent. But the fact that he could place true consent did not argue for his psychic ability to contract marriage validly, for some decisions declaring nullity were handed down in spite of the defendant's ability to construct true consent.

With the coming of the new test — *capacitas ad sese obligandum seu ad obiectum contractus implendum* — the notion of due discretion receded from its centuries-old attachment to the notion of sufficient consent and settled about the idea of natural capacity or fitness of the subject for the state of matrimony. The earlier test (ability to understand and will marriage) was merely a general test and might well be applied to almost any type of juridical act. Thus, in civil law, the legal test of testamentary capacity or of criminal imputability of the mentally ill is based on the person's ability to know the nature and quality of the act he is performing. Such is the test of moral imputability that the confessor often reduces to the famous two questions: (a) "Did you realize fully that it was a mortal sin?" and (b) "Could you have resisted?" The influence of mental illness on civil capacity, criminal and moral imputability, is entirely resolved in its influence on the person's mental attitude in consenting or performing these present acts.

Marriage, however, is a contract which involves the assumption of serious obligations, without which the marriage is invalid. Disabilities can invalidate the marriage contract by reason of the natural law from two sources: (a) by precluding the necessary consent; (b) by rendering the person an unfit subject of these rights and obligations. An example of the first disability is seen in the five-year-old child; an example of the second is the impediment of incurable impotence. Mental illness, however, can provide examples of both.

The notion of due discretion uncovered in the most recent evolution of Rotal jurisprudence has therefore disengaged the *caput nullitatis* in insanity cases from the *caput nullitatis* in cases of *mentis exturbatio.* The ultimate source of nullity in *amentia* cases now is seen akin to that of impotence, springing from an abiding natural defect in the subject whereby he is radically unfit for marriage, incapable of binding himself to the specific obligations of the marriage contract. In its efforts to pinpoint the ultimate invalidating force of mental illness on the marriage contract, the Sacred Roman Rota, we believe, has delineated the fundamental notion of due discretion and has provided a truly positive norm of mental competence for valid marriage.

Section A. Due Discretion According to St. Thomas

The evolution of the concept of "due discretion" in Rotal jurisprudence — *ad actum humanum ponendum, ad matrimonium intelligendum et volendum, ad sese obligandum* — has, if we are not mistaken, ultimately brought us back to St. Thomas's notion of "due discretion" for valid marriage. The Rota itself has continually appealed to St. Thomas in explaining "due discretion" to the extent that two Thomistic passages, appearing among the *motiva in iure* of so many Rotal decisions since 1919, can now be considered standard and authoritative in jurisprudence:

> Et ideo dicendum, quod ad peccatum mortale sufficit etiam consensus (in) praesens; sed in sponsalibus est consensus in futurum. Major autem rationis discretio requiritur ad providendum in futurum quam ad consentiendum in unum praesentem actum; et ideo ante potest homo peccare mortaliter quam possit se obligare ad aliquid (in) futurum.[127]

[127] *Summa theologica,* III, *suppl.,* q. 43, a. 2, *ad* 2; IV. *Sent.,* d. 27, q. 2, a. 2, *ad* 2.

> Ad primum ergo dicendum, quod in illis ad quae natura inclinat, non exigitur tantus vigor rationis ad deliberandum sicut in aliis; et ideo ante potest in matrimonium sufficienter deliberans consentire, quam possit in contractibus aliis res suas sine tutore pertractare.
>
> Et similiter est dicendum ad secundum, quia votum religionis est de his quae sunt sine inclinatione naturae, quae majorem difficultatem habent quam matrimonium.[128]

These two passages, admittedly quite general, reveal, however, the mind of St. Thomas rather clearly:

1. Discretion is not the same as knowledge or the possession of a certain amount or type of knowledge (nor, conversely, would lack of discretion to be same as ignorance); discretion is, rather, a quality of the spiritual faculties. The Angelic Doctor calls it a *vigor*, that is, a maturity, soundness, aptitude of the psyche. The Rota seems to understand discretion as a quality in its oft-repeated phrase, " *debita discretio seu maturitas iudicii* ". It is clear also that discretion is not the same as the natural virtue of prudence or wisdom.

2. This mental vigor or maturity admits of varying degrees; the required degree is proportionate to the act in question. "*Maior autem rationis discretio requiritur.... non exigitur tantus vigor rationis...*" Hence we speak of due discretion.

3. Regarding acts which require different degrees of discretion, St. Thomas draws a fundamental distinction between acts by which a person binds himself to an abiding obligation (*ad providendum in futurum*) and acts which do not generate obligations for the future (*actus praesens*).

4. A greater degree of discretion is demanded that a person bind himself for the future ("*ut possit se obligare ad aliquid in futurum*") than that he simply consent "*in actum unum praesentem*", being capable thereby of mortal sin.

5. Thus, due discretion is that psychic maturity or vigor whereby simple present acts are truly human acts, hence imputable as meritorious or mortally malicious — or whereby acts involving future obligations are really binding and do, in fact, generate the obligations.

---

128 *Summa theologica*, III, *suppl.*, q. 58, a. 5, *ad* 1, 2.

6. Specifically, therefore, it requires a greater degree of discretion to bind oneself to an engagement contract than to place a simple human act with mortal malice. Canonical doctrine and jurisprudence are uniform in drawing the corollary that, *a fortiori,* the discretion required to bind oneself to the marriage contract is greater than that required to bind oneself to an engagement contract.

7. A greater degree of discretion is required to bind oneself to the vows of religious profession than to the marriage contract. *"In illis ad quae natura inclinat..."*

For the sake of illustration it would be well to apply these observations to some concrete examples:

A) A child at five years of age, let us say, is generally considered devoid of sufficient mental maturity and corresponding personal responsibility required to make his simple acts truly human acts and hence liable to mortal guilt. *A fortiori* he lacks sufficient discretion to incur obligations for the future.

B) A child of seven, upon attainment of the use of reason, is generally considered to be endowed with sufficient discretion to consent *"in unum actum praesentem"* and hence he can commit mortal sin. But this degree of discretion does not suffice that he effectively bind himself to an obligation, v. gr., by making a contract.

C) A lad of fourteen may have the psychic maturity required to enter the marriage contract, but this degree of *"vigor rationis"* may not suffice that he be able to bind himself to the obligations of religious profession.

From what has been stated above, an all-important point should already be clear: the basic question of due discretion for valid marriage does not concern a person's psychic aptitude to place the psychological act of marital consent, a qualified human act which, as a human act, is morally imputable before God; rather, it concerns the psychic aptitude *to bind oneself* to the obligations of the marriage contract. The fact that the contractant was able to commit a mortal sin, that his act of consent was integral and a morally imputable human act, is irrevelant. The crucial question is whether he enjoyed *the greater degree of discretion* required that he be able to assume effectively the obligations which would normally arise from an integral act of consent. The reason why the greater degree of discretion is required for acts generating future obligations, according to St. Thomas, is not that the psychological act of the one is more difficult than the other. It is not that consent in future obligations must be psychologically more informed, more intense, or more deliberate as a human act. Rather, greater aptitude of the psyche is required to sustain the obligations to be incurred. Less discretion is required in consenting for marriage than for religious vows — not because the act of consent in the vows is more difficult to place, but because the religious life, its burdens and obligations, are more difficult to bear; for nature does not incline us to this type of life as it inclines us to marriage. The object of the religious vow is much harder to observe than the object of the marriage contract because married life has the inclination of nature to sustain it and help it along. The "greater difficulty" and the "inclination of nature" have not to do with the ability of understanding the object of the vow or of the contract, but with the ability to undertake, realize, fulfill, observe the object of the vow or contract.

Thus, a lad of ten years, having read the life of some great saint, might make a free and deliberate promise to God to remain celibate for the rest of his life. The act of promising was a human act, perhaps highly meritorious in the sight of God; yet he incurred no obligation of celibacy because he lacked sufficient discretion "*ad providendum in futurum... ut possit se obligare ad aliquid in futurum*".

In Decretal Law a child of seven might make a promise to marry, but only at puberty upon ratifying his promise did he incur the strict moral and juridical obligation from which he could not freely recede thereafter. This, however, does not argue to the fact that his original act of promising was not a morally imputable human act. To place a human act is one thing; to assume an obligation is another.

Canon 214, § 1, states that a cleric who receives sacred orders under grave fear is indeed validly ordained but he does not incur the obligations attached to the orders.[129]

---

[129] "Clericus qui metu gravi coactus ordinem sacrum recepit nec

Thus, the minimum degree of liberty which allows the requisite intention on his part and valid ordination does not suffice to allow the incurrence of the obligations attached.

Examples from recent Rotal decisions cited in the preceding article indicate that the same situation may apply in insanity cases. A person may freely and deliberately place an act of marital consent which is structurally integral, psychologically sufficient to generate the bond, a truly human act and morally imputable.... and yet, willy-nilly, he cannot contract the obligations of marriage. Endowed with sufficient discretion to place human acts, to sin mortally, even to elicit an integral act of consent, he may still lack the *greater* discretion required "*ad sese obligandum*". Due discretion for valid marriage does not mean merely the relative aptitude of the psychic powers which is necessary and sufficient to elicit naturally sufficient consent. It is rather the minimum relative aptitude, maturity, integrity of the psychic powers which is necessary that a person, by dint of the natural law, can effectively oblige himself by the marriage contract.

Section B. Actus Naturaliter Exsistens sed Iuridice Inefficax

The distinction of *actus naturaliter exsistens sed iuridice inefficax* as applied to marital consent has been gradually clarified, especially in the elaboration of the institute of *sanatio in radice.* Though the terminology varied, the distinction was solidly accepted by canonical doctrine and clearly upheld in the Code of Canon Law. Canon 1139, treating of the sanation of invalid marriages, speaks of "naturally sufficient" consent which was, however, "juridically inefficacious" because of a dispensable obstacle of ecclesiastical law. Although in other sections of the Code the Legislator is not so explicit in delineating the

---

postea, remoto metu, eandem ordinationem ratam habuit saltem tacite per ordinis exercitium, volens tamen per talem actum obligationibus clericalibus se subiicere, ad statum laicalem, legitime probata coactione et ratihabitionis defectu, sententia iudicis redigatur, sine ullis coelibatus ac horarum canonicarum obligationibus."

precise source of nullity of juridical acts, the distinction of *inexsistentia* and *invaliditas* is equally applicable and, we think, highly useful in explaining the fundamental notion of due discretion for valid marriage.[130]

Within the framework of this distinction, we might say for the sake of illustration that there are three possible sources of nullity in marriage. The act of marital consent might be:

1. *Actus inexsistens,* because of a defect or vitiation of the consent itself. It is therefore naturally insufficient to generate the marriage bond, for the effect would be intrinsically beyond the capacity of the cause. As far as its juridical relevance is concerned, the act of vitiated or defective consent is non-existent, lacking an essential constitutive element of true matrimonial consent. It is *actus inexsistens* either because it was not even a human act (e.g., due to drunkenness, hypnosis, narcotics, etc.) or because, in spite of being a human act, it was not the *qualified human act* of genuine marital consent (e.g., due to ignorance, error, simulation, condition, fear, etc.). In both cases, of course, marriage is null for want of an adequate efficient cause. Since marital consent cannot be supplied by any human power, and since marriage of necessity must be constituted by true matrimonial consent (*actus naturaliter exsistens*), it is clear that such a union cannot be rectified without the renovation, or rather, the eliciting of genuine consent. Sanation is out of the question (canon 1140).

2. *Actus naturaliter existens sed iuridice inefficax* because of an extrinsic obstacle placed by positive church law. That is, the act of consent was sufficient in itself to generate the bond, but failed to do so because, for example, of a defect of canonical form, the presence of a diriment impediment of ecclesiastical law, the omission

---

[130] C. Lamas (Chicagien.), Mar. 15, 1956, *in iure*: "Accurate distinguendae sunt causae nullitatis ex parte ipsius consensus ab illis quae se tenent ex parte personae, quae inhabilis est. Haec personae inhabilitas non excludit consensum, qui erit nullus *iuridice* seu *invalidus*, neutiquam autem per se est nullus *physice* (GASPARRI, *De matrim.*, II, n. 811, contra SANCHEZ, *De matrim.*, lib. II, disp. 35). Quod obtinet etiamsi agatur de impedimento juris divini (GASPARRI, *ibid.*, n. 813), ut est impotentia vel ligamen." This was a case involving homosexuality.

of the solemnities required by church law for valid proxy marriage, etc. That true marital consent can be elicited while a person is under a diriment impediment of ecclesiastical law, or while failing to observe due canonical form, is undeniable. The practice of the Church of sanating such unions according to canon 1139, § 1, provides ample evidence:

> Quodlibet matrimonium initum cum utriusque partis consensu naturaliter sufficiente, sed iuridice inefficaci ob dirimens impedimentum iuris ecclesiastici vel ob defectum legitimae formae, potest in radice sanari, dummodo consensus perseveret.

3. *Actus naturaliter existens sed iuridice inefficax* because of a non-dispensable obstacle placed by divine law. Examples would be the diriment impediments of previous marriage bond and irreparable impotence. An integral act of consent is prevented by divine law itself from generating an effective exchange of marital rights and obligations. It is the common opinion of canonists that true matrimonial consent can be emitted while a person is under such an impediment.[131] With regard to the impediment of *ligamen,* the Church can and does sanate the second union when the impediment ceases with the death of the first spouse.[132] With regard to the impediment of antecedent and perpetual impotence, the doctrine of Cardinal Gasparri is generally held in canonical doctrine:

> Igitur in subiecta materia non est differentia inter impedimentum iuris ecclesiastici et impedimentum iuris divini; utrumque excludit *efficaciam* consensus, sed per se non excludit *consensum ipsum.*[133]

---

131 GASPARRI, *De matrimonio,* II, n. 813; CONTE A CORONATA, *Institutiones,* III, *De matrimonio,* n. 689; WERNZ-VIDAL, *Ius canonicum,* V, *Ius matrimoniale,* n. 658; JEMOLO, *Il matrimonio nel diritto canonico,* n. 168; VLAMING-BENDER, *Praelectiones iuris matrimonii,* p. 534; PALAZZINI, "De sanatione in radice," *Casus conscientiae,* I, *De matrimonio,* p. 167; and especially, BENDER, "Sanatio matrimonii invalidi ob impedimentum iuris divini," *Ephemerides Iuris Canonici,* XIII (1957), pp. 19-44.

132 Cf. the cases reported in *The Jurist,* XX (1960), pp. 78-79, and BOUSCAREN-O'CONNOR, *Canon Law Digest,* 1958 Supplement, under canon 1139.

133 *De matrimonio,* II, n. 813.

To illustrate his point he supposes a case. A woman knows that she is impotent but that she can again become potent through an operation which involves danger of death. Hoping to undergo the operation later, she marries. The marriage is null, of course, because of the impediment. Afterwards she undergoes the operation, which proves successful. This union can now be sanated by the Church, for true marital consent can coexist with a diriment impediment of the natural law.

Some authors, however, argue from the fact that since the *ius ad actus per se aptos* belongs to the essential object of the contract and was impossible of fulfillment, consent was necessarily destroyed. Answers Cappello: "Quod vero huiusmodi consensus sit *iuridice* inefficax, id pendet ex inhabilitate personae, non autem ex defectu *qua tali* voluntatis."[134] Cappello here reflects the more common opinion of canonists.[135]

Where in this tripartite framework does the *caput nullitatis* in insanity cases belong? As stated elsewhere at some length, the Roman Rota traditionally had placed the *caput nullitatis* in the first category, making the psychological integrity of the act of consent (*actus existens vel inexistens*) the unique criterion of valid marriage.

Apparently insanity cases do not belong to the second category, i.e., *actus existens sed iuridice inefficax* because of a purely positive obstacle of church law. However, Cappello would, were he to make a logical extension of his principles, have to place in the second category the invalidating force of *amentia* intervening between the granting of the mandate and the celebration of the marriage by proxy. Treating of the possibility of a *sanatio in radice* after supervening insanity, Cappello states that the original consent is not thereby destroyed and that, therefore, a sanation is possible:

> Sanatio ex dictis id unum exigit, scil. quod consensus coniugalis revera praestitus fuerit et adhuc perseveret seu numquam fuerit revocatus. Iamvero eo ipso quod pars incidit in amentiam, nullatenus mutatur eius voluntas et revocatur consensus, qui naturaliter ac iuridice perseverat.[136]

---

[134] *De sacramentis,* V, *De matrimonio,* n. 589, 1°.
[135] Cf. CONTE A CORONATA, *loc. cit.;* BENDER, *loc. cit.*
[136] CAPPELLO, *op. cit.,* n. 853, 3°.

If there is no obstacle stemming from consent, neither is there an impediment of the natural law present; otherwise, a sanation would be out of the question:

> Nam in iure divino sive naturali sive positivo Ecclesia nequit dispensare; proinde neque efficere potest ut vinculum *ex nunc* exsurgat, neque convenienter potest fingere illud *ex tunc* adfuisse.[137]

Logically, then, the disposition of canon 1089, § 3, would be strictly an obstacle of positive ecclesiastical law.[138]

The elucidation of the concept of due discretion made in the recent tendency in Rotal jurisprudence seems to make it certain that the proper *caput nullitatis* in insanity cases belongs in the third category wherein the invalidity stems from a non-dispensable obstacle to efficacy placed by the natural law itself. *Amentia* seems then to resemble the impediment of impotence and to constitute, like impotence, a strict diriment impediment which renders the person *subiectum inhabile iurium et obligationum contractus maritalis*, prescinding from the psychological integrity of the act of consent. Hence, it would seem that there are three types of nullity cases deriving from mental impairment of all kinds:

1. Those wherein nullity stems solely from a defective act of consent (*actus naturaliter inexistens*), due discretion remaining intact. For example, marriages contracted while the contractant is under the influence of alcohol or narcotics, or is in an hypnotic trance, etc. In these cases of *mentis exturbatio* the act of consent was deficient either in its internal formation or at least its external manifestation; it was *actus naturaliter inexistens.* In spite of the temporary suspension of his faculties, the contractant possessed the habitual mental maturity to assume validly the obligations of the contract. Because he temporarily lost command of his faculties he could not place the efficient cause of the bond — *actus naturaliter existens.*

2. Those wherein the act of consent was integral, *ac-*

---

[137] *Ibid.*, 1°.

[138] However, Cappello, commenting on canon 1089, § 3, seems to suppose that intervening insanity automatically extinguishes consent: "Ut *valide* autem procurator munus suum exerceat, iure *communi*, i.e. ex praescripto can. 1089, requiritur... ut cum mandatarius nomine mandantis contrahit, hic mandatum *non revocaverit* aut *in amentiam non inciderit;*

tus existens, of itself sufficient to generate the bond, but *actus iuridice inefficax,* because the person lacked that greater degree of mental maturity, integrity, vigor, etc., required to effectively bind himself. The Rota cases mentioned previously as examples of the recent tendency illustrate the point.

3. Those wherein the person was under the diriment impediment of defect of due discretion and was also unable to place sufficient marital consent. A parallel case would be that of the incurably impotent man who moreover makes an intention *contra bonum prolis* in his attempt to marry. The combination is much more frequent in insanity cases and will often flow from the very nature of the impediment, for the faculties whose maturity is required to assure a binding obligation are the very faculties employed to place marital consent.

In this third case, it seems that the ultimate *caput nullitatis* is the diriment impediment and not the defect of consent. For, *a priori* to the placing of any consent, such a person is *subiectum inhabile ad matrimonium* whether or not he ever attempt marriage. His defective act of consent has no bearing on the invalidity of the bond. To declare a marriage null by reason of defect of consent necessarily supposes the natural fitness or capacity of the contractants.[139] Hence, if a court rules such a marriage null by reason of defect of consent, it is partly right and partly wrong, it would seem. The marriage is indeed null, but not because of the defective consent any more than the marriage of the impotent man who made the contrary intention is null by reason of simulation.[140] It is for this reason that the Rota will treat of the grounds of defect of consent only subordinately, that is, if the grounds of diriment impediment are found insufficiently supported for an affirmative decision. The court will investigate grounds of defective consent only on the supposition of the natural fitness of the parties.[141]

---

nam consensus matrimonialis nullimode suppleri potest, ut fit in reliquis contractibus." — *Ibid.,* n. 619, 3, 3°.

[139] Cf. *supra,* Chapter I, footnote 64.

[140] Cf. *infra,* footnote 169.

[141] Cf. supra, "*Contradictory Capita,*" pp. 22-26.

Article 3. THE DIRIMENT IMPEDIMENT OF MENTAL INCOMPETENCE

Relevant not only to the theoretical ascertainment of the ultimate source of the invalidating force of mental impairment upon the marriage contract, but also to the practical structure of judicial proof, is the disputed question whether insanity invalidates as a strict diriment impediment or as a defect of marital consent. According to the long-traditional jurisprudence of both secular and ecclesiastical courts, the invalidating force of mental impairment stems from an inability to elicit naturally sufficient consent. Marriage attempted by the mentally incapacitated is null for lack of consent; hence, there was no effective cause of the marriage bond.

Authors who posit the question whether insanity be a diriment impediment or a defect of consent are considering mental impairment only in this light as the natural inability to elicit sufficient consent. D'Avack states that because insanity constitutes a defect of natural capacity and only in its effects is resolved in a defect of consent, it is rather a diriment impediment, for the invalidity stems more from the level of "*non posse*" of the contractant than from the resultant level of "*non esse*" of true and sufficient consent. Hence, he says, the simple convalidation of marriages null by reason of mental impairment should be carried out according to the norms of canons 1133-1135 (diriment impediment), and not according to canon 1136 (defect of consent).[142] Jemolo, in a footnote, approves the reasoning of d'Avack and states that, therefore, *defectus discretionis iudicii* is a strict diriment impediment in the language of the Code.[143] Ravà, too, cites d'Avack in support of the thesis that the defect of due discretion is a defect of natural capacity and a diriment impediment of the natural law.[144] Graziani[145] and Conte a Coronata[146] hold

[142] D'AVACK, *Cause di nullità e di divorzio*, pp. 115-117.

[143] JEMOLO, *Il matrimonio nel diritto canonico*, n. 46, nota 1: "Non ci pare dubbio, malgrado l'espressione del detto can. 1982, che in sé l'infermità mentale costituisca un difetto di capacità e così un impedimento, nel linguaggio del *Codex*."

[144] RAVÀ, "Il *defectus discretionis iudicii* come causa di nullità del matrimonio nella giurisprudenza rotale," *Il Diritto Ecclesiastico*, LXVIII (1957), pp. 359, 383.

that *amentia* or *dementia* can, with equal legitimacy, be catalogued with the diriment impediments or with the defects of consent. Although they do not explicity place *amentia* among the diriment impediments, Giacchi [147] and Bánk [148] state that one cannot speak of a defect of consent unless the natural capacity to consent is already supposed.

The common doctrinal opinion, however, considers the psychic inability to elicit sufficient consent simply in its effect of a *de facto* defective act of consent, hence placing this *causa nullitatis* somewhere among the defects of consent as listed in *Caput V* of the matrimonial law of the Code. Nearly all the manuals treat of insanity in their commentary on *Caput V*, and most often, under canon 1082. De Smet's third edition of *De sponsalibus et matrimonio*, appearing after the Code when the notion of impediment was narrowed from its previous acceptance, said of *amentia* that it *"constituit impedimentum dirimens matrimonii."* [149] These words were changed to *"substantialiter vitiat consensum"* in the fourth edition appearing in 1927. Writing in the *Dictionnaire de Droit Canonique* De Smet

---

[145] GRAZIANI, *Volontà attuale e volontà precettiva nel negozio matrimoniale canonico*, p. 92: "Giova soltanto aver richiamato l'attenzione sul fatto che l'*amentia* (o la *dementia*) e, sotto certi aspetti, anche l'incapacità attuale d'intendere possono essere catalogate, con pari legittimità, tra gli impedimenti propriamente detti e tra le cause di mancanza del consenso, per essere e una condizione personale del soggetto e un fatto direttamente impeditivo del formarsi del consenso, come *actus humanus*."

[146] CONTE A CORONATA, *Institutiones iuris canonici, De sacramentis*, III, *De matrimonio et de sacramentalibus*, n. 437, nota 5: "Dubium moveri potest utrum amentia et dementia inter impedimenta proprie dicta enumerandae sint, an solummodo ut vitium consensus. Menti Codicis melius convenire videtur eas inter vitia consensus enumerare, ut clare innuit c. 1982, quamvis non incongrue etiam inter impedimenta proprie dicta enumerari possint, quia ut verae inhabilitates considerare possunt."

[147] GIACCHI, *Il consenso nel matrimonio canonico*, p. 47: "Che un matrimonio sia nullo per mancanza del consenso presuppone la capacità psichica a consentire, senza la quale non si può evidentemente scendere ad esaminare se consenso vi fu o no."

[148] BÁNK, *Connubia canonica*, p. 341: "Codex expressis verbis de impedimento amentiae non loquitur in iure matrimoniali, neque in tractatu de habilitate contrahentium (impedimenta), neque inter vitia consensus. Haec enim quaestio magis ad *capacitatem naturalem* personarum pertinet, de qua in locis diversis disserit lex. De vitiis consensus enim vix moveri potest quaestio, nisi supponetur capacitas seu habilitas naturalis contrahentium." Bánk seems to exclude *amentia* both as a defect of consent and as a strict diriment impediment.

[149] DE SMET, *De sponsalibus et matrimonio*, editio tertia (Brugis: Car. Beyaert, 1919), n. 522 bis.

explained: "Insanity or dementia is not to be counted among matrimonial impediments if one wishes to abide by the spirit of the Code. One must rather treat it as a defect of consent..." [150] Most writers who have raised the question have, usually without explanation, simply repeated the observation of De Smet. [151]

Indeed it seems that, considering the perspective given it in canonical commentaries generally, and considering the settled jurisprudence of the Rota (which has traditionally sought the invalidating force of mental impairment in a defective act of consent), the common opinion is the more acceptable, i.e., that inability to consent may not be considered a diriment impediment in the language of the Code, but rather as a cause of defective consent. The mere fact that this disability is a "defect of personal capacity" does not automatically make it a diriment impediment. For one thing, it is questionable that "defect of personal capacity" is a peculiar characteristic of a diriment impediment. [152] Secondly, this disability presents too many differences from the concept of a diriment impediment as envisioned by the Code. It would be the only "impediment" representing a disability which affects *matrimonium in fieri* (the positing of consent) and not *matrimonium in facto esse* (unfitness for the state of marriage either in general or with a particular person or class of persons). It would be the only impediment which the normal person would incur and shed hundreds of times a year, as often as he falls asleep, becomes drunk, etc. If it be considered an impediment, then ignorance, error, and fear should also be called impediments, for they too cause an incapacity to place true and sufficient marital consent; however, the Code regards them simply as causes of defective consent and nullity is declared on the grounds of the defective act rather than on the grounds of an incapa-

---

150 De Smet, "Aliénation mentale en matière de consentement matrimonial," *DDC*, Tom. I, col. 416.

151 Castañeda, *La locura y el matrimonio*, p. 1, nota 1; Van Ommeren, *Mental Illness Affecting Matrimonial Consent*, p. 172; Pickett, *Mental Affliction and Church Law*, p. 144; Klemme, *Lucid Intervals and Matrimonial Consent*, p. 18.

152 Jaime Mans, "En torno a la naturaleza jurídica de los impedimentos matrimoniales," *Revista Española de Derecho Canónico*, XIV (1959), pp. 793-804.

ble or unfit person. Mans makes a keen observation on the difference between *amentia* and the diriment impediments of the Code, relying on the distinction between *actus naturaliter existens* and *actus juridice inefficax*:

> We must insist that the diriment impediments of matrimony are one thing, and the incapacity to give true marital consent is another. The absence of diriment impediments is required for the *efficacy* of consent, that is, that it produce a valid marriage; the capacity of the parties is required so that there can be true marriage consent, that is, for the very *existence* of the consent. Impediments and capacity both refer to the persons of the contractants, but the impediments refer to the contractants as the material object of the contract; capacity refers to them as subjects of the contract.[153]

However, recent Rotal jurisprudence has begun to investigate the invalidating force of mental impairment not merely in its effect of precluding sufficient marital consent at the time of the wedding (*causa efficiens*)[154] but also in its effect of rendering the person objectively incapable of assuming one or another, or all, of the essential rights and obligations of the marriage contract (*causa materialis*). It seems that mental impairment can thus invalidate the contract in exactly the same way as the diriment impediment of impotence; according to this conception, therefore, insanity is a strict diriment impediment in the language of the Code, *aequo iure* with impotence.

---

153 MANS, *El consentimiento matrimonial*, p. 24; MANS-BERNÁRDEZ, *Derecho matrimonial canónico*, I, p. 316.

154 The ability to place psychologically sufficient consent seems to be a natural presupposition or an essential preamble to marriage, much like the supposition that marriage is between a man and a woman. We do not consider every adult man as continually under a "diriment impediment" to marriage in relation to irrational animals or to members of his own sex. One man cannot marry another man; certainly there is a natural incapacity there, but this is hardly the Code's sense of a diriment impediment. Unless marriage be between a man and a woman and between people who are capable of constructing its efficient cause, there is no use even thinking about the state of marriage... the plane on which the Code conceives the diriment impediments. This seems to be why Bánk states as reasonable the legislator's failure to assign *amentia* either to the list of diriment impediments or to the defects of consent. Cf. *supra*, footnote 148.

Section A. The Invalidating Force of Impotence

Marriage is a contract and as such is subject to the conditions of contracts according to the natural law. Moreover, it is a contract *sui generis* whose essential formal object has been determined immutably by nature.[155] It is bilateral so that the rights and obligations of the contract cannot arise in one party unless they arise simultaneously in the other. It is indivisible so that if only one essential obligation is excluded from the negotiation, the entire contract is null. It is irrescindable so that a substantial defect concomitant with the negotiation renders the contract null from the beginning, but if subsequent to the negotiation it does not dissolve the valid contract.

In themselves, potency and impotency are irrelevant at law; they become relevant in Canon Law only in their bearing on the ability of a person to enter validly the marriage contract, that is, only in their consideration in the order of *rights and obligations.* It is inaccurate to define the impediment of impotence as the *physical* inability to place *actus per se aptos ad prolis generationem;* it is rather the *moral* inability to assume the right and obligation to place *actus per se aptos ad prolis generationem.*[156]

---

155 Cf. Michiels, "Mariage-contrat ou mariage-institution?" *Apollinaris,* XXXIII (1960), pp. 105-106.

156 "Nullus potest se obligare ad impossibile. Sed in matrimonio homo se obligat ad copulam carnalem, quia ad hoc dat alteri sui corporis potestatem. Ergo frigidus, qui non potest carnaliter copulari, non potest matrimonium contrahere... In matrimonio est contractus quidam quo unus alteri obligatur ad debitum carnale solvendum. Unde sicut in aliis contractibus non est conveniens obligatio si aliquis se obliget ad hoc quod non potest dare vel facere, ita non est conveniens matrimonii contractus si fiat ab aliquo qui debitum carnale solvere non possit. Et hoc impedimentum vocatur impotentia coeundi, nomine generali..." — St. Thomas, *Summa theologica,* III, *suppl.,* q. 58, a. 1.

McCarthy writes: "When we say that conjugal impotence is a diriment impediment of the natural law we mean that one who is impotent is, in the very nature of things, incapable of entering the marriage contract. Something essential to that contract is necessarily excluded in the circumstances. The person who is impotent is incapable of doing something which it is essential to the marriage contract that he be capable of doing... But what is the metaphysical basis of all this?... The man obliges himself to give to the woman the use of his body in a particular way — precisely the right to have with him acts of sexual intercourse. The woman undertakes similar obligations to the man regarding

Hence, a person who is physically incapable of placing perfect copula may well be able to enter the marriage contract, for if his condition is curable by ordinary measures, he is still capable of assuming the right and obligation *sub gravi* of placing *actus per se aptos ad prolis generationem.* On the other hand, a person might be physically capable of arriving at sexual union, and yet be incapable of assuming the right and obligation to conjugal copula because he can attain to sexual union only by sinful means. Traditional doctrine has always conceived the impediment of impotence in the moral order of rights and obligations. That is why incurable (perpetual) impotence invalidates, while curable (temporary) impotence does not.[157] That is why traditional doctrine has considered as "incurable" those cases of impotence which can be remedied only by extraordinary or sinful means (the classic examples: mortally dangerous operation, operation involving extraordinary damage to health or to one's salvation, a miraculous remedy).[158] For no one can be said to assume an obligation *sub gravi* which can be honored only by sinful or extraordinary measures. Nor can the partner be said to possess a right which can be honored only through the heroic or sinful cooperation of his spouse. Thus a Rotal sentence could declare a marriage null on the grounds of impotence even though the partners arrived at material union, but could do so only through intolerable

---

the use of her body. Clearly, if a man is incapable of sexual intercourse he cannot give to a woman the right to have this intercourse with him. And viceversa. In these circumstances, any attempt to give this right is futile. It involves a contradiction. It can originate no obligation regarding the conjugal act. *Nemo tenetur ad impossibile.* Accordingly the whole contract is, in the very nature of things, invalid." — JOHN McCARTHY, "The Impediment of Impotence in the Present-day Canon Law," *Ephemerides Iuris Canonici,* IV (1948), pp. 96-130 at pp. 100-101.

[157] "Impotentia temporanea juri coeundi non adversatur, sed hujus juris exercitium tantum afficit; usus vero matrimonii non est de ejus essentia et sufficit matrimonii consummationem fuisse possibilem, quo tempore contractum fuit, vel possibilem futuram." — HOLBÖCK, *Tractatus de jurisprudentia Sacrae Romanae Rotae,* p. 59.

[158] HOLBÖCK, *ibid.;* PALAZZINI, "De impedimento impotentiae," *Casus conscientiae,* I, *De matrimonio,* p. 70: "*Perpetua* quae sine mediis inhonestis vel sine probabili vitae periculo aut gravi damno salutis vel sine miraculo auferri nequit. Aliter, licet forte grave incommodum, v.g. gravis operationis, subeundum sit, est *temporanea.*"

pain on the part of the woman.[159] Thus, too, a recent Rotal sentence could state as a principle that a person is impotent if he can arrive at sexual union only by sinful means.[160] An early Rotal sentence declared a marriage null on the grounds of impotence even though the woman's disability *de se* was perhaps curable by ordinary means, but it so happened that she dwelt *"in barbaris et dissitis regionibus, quae, ex declaratione Iudicis, medicis in gyneologica scientia peritis et artis salutaris praesidiis necessariis, carent omnino..."*[161]

From what has been said, one can ascertain what is to be thought of some recent notions of the impediment of impotence which reduce it to the stark physical ability to perform coitus. Lazzarato holds that potency is the capacity to arrive at physical union under whatever circumstances; therefore, the pervert who can arrive at material union only by torturing his wife is potent.[162] According to Misuraca, impotence should be defined in biological terms to signify any impediment rendering impossible the biological end of marriage intended by nature.[163] According to Oesterle, a woman suffering from vaginism which allows material union only with intolerable pain is indeed potent but under no obligation to render the debt.[164]

Canonical doctrine, however, overwhelmingly conceives the impediment of impotence to coincide, not with the sheer physical inability to arrive at perfect copula, but with the moral impossibility of binding oneself *sub gravi* to place such acts.

---

[159] C. Heard (Mediolanen.), Dec. 30, 1949. The decision states *in iure*: "Talis enim inhumanus modus agendi, etsi materialem matrimonii consummationem causat, impotentiae impedimentum excludere nequit; nam sicut nemo iure tenetur ad operationem chirurgicam subeundam quae secum fert periculum vitae, ita nemo iure tenetur ad copulam admittendam quae necessario secum fert dolores qui intolerabiles sunt." — *Ephemerides Iuris Canonici*, VII (1951), p. 363.

[160] C. Mattioli (Chicagien.), Mar. 24, 1960: "Ideo, vere impotens dicendus esset: nam, id re vera nos posse teneri debet, quod jure possumus, scilicet absque Dei offensione et legis moralis injuria."

[161] C. Persiani, Nov. 15, 1909 (Vol. I, 141).

[162] D. Lazzarato, "De copula artificiosa semel tantum admissa," *Ephemerides Iuris Canonici*, IV (1948), pp. 470-472, at p. 472.

[163] Salvatore Misuraca, "L'impotenza canonica dal lato urologico," *Ephemerides Iuris Canonici*, XVII (1961), pp. 258-303, at pp. 276-279.

[164] Gerardus Oesterle, O.S.B.. "Vera impotentia a parte mulieris?" *Il Diritto Ecclesiastico*, LXIII (1952), pp. 43-51, at p. 48.

Section B. The Invalidating Force of Psychic Defect

Both canonical doctrine and ecclesiastical jurisprudence hold that psychic defect or disorder can, even without precluding true and sufficient consent, prevent the assumption of an essential right and obligation of the marriage contract, thereby rendering the contract null. This is precisely the juridical figure of psychic impotence. The irreparably impotent person (by reason of psychic disorder) who attempts marriage is attempting to bind himself to an obligation which cannot be fulfilled; he attempts to grant a right which cannot be honored. His marital consent is bound to be inefficacious. A decision of the Etruscan regional tribunal in Italy, in declaring a marriage null because of psychic impotence arising from acute paranoia, explained the source of invalidity in this way:

> In Iure: Cum obiectum essentiale matrimonialis contractus sit iuxta can. 1081, § 2, mutua traditio et acceptatio iuris in corpus in ordine ad actus per se aptos ad prolis generationem, patet quod, si unus contrahentium in impossibilitate versetur tale ius alteri concedendi, per se deficit obiectum ipsum essentiale contractus, ideoque contractus ipse necessario irritus atque invalidus vadit. Ius enim ad impossibile ne concipi quidem potest. Hinc consequitur ut impotentia, quam antiqui doctores significabant nomine defectus corporis vel impossibilitatis conveniendi corpore, constituat impedimentum iuris naturalis...
>
> Ut contingit in quibusdam formis psychopathiae, quamvis non omnes psychopathiae, ne paranoia quidem, secumferant necessario impotentiam. Sed in illis casibus, quibus omnia in favorem impotentiae functionalis in subiecto concurrant, et agatur de subiecto pathologico seu psychopathico, medicorum erit edicere utrum impotentia vere exsistat necne, et quatenus cum vitio congenito connectatur, itemque utrum perpetua habenda sit necne.[165]

If the Roman Rota prefers to handle cases of psychic impotence rather as cases of nonconsummated marriage with a view to the papal dispensation *super rato*,[166] it is not

---

[165] Tribunale Regionale Etrusco (Florentina), 9 giugno, 1942, Sanesi *ponente*. Reported in *Il Diritto Ecclesiastico*, LIV (1943), pp. 147-156, at pp. 147 and 151.

[166] D'Avack speaks quite strongly against this practice of the Rota: "In sè e per sè considerate, tali giustificazioni sono, a mio sommesso avviso, tutt'altro che convincenti e denotano piuttosto un prestabilito

because the Rota denies the juridical figure of psychic defect rendering a person impotent; the reason is because of lack of sufficient proof of the antecedence and incurability of the condition in a given case.[167]

Why not extend this principle to *all* the essential rights and obligations of the marriage contract, any one of which, if it is lacking, invalidates the contract? Certinly the right to place conjugal copula is not the only essential right whose exclusion renders the contract null. Just what exactly are the essential, indispensable rights and obligations of the marriage contract cannot be ascertained by mere logical deduction from the essence of marriage, for the concept of matrimony is not immediately evident. Writes Huizing:

> Etenim vera conceptio matrimonii non a priori, ope logicae cuiusdam deductionis, statui potest, sed tantum per viam inductivam seu analysim realitatis matrimonii prout conscientia christiana de ea iudicat et semper iudicavit.[168]

Fortunately the Christian conscience of tradition offers us a fairly clear delineation of the essential formal object of marriage. It must be recalled that a particular right and obligation of the substance of marriage might be excluded in one of two ways by virtue of the natural law: (1) by

---

proposito a non volersi addentrare su di un terreno indubbiamente infido e irto di innegabili difficoltà, quale è quello delle impotenze psichiche, che non un'accertata impossibilità obbiettiva di affrontarlo, vagliarlo e risolverlo nei singoli casi con una *moralis saltem certitudo.* Gli argomenti invero, addotti per negare *a priori* tale possibilità, si rivelano privi di ogni consistenza, se non addirittura infondati... Ma in realtà la spiegazione di tale fenomeno va, a mio avviso, collocata in due concorrenti ragioni pratiche: nell'abbandono cioè da un lato dell'*experimentum triennalis cohabitationis,* e nello sviluppo dall'altro dell'istituto della *dispensatio pontificia a matrimonio rato et non consummato.*" — *Cause di nullità e di divorzio,* pp. 563-564.

[167] As far as the principle is concerned, Sheehy states: "This same doctrine is clearly discernible in the jurisprudence of the Sacred Roman Rota, which recognizes Functional (and Psychical) impotence as an established ground on which the validity of a marriage may be impugned." — GERARD SHEEHY, "Male Psychical Impotence in Judicial Proceedings," *The Jurist,* XX (1960), 253-294, at p. 259. He refers to the important article of Szenwic, "L'impotenza nella recente giurisprudenza rotale," *Il Diritto Ecclesiastico,* LXV (1954), I, Pt. 2, pp. 41-46, 96-101.

[168] PETRUS HUIZING, S.I., "Bonum prolis ut elementum essentiale obiecti formalis consensus matrimonialis," *Gregorianum,* XLIII (1962), 657-722, at p. 714.

exclusion from the act of consent; (2) because of objective inability to assume said right and obligation. Thus, for example, the *ius-debitum* to conjugal copula might be excluded either by deliberate simulation or by the diriment impediment of impotence.[169] Hence, a survey of traditional canonical doctrine on invalidating contrary conditions and intentions will reveal what particular rights and obligations are indispensable to a valid contract so that their exclusion, even by objective inability to assume them, will necessarily nullify the marriage.[170]

With regard to the *bonum fidei* it is certain that the exclusion of the obligation to observe marital fidelity, at least to the extent of refraining from adultery, invalidates the contract. It is not quite so clear whether to reserve to oneself the right to carry on sodomitic practices with a third person substantially violates the *bonum fidei* and

---

[169] It seems to us that the impotence is prior to the simulation in the order of causality so that if an incurably impotent man, in order perhaps to hide his disability, makes a pact with his fiancée to exclude the mutual right and obligation of conjugal copula, the ensuing marriage is null, to be sure, not because of simulation but because of impotence. For the right and obligation was already, by reason of antecedent impotence, objectively non-transferable; the positive act of exclusion was not the cause of the non-transference; that is, it was not the cause of marital nullity.

[170] Except for the *ius-debitum ponendi actus per se aptos ad prolis generationem* and its exclusion by the impediment of impotence, canonical doctrine has not considered the objective inability to assume the specific rights and obligations of the marriage contract. Jemolo seems to be the first to ask whether *jus ad fidem* might be excluded not merely by simulation but also by the objective inability to sustain the obligation: "Poichè è nullo il matrimonio nel quale alcuno neghi il bene della fedeltà, è possibile chiedersi se sia idoneo al matrimonio chi si trovi in condizioni psichiche tali da essere incapace a restare fedele... sembra che debba dirsi mancare in essi la capacità matrimoniale, non potendosi promettere la fedeltà, se per una propria alterazione morbosa non siasi in grado di restare fedeli. Non consta però di decisioni che affrontino la questione in tali termini." — A. C. Jemolo, *Il matrimonio nel diritto canonico*, n. 49.

Conte a Coronata takes up Jemolo's question and answers by denying the supposit, i.e., that such persons could exist. But in the supposition that they exist, he grants that they would be incapable of marriage. Cf. *Institutiones, De Sacramentis*, III, n. 441.

Such persons do exist and Rotal jurisprudence has treated not a few cases involving the sexual psychopathy of nymphomania. In the decision *coram* Sabattani (Neapolitana), June 21, 1957, the invalidating force of nymphomania was considered exactly as Jemolo had conjectured, i.e., as arising from an objective inability to fulfill the obligation.

invalidates the contract. Rotal jurisprudence in cases of homosexuality holds to the opinion that such intention is not against the substance of marriage.[171] With regard to the *bonum sacramenti* a marriage is null if essential marital rights are restricted to a trial period of temporary duration, to a period to begin after initial suspension of rights, or to stated intervals during the union, e.g., restricted to sterile periods.[172]

In his monumental article "Bonum prolis ut elementum essentiale obiecti formalis consensus matrimonialis", Huizing surveys the Christian tradition regarding the indispensable rights and obligations of the *bonum prolis* as constituting an essential element of the formal object of matrimonial consent, "*...seu quaenam sint iura et obligationes coniugum circa prolem quorum exclusio irritat consensum*".[173] Although some rights and obligations of

---

[171] Cf. c. Parrillo, Aug. 12, 1929 (Vol. XXI, 440); c. Massimi, May 29, 1935 (Vol. XXVII, 358); c. Lamas (Chicagien.), Mar. 15, 1956, *in iure;* c. Brennan (Parisien.), Mar. 27, 1958, *in iure;* c. Mattioli (Clevelanden.), Dec. 11, 1958, *in iure.* This last sentence states *in iure*: "Quidquid tenendum sit de jure coniugis obtinendi separationem perpetuam ex sodomia alterius (quae, ad effectum de quo agitur, adulterio aequiparanda esset), remanet haud certam ac tutam posse haberi sententiam, vi cuius, per sodomiam ac per bestialitatem, ita *coniugalis fides* plene detrectata habenda esset.

"Sunt, ex praeclaris AA., qui id affirmant; sed etiam non desunt qui, optimis fundamentis innixi, absolutissime negant. Ideo, Tribunal hoc Apostolicum renuit, in similibus, pro vinculi nullitate sententiam ferre, etiam ubi apparuerit nupturientem reservasse sibi jus prosequendi, post initas nuptias, commercium sodomiticum jam antea instauratum."

Oesterle, failing to distinguish between the fact of sodomy as a cause of perpetual separation (likened to adultery) and the intention to carry on sodomitic practices as a possible invalidating intention, adamantly rebukes the Rota on this point: "...ius canonicum saltem ex tempore S. Thomae, paucis exceptis auctoribus, sodomiam ante et post Codicem aequiparavit adulterio..." — "De relatione homosexualitatis ad matrimonium," *Revista Española de Derecho Canónico,* X (1955), 7-60, at p. 60.

[172] Cf. Pope Pius XII's Allocution to a Convention of Italian Catholic Midwives of October 29, 1951 (*AAS*, XLIII: 835). Among other things the Pope stated: "If already at the contracting of the marriage one at least of the parties had the intention of limiting to the sterile periods the marriage right itself, and not merely its use, so that outside those periods the other party should not have even the right to demand the act, that would imply an essential defect of matrimonial consent, which would entail the invalidity of the marriage itself, because the right which arises from the matrimonial contract is a right of each party in regard to the other, which is permanent, uninterrupted, not intermittent." (Translation of Bouscaren, *Canon Law Digest,* III, p. 441).

[173] HUIZING, *op. cit.*, p. 658.

the *bonum prolis* are accidental and can be excluded without invalidating the contract, the following are absolutely essential:

(1) ius et debitum circa actus coniugales perfectos;
(2) ius et debitum ad non impediendam conceptionem;
(3) ius et debitum ad abortum non procurandum;
(4) ius et debitum ad neonatum non mutilandum vel necandum; seu ad conceptionem et physicam exsistentiam conservandam.[174]

As Hervada has recently pointed out, therefore, the perduring contractual relationship of the spouses, *matrimonium in facto esse,* the marriage bond itself, does not consist merely in the *ius ad actus coniugales,* but is constituted of a whole network of mutual rights and obligations, some principal and indispensable, others secondary and derived.[175]

Section C. The Psychic Inability to Bind Oneself

In the line of theory, we might make some suppositions which seem to represent an objective inability to bind oneself to an essential obligation of the marriage contract. First of all, it must be recalled that the essential obligations of marriage are not assumed unless they be assumed *sub gravi;* that is, one must not only duly intend to, but

[174] "Bonum physicum prolis comprehendit certo *exsistentiam* eius *non impediendam.* Quocumque modo illicito iura et obligationes circa conceptionem, nativitatem et vitam prolis admittendam e vinculo matrimoniali excludantur, vinculum irritum est. Haec doctrina, primum a S. Agustino proposita, recepta a doctoribus scholasticis medii aevi, sancita a papa Gregorio IX in decretali *Si conditiones,* omnino communis manebat usque ad annum 1927, in quo De Smet novam suam sententiam publici iuris fecit; at postea quoque non desinit esse longe communior, quam constans iurisprudentia romana strenue sustinet. Exemplum classicum huiusmodi exclusionis est formula quam adhibuit Gregorius IX: Si generationem prolis evites. In specie huc spectant condiciones seu intentiones: procurandi sterilitatem; evitandi conceptionem; procurandi abortum; prolem conceptam vel natam necandi." — Huizing, *op. cit.,* p. 716, conclusio 3.

[175] Cf. J. Hervada, "El matrimonio *in facto esse* su estructura jurídica," *Ius Canonicum,* I (1961), pp. 135-175.

also be psychically able to, bind oneself to do or omit something under pain of subjectively grave guilt. Should a person exclude a *serious* obligation on his part in the observance of marital fidelity, he is excluding the obligation itself. Equally true is the axiom that he who is incapable of a human act (i. e., of mortal sin) is likewise incapable of binding himself to serious obligations. Thus, the idiot is incapable of marriage not only because he cannot place the human act of consenting in marriage, but also because he cannot sustain obligations, honor others' rights, or incur moral guilt. Hence, the idiot is simply incapable of the marriage contract.

With regard to the inability to assume a particular obligation of the contract, the axiom holds strong in ecclesiastical jurisprudence as a dictate of the natural law itself: *Nemo ad impossibile obligari potest.*[176] Thus, a person who is incapable of fulfilling an essential obligation of the marriage contract must be said to be incapable of assuming said obligation. This holds true for the physically impotent as well as for the psychically incompetent. Rotal jurisprudence has treated of psychic defect in this regard, both in precluding the obligation of conjugal copula (psychic impotence) and the obligation of marital fidelity (nymphomania). The same principle is applicable to *all* the essential obligations of the contract.

Canonical doctrine and jurisprudence are also firmly agreed on the principle that he who is incapable of sustaining an essential obligation except by sinning or by altogether extraordinary means, is likewise incapable of binding himself *sub gravi* to such an obligation; a correlative right in his partner is simply unintelligible in such circumstances.

Without saying whether or not such persons actually exist, we think that the following suppositions are theoretically true and consistent with the principles already stated:

A. They are psychically incapable of assuming the essential rights and obligations of the *bonum prolis*:

---

[176] Reg. 6 in VI°. Cf. M. STOCKHAMMER, "Ultra posse nemo obligatur," *Rivista Internazionale di Filosofia del Diritto*, XXXVI (1959), pp. 25-35.

(1) who, at the time of the wedding, are afflicted by a serious mental defect or disorder whereby they can attain to material sexual union *only* by inflicting pain and mutilation on the partner; (2) who can attain to material union *only* through intolerable horror, trauma, or violence; (3) who can attain to material union *only* through self-mutilation; (4) who can attain to material union only through intrinsically evil means; (5) who, out of a morbid compulsion-obsession, irresistibly seek to prevent conception by, e. g., the use of douches; (6) who, out of a maniacal fear of giving birth, compulsively procure abortion; (7) who insanely kill their offspring, e. g., by cannibalistic behavior.

B. They are psychically incapable of assuming or binding themselves to the *bonum fidei* who are irresistibly drawn to indulge in extra-marital affairs involving adultery. It is doubtful whether he is capable of the *bonum fidei* who compulsively practices sodomy with a third person whether of the same or opposite sex.

C. They are psychically incapable of binding themselves to the *bonum sacramenti*: (1) who, by true psychopathy, are compulsive bigamists; (2) who, because of a psychopathic *horror feminae* are incapable of sustaining a permanent union; (3) who, because of psychopathic moral anesthesia, cannot base their behavior on anything other than sheer, immediate expediency, making the observance of permanent and abiding serious obligations a moral, if not a physical, impossibility.

These statements are made only in the line of principle. Whether they reflect actual human beings is a question of fact; it must be noted, however, that the principles understand persons who are afflicted by real mental illness affecting personal responsibility, not merely normal people in difficult external circumstances.

It might be objected that the eventual non-observance of an essential obligation, or the mere material violation of an essential right, does not argue to an incapacity to assume the right and obligation which one proposes, or at least, knows, he will not fulfill. As in the case, however, of the incurably impotent (of whom the same objection could be made), the answer is that to grant a right or to assume an obligation the person must necessarily enjoy liberty regarding the object of the right and obligation. St. Thomas writes:

> Quamvis actus carnalis copulae non sit de essentia matrimonii, tamen potentia ad actum est de eius essentia, quia per matrimonium datur utrique coniugum potestas in corpus alterius respectu carnalis copulae.[177]

Thus, although marital fidelity is not of the essence of marriage (for a marriage can exist without fidelity), yet the power to be faithful is of the essence of matrimony; in the marriage contract there is given to each of the partners the right and obligation of marital fidelity. The same can be said of the permanence of the bond, of abstaining from what prevents conception or birth, of positively contributing to the physical conservation of the fetus or newborn.[178]

Must the psychic condition which renders a person incapable of honoring the essential rights and obligations of matrimony be incurable in order to invalidate the contract? Or, perhaps, does temporary or curable incompetence invalidate? Certainly, with regard to the psychic competence required to elicit psychologically sufficient consent during the wedding, even a temporary or curable condition invalidates for it prevents the efficient cause of the contract. But prescinding from this source of nullity and treating solely of psychic inability to observe essential obligations, we think a distinction must be made. One must distinguish between positive and negative essential obligations. Certainly, with a positive obligation, e. g., placing *actus per se aptos ad prolis generationem,* the condition must be incurable, for if the physical inability is temporary, the right and obligation can be assumed. "*Lex affirmativa obligat semper at non pro semper,*" is the famous axiom.

---

177 ST. THOMAS, *Summa theologica,* III, *suppl.,* q. 58, a. 1, *ad* 1. A Rotal sentence states: "Ex ipsa natura rei et ex institutione divina descendit, quod matrimonium, quo coniugalis initur societas per coniunctionem animorum cum mutua obligatione mutuoque iure perpetuo et indissolubili, nonnisi mutuo consensu perficitur, cum agatur de obiecto in personali dominio et in personali arbitrio utriusque partis." — c. QUATTROCOLO, Apr. 16, 1935 (Vol. XXVII, 254).

178 The *libertas disponendi de obiecto iuris et obligationis* must be enjoyed at the very moment of contracting, for it is at that moment when the rights and obligations are actually assumed.

It is enough if perfect conjugal copula can be placed *suo tempore,* and not every moment.

On the other hand, "*Lex negativa obligat semper ac pro semper.*" Hence, even if the condition is temporary and curable by ordinary means, as long as it lasts, the negative obligation is simply unassumable. Therefore, it seems to us that curable nymphomania simply prevents the nymphomaniac from binding herself to the obligation of marital fidelity. Hence, too, the condition of psychopathic cannibalism, by which the mother is driven out of false sense of devouring love to eat her newborn, invalidates the contract, even should the condition be curable by ordinary means.

Section D. On Possible Ecclesiastical Legislation

As can be seen, the concept of inability to assume the rights and obligations of the marriage contract is nothing more than the impediment of impotence extended to all the essential *iura-debita* of the contract. Hence, one might call such a general impediment that of "moral impotence," i. e., the moral inability to bind oneself to the substance of the marriage contract. If the canon on physical impotence (canon 1068) were slightly altered, it could well include the impediment of "moral impotence."

But the ability to bind oneself to an observance of the substance of the marriage contract does not exhaust the concept of "due discretion." In our study we have discovered, we believe, three distinct sources of nullity of the marriage contract by reason of mental impairment of all kinds. The first two have to do with a defect of sufficient consent; the third prescinds from the natural integrity or sufficiency of the act of consent:

1) *Incapacitas legitime manifestandi voluntatem actu vere humano.* Thus, even if there be true internal consent, some are prevented from validly manifesting it because actually incapable of placing a human act, a juridical act. This seems to be the proper *caput nullitatis* in cases of *mentis exturbatio* wherein the habitually normal person attempts to marry while drunk, hypnotized, sonambulating, delirious, etc.

2) *Incapacitas efformandi verum consensum internum qui sit naturaliter sufficiens ad matrimonium constituendum.*

3) *Incapacitas assumendi essentiales obligationes maritalis contractus ex obiectiva ineptitudine ad illas servandas.*

If it be permitted to us to suggest what legislation might be instituted to clarify the sources of nullity by reason of mental impairment, we would suggest that a third paragraph be added to canon 1081:

> § 3. Ipso naturae iure incapaces sunt valide contrahendi matrimonium qui consensum nequeunt exterius manifestare actu vere humano, vel qui ob morbum mentis verum consensum matrimonialem interius nequeunt efformare.

Among the diriment impediments strictly so called in *Caput IV*, perhaps after canon 1068 on impotence, a formulation of the impediment of mental incompetence or "moral impotence" might be inserted along these lines:

> § 1. Inhabilis ad validum matrimonium ineundum est qui ob defectum discretionis matrimonio proportionatae incapax redditur assumendi omnia et singula iura et debita essentialia contractus nuptialis.
>
> § 2. Si talis incapacitas dubia sit, sive dubio iuris sive dubio facti, matrimonium non est impediendum.

Scholion I: On Psychopathic Personality

The psychopathic personality, "that strange actor in the arena of crime," [179] stands as an enigma too in the matrimonial forum. As far as this writer knows, although a number of cases have been tried, no case of a psychopath, pleaded precisely on the invalidating nature of this disorder, has been judged affirmatively by the Rota.

Guttmacher writes:

> There is the sociopathic type, described so fully in Hervey Cleckley's *Mask of Sanity*. They have shown evidences of life-long social maladjustment reaching back into early

---

[179] Dr. Henry A. Davidson, "The Psychiatrist's Role in the Administration of Criminal Justice," *Criminal Psychology* (ed. Richard W. Nice), pp. 13-39, at p. 14.

> childhood. Dr. Robert Lindner used the very apt phrase, "rebel without a cause", to describe them. They are in conflict with society in all areas. Benjamin Rush, the first psychiatrist in America and one of the signers of the Declaration of Independence, called the condition "anomia", a term derived from the Greek word for lawlessness. He postulated the existence of a congenital defect of the moral sense in conjunction with normal, or even superior, intellectual powers. English writers have designated these individuals "moral imbeciles" or "moral defectives."
>
> They are often very bright, attractive, and superficially ingratiating. But this amiability is a skillful masking of an overwhelming hostility. They are socially irresponsible. Other persons are merely objects to be manipulated for their own hedonistic purposes. Distant goals are sacrificed for immediate expediency. It has been suggested that they possess a peculiar incapacity to conceptualize, particularly in regard to time. They possess no loyalties and are suspicious of others.[180]

What is called moral insanity and constitutional immorality on the Continent is what the American school refers to as psychopathic personality or simply, the sociopath. Marriage cases of nullity involving a sociopath present thorny problems for ecclesiastical judges.

In the celebrated Rotal case *coram* Wynen in 1941 it was argued that the psychopath lacks a conscience; though he have conceptual knowledge of what he is doing and knows conceptually right from wrong, yet he lacks evaluative knowledge. He acts without an appreciation of the import of his deeds; he is irresponsible and antisocial. It was alleged that Titus, in order to elicit sufficient marital consent, must enjoy not only the notional knowledge of marriage, but also an evaluative knowledge of marriage, a sense of its values, especially regarding its ethical aspect. The concurrent opinion of seven experts was that this particular man, though an intelligent professional man, suffered from constitutional immorality, lacked the requisite evaluative knowledge, and hence contracted marriage invalidly. The decision, however, was negative.[181]

---

180 Dr Manfred S. Guttmacher, "The Psychiatric Approach to Crime and Correction," *Criminal Psychology* (ed. Richard W. Nice), pp. 112-141, at p. 120.

181 Cf. *supra* the analysis of the doctrine of values in this chapter under "A Survey of Rotal Jurisprudence," pp. 116-119.

The effort to seek an invalidating force in behavioral or characterological disorders (psychopathies) by reducing the disorder to a necessary defect of marital consent has not met with success. As the doctrine of values was enunciated to establish invalidity in the marriages of the morally insane, so Villeggiante has argued to show a necessary defect of psychological consent in the case of nymphomaniacs [182] and Oesterle reduces constitutional homosexuality to a necessary, compulsive, simulated act of consent. [183]. It seems to us, however, that the perspective employed to ascertain the marriageable status of the psychopathic personality is misplaced when it seeks to reduce a behavioral disorder, by means of a dubiously valid inference, to a necessary anomaly in the act of consent. [184] The disorder of the psychopath is in the area of behavior, not of thought and perception; the compulsion of the nymphomaniac is towards carnal acts regardless of a marriage bond, and not towards marital consent; the homosexual is driven to sodomitic acts with members of his own sex, not necessarily to a positive exclusion of marital rights when he says,

---

182 SEBASTIANO VILLEGGIANTE, "Ninfomania e cause di nullità matrimoniale," *Il Diritto Ecclesiastico,* LXXI (1960), II, pp. 162-184; "Ninfomania e difetto di consenso," *ibid.*, pp. 315-322.

183 GERARDUS OESTERLE, O.S.B., "De relatione homosexualitatis ad matrimonium," *Revista Española de Derecho Canónico,* X (1955), pp. 7-60; "Welchen Einfluss hat die Homosexualität auf die Ehe?" *Oesterreichisches Archiv für Kirchenrecht,* XII (1961), pp. 305-337.

184 C. Wynen, Feb. 25, 1941 (Vol. XXXIII, 156): "Ex omnibus rationibus adductis apparet, quam caute perpendere oporteat peritias asseclarum doctrinae expositae, iuxta quam certus quidam homo, qui se maculavit repetitis delictis iisque gravibus, incapax declaratur ad validum consensum matrimonialem eliciendum." C. Sabattani (Neapolitana), June 21, 1957, *in iure*: "Ubi asseveratur voluntatis perturbationem oriri ex quadam psychica infirmitate, manifeste constare debet de facto morbi physici deque influxu eiusdem in vita psychica subiecti: relatio effectus et causae inter anomaliam physicam et psychicam perturbationem indubitanter exsistat necesse est." C. Mattioli (Chicagien.), Mar. 24, 1960, *in facto*: "Quod autem statuta ac decreta eius saepe saepius exsecutionem non attingant, nihil interest ad effectum de quo agitur [scil. ad probandam inhabilitatem ponendi consensum sufficientem]. Id enim spectat obligationis jam contractae adimplementum, ideo nullo modo consensum ingreditur illumque laedit." Parenthetic explanation ours. C. Filipiak (Davenporten.), Feb. 14, 1958, *in iure*: "Unde matrimonium psychopaticorum, etsi saepissime infelix, declarari non potest invalidum ex capite defectus consensus propter amentiam, nam eiusmodi psychopaticorum consensus matrimonialis pathologicis impulsibus per se non afficitur."

"I will." A recent Rotal decision stated clearly that psychopathic impulses do not *per se* affect marital consent:

> Itaque sunt qui laborant cogitationum occupatione seu, ut aiunt, ideis coactivis vel obsessionibus (idées obsédantes), vel impulsibus (ex. gr., poromania, pyromania, cleptomania, oniamania, etc.), vel sexus perversitatibus (onanismo, fetichismo, exhibitionismo, homosexualitate, immo sadismo, antropophagia, masochismo, etc.), aliisque statibus abnormibus, ex quibus varii effomantur psychopatiarum typi, ut ex. gr. impulsivi, contradictorii, mendaces, phantastici, antisociales, etc. Unde matrimonium psychopaticorum etsi saepissime infelix, declarari non potest invalidum ex capite defectus consensus propter amentiam, nam eiusmodi psychopaticorum consensus matrimonialis pathologicis impulsibus per se non afficitur. [185]

It seems, rather, that the possible invalidating force of a deep-seated characterological disorder should be investigated in its own field, i. e., that of behavior and adherence to a norm. The question of the psychopathic personality, it seems, is not centered about whether or not he could give psychologically sufficient consent, but whether he was capable of assuming *sub gravi* the essential obligations of the marriage contract which would normally arise from sufficient consent. The case of the physically impotent, for example, is not reduced by some nebulous inference to a defective act of consent, but is left in the order of ability to assume rights and obligations. The question regarding the impotent as well as the sociopath is not whether his consent was *actus exsistens*, but why it is that the *actus exsistens* be necessarily *actus inefficax*.

Was this sociopath able to assume each and every essential obligation of the marriage contract? These obligations cannot be validly assumed unless *sub gravi*, i. e., the person must make a perduring commitment to place certain acts and to abstain from certain acts under pain

---

[185] C. Filipiak (Davenporten.), Feb. 14, 1958, *in iure*. Reported in *Monitor Ecclesiasticus*, LXXXIV (1959), 611-615, at p. 612. Dr. Henry A. Davidson writes: "A psychopath may be anything else, but he is *not* insane. A psychopath is a person who lacks a conscience. He is a rebellious, antisocial individual who gets that way because of some personality quirk, not because of any mental disease. He is a psychopath not by reason of what he says or thinks but by reason of what he does." — "The Psychiatrist's Role in the Administration of Criminal Justice," *Criminal Psychology*, pp. 16-17.

of subjectively grave culpability. Is the sociopath capable of this? The answer is not altogether clear. Ford and Kelly write:

> The responsability of the psychopath for his deeds is highly problematical. In *The Mask of Sanity,* Dr. Hervey Cleckley gives a fascinating account of these numerous, unfortunate, extremely trying and baffling personalities. He considers psychopaths to be psychotic and largely irresponsible for their erratic behavior. Cavanagh and McGoldrick would probably endorse this view while recognizing the practical difficulties of having it acknowledged for juridical purposes at the present time. Dr. Henry C. Schumacher is of the opinion that psychopaths are "semi-insane and semi-responsible." At any rate this is the type of case on which expert psychiatric testimony is very likely to disagree. And nothing would be more likely to prejudice a case in the ecclesiastical courts than to appeal to a theory of "moral insanity." [186]

We think, in the theoretical order, that if a person, by dint of a deep-seated psychopathy, lacks moral conscience and responsibility to such an extent that his acts within a disordered nucleus are not subject to grave moral guilt, he is incapable of binding himself to serious, abiding, pertinent obligations. Hence, in the last analysis, we think the critical point regarding the marriageable status of the psychopathic personality is not with the imputability or sufficiency of the act of marital consent, but with his morally imputable adherence to the essential obligations inherent in the marriage bond.

Scholion II: On Constitutional Homosexuality

Nullity cases involving a constitutional homosexual present especially perplexing problems mainly because it is not clear on what precise grounds, as a necessary consequence of this peculiar sexual psychopathy, such a marriage might be null. Usually the validity of the marriage will be attacked on the following grounds: (1) exclusion of the *bonum fidei;* (2) exclusion of the *bonum sacramenti;* (3) mental defect; (4) psychic impotence.

---

[186] Ford-Kelly, *Contemporary Moral Theology,* p. 270.

Even with the psychically normal contractant, of course, simulation or impotence might be verified in a given case. And, *per accidens* at least, the homosexual might be impotent or at least fail to consummate his marriage, although this might not necessarily follow from his disorder.[187] Or, conscious of his disorder, the homosexual might *per accidens* make a condition or intention against permanence so that he in no way intends to bind himself to a lasting union if he finds that married life is intolerable for him after the initial trial; or he might reserve to himself the right to carry on his ingrained habits of sodomy with members of his own sex during his married life. Such intentions or conditions, although not the fatal outcome of his disorder, might, however, be more likely in the case of the homosexual, since he seems to have a stronger *causa simulandi* than the normal person.[188]

Oesterle has written strongly in favor of the thesis that constitutional homosexuality leads the afflicted party to a compulsive and unavoidable act of simulation when eliciting marital consent.[189] Given his *horror feminae* or *horror copulae*, the homosexual cannot but intend a union which excludes rights and obligations to conjugal acts, to marital fidelity, or to marriage itself. Hence, the marriage of the constitutional homosexual is null in virtue of canon 1086, §2. This thesis, however, if we are not mistaken, contains some crucial points which are doubtfully valid:

1. "The homosexual necessarily makes a positive will act excluding some essential property of marriage."

---

187 C. Doheny (Mediolanen.), June 7, 1961, *in facto*: "Scientia enim medico-legalis docet ex homosexualismo posse, aliquando, impotentiam ad heterosexualia consequi, non autem, necessario ac infallibiliter debere." C. Pasquazi (Rhedonen.), Oct. 26, 1961, *in iure*: "Plures dari possunt causae psychicae, quae impediunt actus coniugales regulares ut e.g. repugnantia, metus, gravis defatigatio, nervorum debilitas, quae, tamen, fere semper constituunt incapacitatem temporaneam et relativam. Quaedam quoque vitia ut masturbatio diu continuata, frequens sodomia et, praesertim, pederastia, causa possunt esse incapacitatis ('Gli invertiti, gli omosessuali, sono degli individui che hanno una vera e incoercibile tendenza verso gli altri dello stesso sesso, mentre per quello opposto hanno una ripulsione incommensurabile o comunque totale frigidità psichica e organica.' Cf. MOGLIE, *Manuale di psichiatria*, p. 233, 2. ed., 1940)."

188 Cf. VINCENT P. COBURN, "Homosexuality and the Invalidation of Marriage," *The Jurist*, XX (1960), 441-459; J. F. HARVEY, "Homosexuality and Marriage," *Homiletic and Pastoral Review*, LXII (1961), 227-234.

189 Cf. *supra*, footnote 183.

In answer we might say that even if this could be proved, then his act of exclusion in giving marital consent is not a human act but the product of a fatal determinism. As such it cannot have efficacy in the intentional order. That this compulsive simulation, though conceivable perhaps in the field of medicine as "simulation", does not generate the canonical figure of "simulation" has been treated elsewhere.[190] If such a marriage is null it is not because of positive exclusion *ad normam can.* 1086, §2.

2. "The homosexual excludes not just the exercise of the right and the fulfillment of the obligation, but the right and obligation itself." This might be difficult to prove except that Oesterle denies any distinction between *ius* and *usus iuris.* Therefore, exclusion of one necessarily would mean exclusion of the other.

3. "Sodomy is equated to adultery and hence it violates substantially the *bonum fidei.*" Oesterle admits that this is contrary to Rotal jurisprudence but adamantly claims that the jurisprudence is contrary to common canonical doctrine both before and after the Code.[191]

Oesterle's conception is not the canonical figure of simulation, but rather points to mental defect. For simulation presupposes the psychic ability to construct and posit naturally sufficient consent, whereas mental defect or *amentia* is the disorder which prevents one from eliciting naturally sufficient consent. What is often lost sight of, we believe, is that a behavioral disorder might generate a fatal determinism, but the determinism is not towards withholding marital consent, but towards the setting of compulsive patterns of conduct. That the disorder argues to a necessary withholding of consent is a gratuitous statement; in fact, as a number of recent Rotal sentences have pointed out, the common hope of the homosexual that marriage will cure his problem argues forcibly to the fact of integral consent.[192]

---

[190] Cf. *supra,* the concluding observations of "Contradictory *Capita*", pp. 25-26.

[191] "De relatione homosexualitatis ad matrimonium," *Revista Española de Derecho Canónico,* X (1955), pp. 57-60.

[192] Cf. c. Pinna (Parisien.), Apr. 22, 1958, *in facto;* c. Doheny (Southvarcen.), Apr. 16, 1962, *in facto.* In an interesting case involving an exhibitionist, the decision stated: "Sed Patres nedum concluserunt virum conventum nullam habuisse causam simulandi consensum, sed profecto

In order to reduce homosexuality to a mental defect one must show that this specific disorder somehow injured the faculties of knowing and willing marriage.[193] But such an inference is weak, for the inability to conform one's conduct in a certain sphere is not easily shown to redound automatically in the fact that the person thereby is prevented from understanding what marriage is or from duly intending marriage thus conceived.[194] Such attempts have been continually repudiated by the Rota.

The correct starting point, we believe, is the one mentioned in a homosexuality case *coram* Lamas of March 15, 1956, among the *motiva in iure.* There the court distinguishes carefully between sufficient consent and the fitness of the person. Personal *inhabilitas* does not exclude consent, which is physically *exsistens* but *iuridice nullus,* and this, even if the *inhabilitas* arises from an impediment of divine law.[195] If constitutional homosexuality invalidates, it seems to us, it is not because of a redundant defect in the act of marital consent, but because of the behavioral disorder itself rendering the person objectively incapable of binding himself *sub gravi* to an essential obligation of the contract of marriage. Thus, for example, his *horror copulae* might prevent the assumption of the right and obligation to perfect conjugal copula (psychic impotence). With regard to indissolubility, if the homosexual, by reason of his *horror feminae,* is constitution-

---

affirmarunt eum habuisse motivum honestum et laudandum ineundi matrimonium christianum. Ipse enim ex tali matrimonio non spernendum bonum expectavit sanationem nimirum suae propensionis ad actus sexuales perversos... Quodsi, hac spe fretus, Mariam duxerit, quam longe abierit conventus ab intentione ficte contrahendi, nemo non videt." — c. Rogers (Chicagien.), Apr. 14, 1961, *in facto.*

193 C. Mattioli (Chicagien.), Mar. 24, 1960, *in iure*: "Nam, veluti sententia appellata luculenter probat, inhabilitas juri tradendo acceptando ad actus heterosexuales tunc tantum, juxta orthodoxa principia, admitti posset, cum probata resultaret laesio superiorum facultatum, ita ut victima practice tamquam 'amens' reputari deberet."

194 Cf. *supra,* footnote 184.

195 C. Lamas (Chicagien.), Mar. 15, 1956, *in iure*: "Accurate distinguendae sunt causae nullitatis ex parte ipsius consensus ab illis quae se tenent ex parte personae, quae inhabilis est. Haec personae inhabilitas non excludit consensum, qui erit nullus *iuridice* seu *invalidus,* neutiquam autem per se est nullus *physice* (GASPARRI, *De matrim.,* II, n. 811, contra SANCHEZ, *De matrim.,* lib. II, disp. 35). Quod obtinet etiamsi agatur de impedimento iuris divini (GASPARRI, *ib.* n. 813), ut est impotentia vel ligamen."

ally incapable of a lasting union with a woman, he cannot conceivably bind himself *sub gravi* to a lasting relationship. As far as the *bonum fidei* is concerned, it seems more probable that inability to abstain from sodomy does not argue to the inability to bind oneself to the *bonum fidei.* Sodomitic acts do not seem to violate substantially the essential obligation of marital fidelity; thus, the homosexual, even if he positively reserves to himself the right to carry on sodomitic practices during his marriage, can nevertheless bind himself to marital fidelity.[196] Hence, the disorder of the homosexual places him in an altogether different category thant that of the nymphomaniac, whose disorder violates the *bonum fidei* substantially. Were sodomy equated to adultery in this matter, then the homosexual, like the nymphomaniac, might be found to be objectively incapable of assuming the essential obligation of marital fidelity.

---

[196] C. Mattioli (Clevelanden.), Dec. 11, 1958, *in iure*: "Ideo Tribunal hoc Apostolicum renuit, in similibus, pro vinculi nullitate sententiam ferre, etiam ubi apparuerit nupturientem reservasse sibi jus prosequendi, post initas nuptias, commercium sodomiticum jam antea instauratum."

BIBLIOGRAPHY

SOURCES

Acta Apostolicae Sedis, Commentarium Officiale. Romae: 1909-1929; in Civitate Vaticana: 1929.

Acta Sanctae Sedis. 41 voll. Romae: 1865-1908.

BOUSCAREN, T. LINCOLN, S. J. *The Canon Law Digest.* 4 vols. (Vol. IV in collaboration with James I. O'Connor, S. J.) Milwaukee: Bruce, 1934-1958.

Codex Iuris Canonici Pii X Pontificis Maximi iussu digestus Benedicti Papae XV auctoritate promulgatus. Typis Polyglottis Vaticanis, 1933.

Corpus Iuris Canonici. 2. ed. Lipsiensis. Post Aemilii Ludovici Richteri curas ad librorum manu scriptorum et Editionis Romanae fidem recognovit et adnotatione critica instruxit Aemilius Friedberg. 2 voll. Graz: Akademische Druck - U. Verlagsanstalt, 1959.

Corpus Iuris Civilis. Vol. I (16. ed. lucis ope expressa), *Institutiones* recognovit P. Krueger; *Digesta* recognovit Theodorus Mommsen, retractavit P. Krueger. Vol. II (11. ed. lucis ope expressa), *Codex Iustinianus* recognovit et retractavit P. Krueger. Vol. III (6. ed. lucis ope expressa), *Novellae Constitutiones*: R. Schoell; opus Schoelli morte interceptum absolvit G. Kroll. Berolini: apud Weidmannos, 1954.

Decretales D. Gregorii Papae IX suae integritati una cum glossis restitutae. Romae: In aedibus Populi Romani, 1582.

Decretum Gratiani emendatum et notationibus illustratum una cum glossis. Romae: In aedibus Populi Romani, 1582.

POTTHAST, AUGUSTUS. *Regesta Pontificum Romanorum inde ab anno post Christum natum 1198 ad annum 1304.* 2 voll. Berolini, 1874-1875; reprinted, Graz: Akademische Druck, 1957.

Sacrae Romanae Rotae Decisiones seu Sententiae quae prodierunt annis 1909-1952. 44 voll. Romae (post 1929 in Civitate Vaticana): Typis Polyglottis Vaticanis, 1912-1962.

Thesaurus Resolutionum Sacrae Congregationis Concilii. 167 voll. Romae: Camerae Apostolicae, 1718-1908.

REFERENCE WORKS

AQUINAS, ST. THOMAS. *Commentum in Quatuor Libros Sententiarum Magistri Petri Lombardi.* 3 tom. Parmae: Typis Petri Fiaccadori, 1856-1858.

——. *Summa theologica.* 4 tom. Parmae: Typis Petri Fiaccadori, 1852-1854.

BÁNK, JOSEPH. *Connubia canonica.* Romae - Friburgi Brisg. - Barcinone: Herder, 1959.

BENDER, LUDOVICUS, O. P. *Normae generales de personis.* Romae, Desclée & C., 1957.

——. *Dubium in Codice Iuris Canonici.* Romae: Desclée & C. 1962.

BONACINA, MARTINUS. *Opera omnia.* Tom. I: *Tractatus de magno matrimonii sacramento.* Venetiis: apud Jacobum Thomasinum, 1721.

BOTTOMS, ARCHIBALD M. *The Discretionary Authority of the Ecclesiastical Judge in Matrimonial Trials of the First Instance.* The Catholic University of America Canon Law Studies, n. 349. Washington, D.C.: The Catholic University of America Press, 1955.

BUCKLEY, MICHAEL J. *Morality and the Homosexual.* Westminster: Newman Press, 1959.

CAMMACK, J.S., S.J. *Moral Problems of Mental Defect.* London: Burns Oates & Washbourne Ltd., 1938.

CAPPELLO, FELIX M., S. J. *Tractatus canonico-moralis de sacramentis.* Vol. V: *De matrimonio.* Editio septima accurate emendata et aucta. Taurini et Romae: Marietti, 1961.

CAPRIO, FRANK S. and BRENNER, DONALD L. *Sexual Behavior: Psycho-Legal Aspects.* New York: Citadel Press, 1961.

CASTAÑEDA DELGADO, EUDOXIO. *La locura y el matrimonio.* Valladolid-Madrid: Editorial Sever-Cuesta, 1955.

Casus conscientiae. Vol. I: *De matrimonio.* 2ª ed., curante P. Palazzini. Romae: Officium Libri Catholici, 1961.

Las Causas Matrimoniales. Trabajos de la cuarta semana de derecho canónico celebrada en el Monasterio de N.ª S.ª de Montserrat. Salamanca: Consejo Superior de Investigaciones Cientificas, Instituto San Raimundo de Peñafort, 1953.

CAVANAGH JOHN R., and MCGOLDRICK, JAMES B. *Fundamental Psychiatry.* 2d ed., revised. Milwaukee: Bruce, 1958.

CHELODI, IOANNES, *Ius matrimoniale iuxta Codicem Iuris Canonici.* 3. ed. Tridenti: Libr. Edit. Tridentinum, 1921.

——. *Ius canonicum de personis.* 4. ed. curavit PIUS CIPROTTI. Vicetiae: Edit. S.A.T., 1957.

CIPROTTI, PIUS. *De iniuria ac diffamatione in iure poenali canonico.* Romae: Apud Custodiam Librariam Pont. Instituti Utriusque Iuris, 1937.

CONINCK, AEGIDIUS DE, S. J. *De sacramentis et censuris ecclesiasticis.* Lugduni: Sumpt. Claudii Landry, 1619.

Crime and Insanity. Edited by RICHARD W. NICE. New York: Philosophical Library, 1958.

Criminal Psychology. Edited by RICHARD W. NICE. New York: Philosophical Library, 1962.

D'ANNIBALE, JOSEPHUS Card. *Summula theologiae moralis.* 5. ed. 3 voll. Romae: Desclée, Lefebvre et Soc., 1908.

D'AVACK, PIETRO AGOSTINO. *Cause di nullità e di divorzio nel diritto matrimoniale canonico.* Vol. I, 2. ed. Firenze: Casa Editrice del Dott. Carlo Cya, 1952.

——. *Corso di diritto canonico: Il matrimonio.* Vol. I. Edizione provvisoria per gli studenti. Milano: Giuffrè, 1961.

Del Giudice, Vincenzo. *Nozioni di diritto canonico.* Undicesima edizione aumentata e interamente aggiornata. Milano: Giuffrè, 1962.

De Luca, Joannes Baptista (Card.). *Theatrum veritatis et justitiae.* Tom IX: *De testamentis.* Lugduni: Cramer & Perachon, 1697.

De Smet, Aloysius, *De sponsalibus et matrimonio.* 4. ed. Brugis: Car. Beyaert, 1927.

Diana, Antoninus. *Omnes resolutiones morales.* Tom. II: *De sacramento matrimonii.* Lugduni: Huguetan-Barbier, 1667.

Doheny, William J. *Canonical Procedure in Matrimonial Cases.* 2 vols. (Vol. I, 2. ed., revised). Milwaukee: Bruce, 1948.

Fässler, Hans Niklaus. *Die Schizophrenie als Ehenichtigkeitsgrund im kanonischen Recht: Versuch einer Bewertung der Schizophrenie nach der Spruchpraxis der Sacra Romana Rota.* Freiburg in der Schweiz: Paulusdruckerei, 1951.

Fazzari, Giuseppe M., S. J. *Valutazione etica e consenso matrimoniale.* Napoli: M. D'Auria, 1951.

Ford, John C., S. J., and Kelly, Gerald, S. J. *Contemporary Moral Theology.* Vol. I: *Questions in Fundamental Moral Theology.* Westminster, Maryland: Newman Press, 1958.

Gasparri, Petrus. *Tractatus canonicus de matrimonio.* 2 voll. 9ª ed. In Civitate Vaticana: Typis Polyglottis Vaticanis. 1932.

Giacchi, Orio. *Il consenso nel matrimonio canonico.* Milano: Giuffrè, 1950.

Gonzalez Tellez, Emanuelis. *Commentaria perpetua in singulos textus quinque librorum Decretalium Gregorii IX.* Tomus IV. Venetiis: ex typis Nicolai Pezzana, 1766.

Graziani, Ermanno. *Volontà attuale e volontà precettiva nel negozio matrimoniale canonico.* Milano: Giuffrè, 1956.

Henriquez, Henricus, S. J. *Summa theologiae moralis.* Tom. I. Venetiis: apud Haeredes Melchioris Sessae, 1600.

Holböck, Carolus. *Tractatus de jurisprudentia Sacrae Romanae Rotae.* Graetiae - Vindobonae - Coloniae: in Officina Libraria "Styria," 1957.

Hostiensis, Henricus Card. *Summa aurea.* Venetiis: ad candentis Salamandrae insigne, 1570.

Jemolo, A. C. *Il matrimonio nel diritto canonico.* Milano: Vallardi, 1941.

Jolowicz, H. F. *Roman Foundations of Modern Law.* Oxford: Clarendon Press, 1957.

Klemme, Dennis C. *Lucid Intervals and Matrimonial Consent: Historical Background and Jurisprudence of the Sacred Roman Rota.* Romae: Pontificia Universitas Lateranensis, 1960.

Kugler, Joannes, S. J. *Tractatus theologico-canonicus de matrimonio.* Norimbergae: Sumpt. Lehmanni, 1713.

Lugo, Franciscus de, S. J. *Tractatus de septem ecclesiae sacramentis.* Venetiis: apud Baba, 1652.

Lugo, Ioannes de, S. J. *Disputationes scholasticae et morales de sacramentis in genere.* Lugduni: Sumpt. Iacobi & Petri Prost, 1636.

MANS PUIGARNAU, JAIME M. *El consentimiento matrimonial: defecto y vicios del mismo como causas de nulidad de las nupcias.* Barcelona: Bosch, 1956.

MANS PUIGARNAU, JAIME M., y BERNÁRDEZ CANTÓN, ALBERTO. *Derecho matrimonial canónico.* 2 voll. Barcelona: Bosch, 1959.

MASCARDUS, J. *Conclusiones probationum omnium.* 3 tom. Venetiis: apud Damianum Zenarium, 1584.

MATTHAEUS CONTE A CORONATA, O.F.M. Cap. *Institutiones iuris canonici.* Vol. III: *De matrimonio et de sacramentalibus.* Editio tertia aucta et emendata. Taurini: Marietti, 1957.

MAYER-GROSS, W., SLATER, ELIOT, and ROTH, MARTIN. *Clinical Psychiatry.* Second edition, fully revised. London: Cassell & C., 1960.

MENOCHIUS, JACOBUS. *De praesumptionibus, coniecturis, signis, et indiciis.* Genevae: Crispini, 1636.

MICHIELS, GOMMARUS, O.F.M. Cap. *Normae generales juris canonici.* 2 voll. Editio altera penitus retractata et notabiliter aucta. Parisiis - Tornaci - Romae: Desclée et Socii, 1949.

——. *Principia generalia de personis in ecclesia.* Editio altera penitus retractata et notabiliter aucta. Parisiis - Tornaci - Romae: Desclée et Socii, 1955.

——. *De delictis et poenis.* 3 voll. (Vol. I, editio altera). Parisiis - Tornaci-Romae-Neo Eboraci: Desclée et Socii, 1961.

MOLINA, LUDOVICUS, S. J. *De iustitia et iure.* Tom. II: *De contractibus.* Moguntiae: Sumpt. Hermanni Mylii, 1614.

NOYES, ARTHUR P., and KOLB, LAWRENCE C. *Modern Clinical Psychiatry.* 5th ed. Philadelphia and London: W. B. Saunders Co., 1961.

O'DEA, JOHN C. *The Matrimonial Impediment of Nonage.* The Catholic University of America Canon Law Studies, n. 205. Washington, D.C.: The Catholic University of America Press, 1944.

O'DONNELL, CLETUS F. *The Marriage of Minors.* The Catholic University of America Canon Law Studies, n. 221. Washington, D.C.: The Catholic University of America Press, 1945.

OESTERLE, GERARDUS, O.S.B. *Consultationes de jure matrimoniali.* Romae: Officium Libri Catholici, 1942.

OJETTI, BENEDICTUS, S. J. *Commentarium in Codicem Iuris Canonici.* Tom. II: *De personis.* Romae: apud Aedes Univ. Gregorianae, 1928.

PALLOTTINI, SALVATOR. *Collectio omnium conclusionum et resolutionum.* Tom. XII. Romae: Typis S. Congr. de Prop. Fide, 1886.

PALMIERI, VINCENZO MARIO. *Medicina legale canonistica.* 2. ed. Napoli: Morano, 1955.

PAYEN, G. *De matrimonio in missionibus ac potissimum in Sinis tractatus practicus et casus,* 2. ed. 3 voll. Zi-ka-wei: Typographia T'OU-SE-WE, 1935-1936.

PELLEGRINI, GERMANUS-JOSEPH, C. P. *Jus ecclesiae poenale.* Tom. I: *De delictis.* Neapoli: D'Auria, 1962.

PICHLER, VITUS, S. J. *Summa jurisprudentiae sacrae universae seu jus canonicum.* Augustae Vindelicorum: Veith, 1758.

PICKARD, WILLIAM M. *Judicial Experts: A Source of Evidence in Ecclesiastical Trials.* The Catholic University of America Canon Law Studies, n. 389. Washington, D.C.: The Catholic University of America Press, 1958.

PICKETT, R. COLIN. *Mental Affliction and Church Law.* Ottawa: The University of Ottawa Press, 1952.

PIRHING, ERNRICUS, S.J. *Jus canonicum.* Tom. IV. Venetiis: ex thipographia Remondiniana, 1759.

The Priest and Mental Health. Edited by E. F. O'DOHERTY and S. DESMOND MCGRATH. Dublin: Clonmore and Reynolds, Ltd., 1962.

REGATILLO, EDUARDUS F., S.J. *Interpretatio et iurisprudentia Codicis Iuris Canonici.* 3. ed. Santander: Sal Terrae, 1953.

——. *Institutiones iuris canonici.* 2 voll. Editio quinta adaucta. Santander: Sal Terrae, 1956.

——. *Ius sacramentarium.* 3. ed. Santander: Sal Terrae, 1960.

REIFFENSTUEL, ANACLETUS, O.F.M. *Jus canonicum universum.* Tom. VI: *Tractatus de regulis juris.* Antverpiae: sumptibus Societatis, 1755.

REYNÉS, LORENZO QUINTANA. *La prueba en el procedimiento canónico.* Barcelona: Bosch, 1942.

ROBLEDA, OLIS, S. J. *La nulidad del acto juridico.* Santander: Universidad Pontificia Comillas, 1947.

SÁNCHEZ, THOMÁS, S. J. *De sancto matrimonii sacramento.* 3 tom. Posterior, et accuratior editio. Viterbii: apud Nicolaum Pezzana, 1737.

SCHMALZGRUEBER, FRANCISCUS, S.J. *Jus ecclesiasticum universum.* Tom. I: *Judex ecclesiasticus.* Romae: ex typographia Rev. Cam. Apostolicae, 1843-44.

SESTO, GENNARO J. *Guardians of the Mentally Ill in Ecclesiastical Trials.* The Catholic University of America Canon Law Studies, n. 358. Washington, D.C.: The Catholic University of America Press, 1956.

SIPOS, STEPHANUS. *Enchiridion iuris canonici.* Editionem septimam recognovit Ladislaus Gálos. Romae - Friburgi Brisg. - Barcinone: Herder, 1960.

SMITH, VINCENT M. *Ignorance Affecting Matrimonial Consent.* The Catholic University of America Canon Law Studies, n. 245. Washington, D.C.: The Catholic University of America Press, 1950.

TAMBURINI, THOMAS, S. J. *Theologia moralis.* Tom. II. Venetiis: apud Nicolaum Pezzana, 1755.

TAPARELLI, LUIGI, S. J. *Saggio teoretico di dritto naturale appoggiato sul fatto.* Ottava edizione riveduta, quinta dell'ultima corretta e accresciuta dall'autore. 2 voll. Roma: La Civiltà Cattolica, 1949.

VANDERVELDT, JAMES H. and ODENWALD, ROBERT P. *Psychiatry and Catholicism.* New York, Toronto, London: McGraw-Hill, 1952.

VAN OMMEREN, WILLIAM M. *Mental Illness Affecting Matrimonial Consent.* The Catholic University of America Canon Law Studies, n. 415. Washington, D.C.: The Catholic University of America Press, 1961.

VICTORIA, FRANCISCUS DE, O.P. *Relectiones XII theologicae. De matrimonio.* Lugduni: Landry, 1587.

——. *Summa sacramentorum Ecclesiae.* Venetiis: S.N.T., 1579.

VLAMING, TH. M. *Praelectiones iuris matrimonii ad normam Codicis Iuris Canonici.* 4. ed. a L. Bender, O.P. Bussum in Hollandia: Paulus Brand, 1950.

WAGNERECK, H. *Commentarius exegeticus SS. Canonum.* 3 tom. Dilingae: apud Joannem Federle, 1672.

WANENMACHER, FRANCIS. *Canonical Evidence in Marriage Cases.* Philadelphia: Dolphin Press, 1935.

WERNZ, FRANCISCUS X., S.J. *Jus decretalium.* Tom. IV: *Jus matrimoniale Ecclesiae catholicae.* Altera editio emendata et aucta. Prati: Giachetti, 1911-1912.

WERNZ, FRANCISCUS X., S.J. et PETRUS VIDAL, S.J. *Ius canonicum.* Tom. V: *Ius matrimoniale.* Editio tertia a P. Philippo Aguirre, S.J., recognita. Romae: apud Aedes Universitatis Gregorianae, 1946.

ARTICLES

ALLERS, RUDOLPH. "Annulment of Marriage by Lack of Consent because of Insanity," in *The Ecclesiastical Review,* CI (1939), 325-343.

——. "Some Medico-Psychological Remarks, on Canons 1068, 1081, and 1087," in *The Jurist,* IV (1944), 351-380.

AMANIEU, A. "Aliénation mentale en matière de nullité de mariage," in *Dictionnaire de Droit Canonique,* Paris: Librairie Letouzey et Ané, 1935, Tome I, coll. 417-440.

ANNÉ, L. "La conclusion du mariage dans la tradition et le droit de l'Église Latine jusqu'au IVe siècle," in *Ephemerides Theologicae Lovanienses,* XII (1935), 513-550.

BENDER, LUDOVICUS, O.P. "Sanatio matrimonii invalidi ob impedimentum iuris divini," in *Ephemerides Iuris Canonici,* XIII (1957), 19-44.

——. "Convalidatio matrimonii et defectus consensus," in *Monitor Ecclesiasticus,* LXXXI (1956), 482-493.

BERNHARD, JEAN, "Propos sur la nature juridique de la *sanatio in radice* dans le droit canonique actual," in *Ephemerides Iuris Canonici,* IV (1948), 389-406.

——. "*La sanatio in radice* et le consentement matrimonial dans le droit canonique moderne (du Concile de Trente au Code de Droit Canonique)," in *Ephemerides Iuris Canonici,* VI (1950), 239-253.

BERTRAMS, WILHELMUS, S.J. "De influxu ecclesiae in iura baptizatorum," in *Periodica de re morali canonica liturgica,* XLIX (1960), 417-457.

——. "De effectu consensus matrimonialis naturaliter validi," in *Apollinaris,* XXXIII (1960), 119-138.

——. "De efficacitate consensus matrimonialis naturaliter validi," in *Periodica de re morali canonica liturgica,* LI (1962), 288-300.

BIDAGOR, RAYMUNDUS, S.J. "Circa ignorantiam naturae matrimonii," in *Periodica de re morali canonica liturgica,* XXIX (1940), 269-289.

BOGANELLI, ELEUTERIUS, "De paranoicorum imputabilitate," in *Apollinaris,* XVI (1943), 88-99.

BRACELAND, FRANCIS J., M.D., Sc.D. "Schizophrenic Remissions." in *The Jurist,* XXI (1961), 362-374.

BURKE, WILLIAM F., JR. "New Light in the Eternal Conflict Between Law and Medicine in Judicial Aspects of Practice." in *Crime and Insanity,* edited by RICHARD W. NICE (New York: Philosophical Library, 1958), 123-135.

CARON, ARTHUR, O.M.I. "Jurisprudence in Canon Law," in *The Jurist,* XVIII (1958), 88-97.

CASTAÑEDA DELGADO, EUDOXIO. "Nulidad por vicio de consentimiento," in *Las Causas Matrimoniales* (Trabajos de la cuarta semana de derecho canonico celebrada en el Monasterio de N.ª S.ª de Montserrat. Salamanca: Consejo Superior de Investigaciones Cientificas, Instituto San Raimundo de Peñafort, 1953), 491-535.

——. "El problema del lucido intervalo en las enfermedades mentales," in *Revista Española de Derecho Canónico,* VIII (1953), 475-503.

——. "Las causas de separación temporal por amencia," in *Revista Española de Derecho Canónico,* X (1955), 383-409.

——. "Comentario" (on the Rotal decision *coram* Felici, Dec. 3, 1957), in *Revista Española de Derecho Canónico,* XIII (1958), 705-718.

CHATHAM, JOSIAH G. "A Primer on Insanity Cases," in *The Jurist,* XX (1960), 343-351.

COBURN, VINCENT P. "Homosexuality and the Invalidation of Marriage," in *The Jurist,* XX (1960), 441-459.

CONNELL, FRANCIS J., C.SS.R. "Conceptual and Evaluative Cognition," (reply) in *The American Ecclesiastical Review,* CXLVII (1962), 422-425.

CROFT, GEORGE, S. J., " Imputability and Mental Abnormality in Canon and Civil Law, " in *The Clergy Review,* XL (1955), 262-271.

D'AVACK, PIETRO AGOSTINO. "L'omosessualità nel diritto canonico," in *Ulisse,* III (1953), 680-697.

——. "Sul *defectus discretionis iudicii* nel diritto matrimoniale canonico," in *Archivio di Diritto Ecclesiastico,* II (1940), 157-178.

DAVIDSON, HENRY A. " The Psychiatrist's Role in the Administration of Criminal Justice, " in *Criminal Psychology,* edited by RICHARD W. NICE (New York: Philosophical Library, 1962), 13-39.

——. "Irresistible Impulse and Criminal Responsibility." in *Crime and Insanity,* edited by RICHARD W. NICE (New York: Philosophical Library, 1962), 29-48.

DEL CORPO, AEGIDIUS. "Actus hominis et actus humanus in consummatione matrimonii," in *Monitor Ecclesiasticus,* LXXXIII (1958), 303-313.

DE MAÑARICUA NUERE, ANDRES ELISEO. "Nulidad pos exclusion de la unidad o de la indisolubilidad," in *Las Causas Matrimoniales* (Trabajos de la cuarta semana de derecho canonico celebrada en el Monasterio de N.ª S.ª de Montserrat. Salamanca: Consejo Superior de Investigaciones Cientificas, Instituto San Raimundo de Peñafort, 1953), 303-329.

De Smet, A. " Aliénation mentale en matière de consentement matrimonial," in *Dictionnaire de Droit Canonique,* Paris: Librairie Letouzey et Ané, 1935, Tome I, coll. 415-417.

Fedele, Pio. "Analisi di recenti sentenze ecclesiastiche in tema di nullità di matrimonio," in *Ephemerides Iuris Canonici,* IX (1953), 347-415.

——. "Un nuovo caso di infermità mentale come causa di nullità del matrimonio?" in *Archivio di Diritto Ecclesiastico,* III (1941), 279-291.

——. "Rassegna ragionata di giurisprudenza rotale in materia matrimoniale," in *Archivio di Diritto Ecclesiastico,* I (1939), 121-150.

Felici, Pericles. "De investigatione psychologica in causis ecclesiasticis definiendis," in *Apollinaris,* XXXII (1959), 202-216.

Flatten, Heinrich. "Ehekonsens und Geisteskrankheit," in *Trierer Theologische Zeitschrift,* LXIII (1954), 266-279.

——. "Qua libertate iudex ecclesiasticus probationes appretiare possit et debeat," in *Apollinaris,* XXXIII (1960), 185-210.

Guttmacher, Manfred S. "The Psychiatric Approach to Crime and Correction," in *Criminal Psychology,* edited by Richard W. Nice (New York: Philosophical Library, 1962), 112-141.

Harvey, John F., O.S.F.S. "Homosexuality and Marriage," in *The Homiletic and Pastoral Review,* LXII (1961), 227-234.

Hayes, John J., "Mental Disease and the Ecclesiastical Courts," in *The Jurist,* XVI (1956), 267-284.

Hervada, F. Javier. "El matrimonio *in facto esse* su estructura jurídica," in *Ius Canonicum,* I (1961), 135-175.

Huizing, Petrus, S.J.. "Bonum prolis ut elementum essentiale obiecti formalis consensus matrimonialis," in *Gregorianum,* XLIII (1962), 657-722.

Hürth, Franciscus, S. J. "Dubia matrimonialia. III: Dubium circa consummationem matrimonii," in *Periodica de re morali canonica liturgica,* XXXVIII (1949), 220-227.

Jullien, Andrea. "Riflessioni sulle responsabilità del giudice e dell'avvocato nel foro ecclesiastico e sulla procedura canonica," in *Monitor Ecclesiasticus,* LXXXIII (1958), 77-96.

Keating, John R. "The *Caput Nullitatis* in Insanity Cases," in *The Jurist,* XXII (1962), 391-411.

Keller, Henricus, S. J. "De usu praesumptionis in iure canonico," in *Periodica de re morali canonica liturgica,* XXIII (1934), 1-47.

Lamas Lourido, Ramón. "Consentimiento matrimonial canónico," in *Nueva Enciclopedia Jurídica,* Barcelona: Francisco Seix, 1953, Tomo V, pp. 126-163.

Lazzarato, Damiano. "De copula artificiosa semel tantum admissa," in *Ephemerides Iuris Canonici,* IV (1948), 470-472.

Lefebvre, Charles. "Debilité mentale," in *Dictionnaire de Droit Canonique,* Paris: Librairie Letouzey et Ané, 1949, Tome IV, coll. 1043-1051.

——. "Demence," in *Dictionnaire de Droit Canonique*, Paris: Librairie Letouzey et Ané, 1949, Tome IV, coll. 1098-1115.

LORENC, F. "De ignorantiae influxu in matrimoniali consensu," in *Apollinaris*, XXVI (1953), 348-388.

LYNCH, JOHN J., S. J. "Notes on Moral Theology," in *Theological Studies*, XVII (1956), 167-196.

MANS PUIGARNAU, JAIME M. "En torno a la naturaleza jurídica de los impedimentos matrimoniales," in *Revista Española de Derecho Canónico*, XIV (1959), 793-804.

MARCONE, JOSEPH. "An matrimonium consummetur actione tantum hominis," in *Monitor Ecclesiasticus*, LXXXII (1957), 631-656.

MCCARTHY, JOHN, "The Impediment of Impotence in the Present-day Canon Law," in *Ephemerides Iuris Canonici*, IV (1948), 96-130.

MCGOWAN, JOHN E. "Fundamentals of Psychiatry in Relation to the Ecclesiastical Tribunal," in *The Jurist*, XVI (1956), 251-266.

MCREAVY, L. L. "Consummation of Marriage — *Actus Humanus* Required?" in *The Clergy Review*, XLIV (1959), 37-40.

——. "Madness and Marriage," in *The Clergy Review*, XLIV (1959), 622-626.

MICHIELS, GOMMAIRE, O.F.M. Cap. "Mariage-contrat ou mariage-institution?" in *Apollinaris*, XXXIII (1960), 103-117.

MISURACA, SALVATORE, "L'impotenza canonica dal lato urologico", in *Ephemerides Iuris Canonici*, XVII (1961), 258-303.

NOVAL, J., O.P. "De semi-amentibus et semi-imputabilitati obnoxiis utrum revera existant aut in iure poenali ecclesiae agnoscantur," in *Jus Pontificium*, IV (1924), 76-86.

OESTERLE, GERARDUS, O.S.B. "Nullitas matrimonii ex capite ignorantiae," in *Ephemerides Theologicae Lovanienses*, XV (1938), 647-673.

——. "Consentement matrimonial," in *Dictionnaire de Droit Canonique*, Paris: Librairie Letouzey et Ané, 1949, Tome IV, coll. 293-354.

——. "De praesumptionibus in jure matrimoniali," in *Revista Española de Derecho Canónico*, IV (1949), 7-33.

——. "Amentia," in *Ephemerides Iuris Canonici*, XI (1955), 284-309.

——. "Von der psychischen Impotenz," in *Ephemerides Iuris Canonici*, XI (1955), 133-155.

——. "De relatione homosexualitatis ad matrimonium," in *Revista Española de Derecho Canónico*, X (1955), 7-60.

——. "De coniecturis in iure canonico," in *Revista Española de Derecho Canónico*, XIV (1959), 393-430, 667-707.

——. "Welchen Einfluss hat die Homosexualität auf die Ehe?" in *Oesterreichisches Archiv für Kirchenrecht*, XII (1961), 305-337.

——. "Vera impotentia a parte mulieris?" in *Il Diritto Ecclesiastico*, LXIII (1952), 43-51.

PALAZZINI, PETRUS. "De impedimento impotentiae," in *Casus Conscientiae*, I, *De matrimonio* 2ª ed., curante P. PALAZZINI (Romae: Officium Libri Catholici, 1961), 68-80.

RAVÀ, ANNA, "Il *defectus discretionis iudicii* come causa di nullità del matrimonio nella giurisprudenza rotale," in *Il Diritto Ecclesiastico,* LXVIII (1957), II, 345-489.

RECKERS, K. L. "De favore quo matrimonium gaudet in iure canonico," in *Ephemerides Iuris Canonici,* VI (1950), 374-425, 510-554.

REGATILLO, EDUARDO F., S. J. "Matrimonio entre bobos," in *Sal Terrae,* XLVIII (1960), 700.

——. "Un caso nuevo de sanación in radice," in *Sal Terrae,* XLIX (1961), 417-427.

RERUM SCRIPTOR (anon.). "Incipit lamentatio vinculi," in *Apollinaris,* XII (1939), 348-389.

ROBLEDA, OLISIUS, S. J. "Nullitas actus iuridici in Codice Iuris Canonici," in *Periodica de re morali canonica liturgica,* XXXV (1946), 29-50.

——. "De conceptu actus iuridici excursus theoricus," in *Periodica de re morali canonica liturgica,* LI (1962), 413-446.

SHEEHY, GERARD, "Male Psychical Impotence in Judicial Proceedings," in *The Jurist,* XX (1960), 253-294.

SPADA, P. "Sanazione in radice ostacolata da impedimento di diritto divino," in *Rivista del Clero Italiano,* XLI (1960), 232-234.

SPINELLI, GIUSEPPE. "In tema d'impotenza femminile per intollerabilità della copula," in *Il Diritto Ecclesiastico,* LXII (1951), 267-271.

STAFFA, DINUS. "De ignorantia naturae matrimonii," in *Monitor Ecclesiasticus,* LXXXII (1957), 426-429.

——. "De impotentia et consummatione matrimonii," in *Apollinaris,* XXVIII (1955), 391-399.

STOCKHAMMER, M. "Ultra posse nemo obligatur," in *Rivista Internazionale di Filosofia del Diritto,* XXXVI (1959), 25-35.

SZENTIRMAI, A. "De consensu matrimoniali ob ebrietatem nullo," in *Periodica de re morali canonica liturgica,* XLIV (1955), 369-384.

SZENWIC, ROMAN. "La schizofrenia nella recente giurisprudenza rotale," in *Il Diritto Ecclesiastico,* LXIII (1952), II, 156-167.

TIBAU, NARCISO. "Nulidad del matrimonio por ignorancia de la sustancia del mismo," in *Las Causas Matrimoniales* (Trabajos de la cuarta semana de derecho canonico celebrada en el Monasterio de N.ª S.ª de Montserrat. Salamanca: Consejo Superior de Investigaciones Cientificas, Instituto San Raimundo de Peñafort, 1953), 187-201.

VILLEGGIANTE, SEBASTIANO. "Ninfomania e cause di nullità matrimoniale," in *Il Diritto Ecclesiastico,* LXXI (1960), II, pp. 162-184.

——. "Ninfomania e difetto di consenso," in *Il Diritto Ecclesiastico,* LXXI (1960), II, pp. 315-322.

VISSER, IOANNES, C.SS.R. "De matrimonio per procuratorem inito," in *Casus Coscientiae,* I, *De matrimonio.* 2ª ed., curante P. PALAZZINI (Romae: Officium Libri Catholici, 1961), 114-119.

WEIHOFEN, HENRY. "The Definition of Mental Illness," in *Criminal Phychology,* edited by RICHARD W. NICE (New York: Philosophical Library, 1962), 194-219.

THE RELEVANT ROTAL DECISIONS CONSULTED IN *SACRAE ROMANAE ROTAE DECISIONES SEU SENTENTIAE*

C. PRIOR, July 10, 1909 (Vol. I, 85-93). Hysteria. *Constat.*

C. MANY, Dec. 23, 1909 (Vol. I, 164-171). Mental deficiency. *Constat.*

C. SEBASTIANELLI Apr. 9, 1910 (Vol. II, 144-148). Hysteria. *Constat.*

C. SINCERO, Aug. 28, 1911 (Vol. III, 430-460). Neurasthenia. *Non constat.*

C. LEGA, Feb. 13, 1913 (Vol. V, 142-159). Manic psychosis. *Constat.*

C. MANY, Aug. 11, 1913 (Vol. V, 562-573). Hysteria. *Non constat.*

C. MANY, Aug. 16, 1913 (Vol. V, 574-586). Schizophrenia: paranoid type. *Constat.*

C. SEBASTIANELLI, Mar. 23, 1914 (Vol. VI, 142-151). Typhoid psychosis. *Constat.*

C. PRIOR, May 15, 1915 (Vol. VII, 215-231). Schizophrenia: paranoid type. *Constat.*

C. MANY, June 27, 1916 (Vol. VIII, 202-212). Post-infective neurasthenia. *Constat.*

C. SEBASTIANELLI, Jan. 7, 1918 (Vol. X, 1-11). Schizophrenia: paranoid type. *Constat.*

C. SINCERO, Dec. 23, 1918 (Vol. X, 142-149). Schizophrenia. *Constat.*

C. PRIOR, Nov. 14, 1919 (Vol. XI, 170-78). Oligophrenia. *Constat.*

C. PRIOR, July 27, 1920 (Vol. XII, 202-215). Schizophrenia. *Non constat.*

C. PRIOR, July, 27, 1920 (Vol. XII, 202-215). Schizophrenia. *Non constat.*

C. ROSSETTI, Mar. 16, 1921 (Vol. XIII, 47-62). Manic-depressive psychosis. *Non constat.*

C. ROSSETTI, May 10, 1921 (Vol. XIII, 85-99). Hereditary schizophrenia. *Non constat.*

C. ROSSETTI, July 1, 1922 (Vol. XIV, 209-217). Neurasthenia. *Non constat.*

C. ROSSETTI, July 3, 1922 (Vol. XIV, 222-228). Schizophrenia. *Constat.*

C. PRIOR, Aug. 17, 1922 (Vol. XIV, 312-320). Schizophrenia: paranoid type. *Constat.*

C. FLORCZAK, June 29, 1923 (Vol. XV, 117-135). Oligophrenia. *Constat.*

C. MANNUCCI, Apr. 8, 1924 (Vol. XVI, 126-138). Schizophrenia. *Non constat.*

C. MASSIMI, Oct. 29, 1924 (Vol. XVI, 371-375). Schizophrenia. *Constat.*

C. GRAZIOLI, Apr. 7, 1926 (Vol. XVIII, 108-116). Compulsion neurosis. *Non constat.*

C. FLORCZAK, May 27, 1926 (Vol. XVIII, 183-190). Manic-depressive psychosis. *Non constat.*

C. GRAZIOLI, June 25, 1926 (Vol. XVIII, 213-221). Oligophrenia. *Constat.*

C. PARRILLO, Feb. 16, 1928 (Vol. XX, 57-81). Schizophrenia. *Non constat.*

C. QUATTROCOLO, June 23, 1928 (Vol. XX, 257-267). Manic-depressive psychosis. *Constat.*

C. MASSIMI, July 28, 1928 (Vol. XX, 317-322). Compulsion neurosis. *Non constat.*

C. MANNUCCI, Jan. 28, 1929 (Vol. XXI, 59-64). Drunkenness. *Non constat.*

C. FLORCZAK, Jan. 31, 1929 (Vol. XXI, 75-84). Drunkenness. *Non constat.*

C. PARRILLO, Feb. 21, 1929 (Vol. XXI, 125-132). Hypnosis. *Non constat.*

C. GRAZIOLI, July 27, 1929 (Vol. XXI, 330-339). Paranoia. *Non constat.*

C. PARRILLO, Aug. 12, 1929 (Vol. XXI, 433-444). Superstitious compulsion. *Non constat.*

C. GUGLIELMI, Feb. 22, 1930 (Vol. XXII, 86-104). Hypnosis, *Non constat.*

C. WYNEN, Mar. 1, 1930 (Vol. XXII, 125-153). Schizophrenia, epileptoid paranoia. *Non constat.*

C. PARRILLO, May 10, 1930 (Vol. XXII, 259-275). Drunkenness. *Non constat.*

C. GRAZIOLI, Apr. 24, 1931 (Vol. XXIII, 150-158). Manic depressive psychosis. *Non constat.*

C. MASSIMI, July 10, 1931 (Vol. XXIII, 273-279). Psychasthenia. *Non constat.*

C. MANNUCCI, Aug. 8, 1931 (Vol. XXIII, 371-378). Schizophrenia. *Constat.*

C. MASSIMI, Nov. 20, 1931 (Vol. XXIII, 462-470). Psychasthenia. *Non constat.*

C. JULLIEN, July 30, 1932 (Vol. XXIV, 364-382). Epilepsy. *Non constat.*

C. QUATTROCOLO, Nov. 17, 1932 (Vol. XXIV, 443-458). Compulsion neurosis. *Non constat.*

C. JULLIEN, Dec. 23, 1932 (Vol. XXIV, 557-578). Manic-depressive psychosis. *Non constat.*

C. QUATTROCOLO, Apr. 25, 1933 (Vol. XXV, 264-270). Drunkenness. *Non constat.*

C. GRAZIOLI, July 1, 1933 (Vol. XXV, 405-419). Schizophrenia. *Constat.*

C. GRAZIOLI, Nov. 27, 1933 (Vol. XXV, 597-606). Psychasthenia. *Non constat.*

C. GRAZIOLI, Nov. 3, 1934 (Vol. XXVI, 708-717). Schizophrenia: hebephrenic type. *Constat.*

C. JULLIEN, Feb. 23, 1935 (Vol. XXVII, 76-90). Morphinism. *Non constat.*

C. QUATTROCOLO, Apr. 16, 1935 (Vol. XXVII, 253-259). Drunkenness. *Non constat.*

C. MORANO, Apr. 30, 1935 (Vol. XXVII, 280-285). Schizophrenia. *Constat.*

C. MORANO, Dec. 21, 1935 (Vol. XXVII, 695-703). Lypemania. *Non constat.*

C. JULLIEN, May 9, 1936 (Vol. XXVIII, 303-319). Schizophrenia. *Non constat.*

C. JULLIEN, Dec. 16, 1936 (Vol. XXVIII, 768-785). Schizophrenia: paranoid type. *Non constat.*

C. WYNEN, Dec. 30, 1936 (Vol. XXVIII, 809-816). Schizophrenia: catatonic type. *Non constat.*

C. WYNEN, Feb. 27, 1937 (Vol. XXIX, 169-196). Morphinism. *Non constat.*

C. Jullien, Mar. 13, 1937 (Vol. XXIX, 197-213). Schizophrenia. *Constat.*

C. Canestri, July 15, 1937 (Vol. XXIX, 525-538). Morphinism. *Non constat.*

C. Quattrocolo, July 31, 1937 (Vol. XXIX, 568-581). Narcotic intoxication (cocaine). *Non constat.*

C. Jullien, Dec. 11, 1937 (Vol. XXIX, 733-740). Drunkenness. *Non constat.*

C. Wynen, Dec. 21, 1937 (Vol. XXIX, 756-770). Paranoia and schizophrenia. *Constat.*

C. Quattrocolo, Dec. 30, 1937 (Vol. XXIX, 810-829). Hysteria and moral insanity. *Non constat.*

C. Heard, Jan. 8, 1938 (Vol. XXX, 13-21). Hysteria. *Non constat.*

C. Wynen, Jan. 13, 1938 (Vol. XXX, 22-37). Schizophrenia: catatonic type. *Constat.*

C. Teodori, June 23, 1938 (Vol. XXX, 350-360). Drunkenness. *Non constat.*

C. Wynen, June 3, 1939 (Vol. XXXI, 371-383). Schizophrenia. *Non constat.*

C. Teodori, Jan. 19, 1940 (Vol. XXXII, 81-92). Sexual hyperesthesia. *Constat.*

C. Caiazzo, July 30, 1940 (Vol. XXXII, 611-627). Manic-depressive psychosis. *Constat.*

C. Canestri, Aug. 3, 1940 (Vol. XXXII, 658-667). Oligophrenia. *Constat.*

C. Wynen, Feb. 25, 1941 (Vol. XXXIII, 144-168). Constitutional immorality. *Non constat.*

C. Heard, June 5, 1941 (Vol. XXXIII, 488-496). Sexual hyperesthesia. *Non constat.*

C. Heard, July 19, 1941 (Vol. XXXIII, 651-658). Schizophrenia: paranoid type. *Constat.*

C. Janasik, July 24, 1941 (Vol. XXXIII, 666-677). Schizophrenia: catatonic type. *Constat.*

C. Teodori, June 9, 1942 (Vol. XXXIV, 466-477). Brain trauma. *Non constat.*

C. Jullien, Oct. 16, 1942 (Vol. XXXIV, 775-781). Sexual hyperesthesia. *Constat.*

C. Canestri, Apr. 12, 1943 (Vol. XXXV, 262-269). Feeble-mindedness. *Non constat.*

C. Wynen, Apr. 13, 1943 (Vol. XXXV, 270-281). Brain trauma. *Non constat.*

C. Quattrocolo, June 16, 1943 (Vol. XXXV, 431-451). Hysteria. *Non constat.*

C. Canestri, July 16, 1943 (Vol. XXXV, 549-612). Psychopathic personality. *Non constat.*

C. Pecorari, Aug. 10, 1943 (Vol. XXXV, 706-724). Schizophrenia. *Constat.*

C. Heard, Dec. 4, 1943 (Vol. XXXV, 885-903). Schizophrenia. *Constat.*

C. Jullien, Dec. 16, 1943 (Vol. XXXV, 948-957). Schizophrenia. *Constat.*

C. Quattrocolo, Mar. 10, 1944 (Vol. XXXVI, 149-161). Schizophrenia. *Non constat.*

C. Teodori, June 20, 1944 (Vol. XXXVI, 434-443). Schizophrenia. *Non constat.*
C. Roberti, Apr. 17, 1945 (Vol. XXXVII, 251-257). Schizophrenia: paranoid type. *Constat.*
C. Teodori, June 25, 1945 (Vol. XXXVII, 405-413). Oligophrenia. *Constat.*
C. Roberti, June 26, 1945 (Vol. XXXVII, 422-428). Hysteria. *Non constat.*
C. Fidecicchi, Dec. 11, 1945 (Vol. XXXVII, 680-688). Schizophrenia. *Constat.*
C. Heard, Apr. 27, 1946 (Vol. XXXVIII, 256-276). Lethargic encephalitis. *Non constat.*
C. Wynen, Dec. 7, 1946 (Vol. XXXVIII, 571-591). Schizophrenia. *Constat.*
C. Jullien (omnibus videntibus), July 5, 1947 (Vol. XXXIX, 397-418). Schizophrenia. *Constat.*
C. Heard, Dec. 30, 1947 (Vol. XXXIX, 617-625). Cerebropathy. *Non constat.*
C. Wynen, Oct. 20, 1948 (Vol. XL, 372-380). Passing state of exaltation. *Non constat.*
C. Pasquazi, May 12, 1949 (Vol. XLI, 218-223). Personality disorder (zelotypia). *Non constat.*
C. Brennan, Nov. 25, 1949 (Vol. XLI, 521-529). Ether intoxication. *Constat.*
C. Pasquazi, Dec. 19, 1950 (Vol. XLII, 675-679). Schizophrenia: paranoid type. *Non constat.*
C. Fidecicchi, May 29, 1951 (Vol. XLIII, 423-429). Personality disorder (zelotypia). *Non constat.*
C. Heard, July 14, 1951 (Vol. XLIII, 526-533). Neuropsychasthenia. *Constat.*
C. Felici, Feb. 26, 1952 (Vol. XLIV, 119-128). Schizophrenia: hebephrenic type. *Constat.*
C. Fidecicchi, May 20, 1952 (Vol. XLIV, 326-336). Hysterical psychopathy from morphine intoxication. *Non constat.*
C. Fidecicchi, July 11, 1952 (Vol. XLIV, 430-442). Schizophrenia: hebephrenic type. *Constat.*
C. Fidecicchi, Oct. 7, 1952 (Vol. XLIV, 517-527). Schizophrenia. *Constat.*

UNPUBLISHED ROTAL DECISIONS

C. Staffa (Quebecen.), Apr. 30, 1953. Schizophrenia. *Non constat.*
C. Mattioli (Quebecen.), May 6, 1953. Schizophrenia. *Constat.*
C. Canestri (Berythen.), July 4, 1953. Schizophrenia. *Non constat.*
C. Heard (Bononien.), Nov. 14, 1953. Psychasthenia. *Constat.*
C. Heard (Quebecen.), Jan. 30, 1954. Encephalitis. *Constat.*
C. Wynen (Mediolanen.), Feb. 25, 1954. Schizophrenia. *Non constat.*
C. Felici (Florentina), Apr. 6, 1954. Paranoia. *Constat.*
C. Canestri (Neo-Eboracen.), May 6, 1954. Schizophrenia. *Constat.*

C. Heard (Romana), May 22, 1954. Manic-depressive psychosis. *Constat.*
C. Caiazzo (Taurinen.), June 22, 1954. Depression psychosis. *Constat.*
C. Pinna (Southvarcen.), Aug. 4, 1954. Schizophrenia. *Constat.*
C. Pasquazi (Rhedonen.), Oct. 19, 1954. Manic-depressive psychosis. *Non constat.*
C. Canestri (Pistorien.), Jan. 11, 1955. Oligophrenia. *Non constat.*
C. Mattioli (Taurinen.), Jan. 26, 1955. Schizophrenia: hebephrenic type. *Constat.*
C. Felici (Ambianen.), Feb. 15, 1955. Lypemania. *Constat.*
C. Brennan (Bostonien.), Feb. 28, 1955. Schizophrenia. *Constat.*
C. Felici (Romana), July 12, 1955. Paranoia. *Constat.*
C. Heard (Nanceien.), July 16, 1955. Nymphomania. *Non constat.*
C. Bonet (Romana), July 27, 1955. Schizophrenia. *Constat.*
C. Brennan (Bruklynien). Nov. 29, 1955. Schizophrenia: hebephrenic type. *Constat.*
C. Mattioli (Taurinen.), Dec. 2, 1955. Syphilitic meningo-encephalitis. *Constat.*
C. Doheny (Angelorum in California), Jan. 23, 1956. Schizophrenia: paranoid type. *Constat.*
C. Lamas (Chicagien.), Mar. 15, 1956. Homosexuality. *Non constat.*
C. Lamas (Romana), Apr. 12, 1956. Manic-depressive psychosis. *Non constat.*
C. Sabattani (Bostonien.), Apr. 20, 1956. Schizophrenia. *Constat.*
C. Canestri (Concordien seu Venetiarum), May 3, 1956. Schizophrenia. *Constat.*
C. Felici (Florentina), May 22, 1956, Constitutional immorality. *Non constat.*
C. Filipiak (Divionen.), June 15, 1956. Psychasthenia. *Constat.*
C. Brennan (Oranen.), July 25, 1956. Psychasthenia. *Non constat.*
C. Felici (Drepanen.), Oct. 16, 1956. Schizophrenia. *Constat.*
C. Doheny (Romana), Oct. 29, 1956. No species indicated. *Non constat.*
C. Mattioli (Quebecen.), Nov. 6, 1956. Syphilitic meningo-encephalitis. *Constat.*
C. Doheny (Philadelphien.), Dec. 10, 1956. Schizophrenia. *Constat.*
C. Brennan (Portlanden. in Oregon), Dec. 13, 1956. Schizophrenia. *Constat.*
C. Lefebvre (Pistorien.), Jan. 31, 1957. Oligophrenia. *Non constat.*
C. Brennan (Campifontis), Jan. 31, 1957. Schizophrenia. *Non constat.*
C. Heard (Quebecen.), Feb. 16, 1957. Mentis debilitas. *Non constat.*
C. Filipiak (Rhedonen.), May 3, 1957. Drunkenness. *Non constat.*
C. Bonet (Romana), June 3, 1957. Schizophrenia: paranoid type. *Constat.*
C. Sabattani (Neapolitana), June 21, 1957. Nymphomania. *Non constat.*
C. Filipiak (Parisien.), Nov. 15, 1957. No species indicated. *Non constat.*
C. Brennan (Drepanen.), Nov. 14, 1957. Schizophrenia. *Non constat.*
C. Mattioli (Romana), Nov. 28, 1957. Schizophrenia. *Constat.*

C. FELICI (Quebecen.), Dec. 3, 1957. Syphilitic meningo-encephalitis. *Constat.*
C. FELICI (Mediolanen.), Jan. 21, 1958. Schizophrenia. *Constat.*
C. FILIPIAK (Davenporten.), Feb. 14, 1958. Psychopathic personality. *Non constat.*
C. BRENNAN (Parisien.), Mar. 27, 1958. Homosexuality. *Non constat.*
C. PINNA (Parisien.), Apr. 22, 1958. Homosexuality. *Non constat.*
C. LEFEBVRE (Nanceien.), Apr. 26, 1958. Nymphomania. *Constat.*
C. HEARD (Oranen.), May 17, 1958. Psychasthenia. *Constat.*
C. LAMAS (Mediolanen.), May 28, 1958. Manic-depressive psychosis. *Non constat.*
C. LAMAS (Bruklynien.), June 25, 1958. Schizophrenia: paranoid type. *Constat.*
C. BEJAN (Atrebaten.), Oct. 25, 1958. Oligophrenia. *Non constat.*
C. PINNA (Parisien.), Oct. 30, 1958. Ignorance in deaf and dumb subject. *Constat.*
C. DOHENY (Oranen.), Nov. 17, 1958. Psychasthenia. *Constat.*
C. MATTIOLI (Bononien.), Nov. 6,, 1958. Schizophrenia. *Constat.*
C. MATTIOLI (Clevelanden.), Dec. 11, 1958. Homosexuality. *Non constat.*
C. HEARD (Rhedonen.), Jan 8, 1959. Manic-depressive psychosis. *Constat.*
C. PINNA (Basileen.), Jan. 13, 1959. Schizophrenia: catatonic type. *Constat.*
C. BEJAN (Quebecen.), Feb. 26, 1959. Schizophrenia: paranoid type. *Constat.*
C. SABATTANI (Januen.), Mar. 14, 1959. Paranoia. *Constat.*
C. PINNA (Romana), Mar. 21, 1959. Manic-depressive psychosis. *Constat.*
C. LEFEBVRE (Rhedonen.), May 9, 1959. Manic-depressive psychosis. *Constat.*
C. HEARD (Sancti Augustini), June 27, 1959. Nymphomania. *Constat.*
C. LEFEBVRE (Drepanen.), Oct. 17, 1959. Schizophrenia. *Constat.*
C. LAMAS (Neo-Eboracen.), Oct. 21, 1959. Schizophrenia. *Constat.*
C. SABATTANI (Neo-Eboracen.), Oct. 22, 1959. Schizophrenia: paranoid type. *Non constat.*
C. BRENNAN (Chicagien.), Dec. 18, 1959. Schizophrenia. *Non constat.*
C. LEFEBVRE (Miamien.), Dec. 18, 1959. Nymphomania. *Constat.*
C. BONET (Campifontis in Illinois), Dec. 21, 1959. Schizophrenia. *Constat.*
C. PINNA (Molinen.), Dec. 21, 1959. Psychasthenia. *Non constat.*
C. MATTIOLI (Chicagien.), Mar. 24, 1960. Homosexuality. *Non constat.*
C. LEFEBVRE (Quebecen.), Apr. 7, 1960. Schizophrenia: paranoid type. *Constat.*
C. PASQUAZI (Quebecen.), May 19, 1960. Schizophrenia: paranoid type. *Non constat.*
C. FILIPIAK (Comen.), July 15, 1960. Schizophrenia: paranoid type. *Constat.*
C. EWERS (Quebecen.), Oct. 29, 1960. Psychasthenia. *Constat.*
C. ROGERS (Neo-Eboracen.), Dec. 1, 1960. Schizophrenia: paranoid type. *Non constat.*

C. PINNA (Liburnen.), Dec. 20, 1960. Schizophrenia: hebephrenic type. *Constat.*
C. FILIPIAK (Rhedonen.), Dec. 23, 1960. Homosexuality. *Non constat.*
C. FILIPIAK (S. Francisci in California), Dec. 23, 1960. Schizophrenia. *Constat.*
C. SABATTANI (Januen.), Feb. 24, 1961. Alcoholic psychosis. *Constat.*
C. ROGERS (Scrantonen.), Mar. 17, 1961. Nervous debilitation. *Non constat.*
C. SABATTANI (Tridentina), Mar. 24, 1961. Schizophrenia: hebephrenic type. *Constat.*
C. ROGERS (Chicagien.), Apr. 14, 1961. Sexual psychopathy (exhibitionism). *Non constat.*
C. FIORE (Romana), May 16, 1961. Oligophrenia. *Non constat.*
C. DOHENY (Mediolanen.), June 7, 1961. Homosexuality. *Non constat.*
C. PASQUAZI (Parisien.), July 20, 1961. Ignorance in deaf and dumb subject. *Non constat.*
C. PASQUAZI (Rhedonen.), Oct. 26, 1961. Homosexuality. *Non constat.*
C. ANNÉ (Campifontis in Mass.), Nov. 25, 1961. Schizophrenia: paranoid type. *Constat.*
C. DE JORIO (Taurinen.), Dec. 19, 1961. Oligophrenia. *Constat.*
C. DE JORIO (Taurinen.), Feb. 28, 1962. Hysteria. *Non constat.*
C. DOHENY (Romana), Mar. 16, 1962. Oligophrenia. *Constat.*
C. DOHENY (Southvarcen.), Apr. 16, 1962. Lesbianism. *Non constat.*

ALPHABETICAL INDEX